LUGMA

LUGMA

ABUNDANT DISHES & STORIES FROM MY MIDDLE EAST

NOOR MURAD

Food photography by Matt Russell
Location photography by Matt Wardle

Cover illustration by Ella Ginn
Script by Karima Sharabi

Quadrille

On Lugma 06

Author's Notes 20

Breakfast and Brunch 24
Mezze, Salads and Soups 56
Rice 114
Vegetarian 142
Fish 186
Meat 204
Halawa (Sweets) 230
Condiments 262

Meal Suggestions 276

Index 280

Acknowledgements 286

About the Author 287

On Lugma

I've always believed that the Middle East should be its own continent. Each country has its unique personality, its own cultural nuances, traditions, dialect and cuisine. It's impossible to paint the whole region with one brush when its history is so rich, its stories so colourful, its offerings so vast and generous. I tend to stick to the battles I'm best equipped to fight, however, which – to no surprise – are food-centred.

The first battle begins with hummus, and the simple fact that I didn't grow up eating it. It was around, sure, but it definitely wasn't part of the family buffet spread. It was *saloonat dajaj* (page 227), *mathrooba* (page 136) and *machboos* (page 132). It was *mehyawa* (page 270), *balaleet* (page 30) and *luqaimat* (page 242). These are dishes you might not have heard of, but they're also dishes I very much deem to be Middle Eastern. As my grandfather rolled up his sleeves and dug into his rice he'd say, '*tabeen lugmat aish* [do you want a bite of rice]?'. The classical Arabic word for rice is actually *aruz*, but in Bahrain it's called *aish*, which means 'living'. In Bahrain there is no table setting without rice because, well, rice is living.

On the other hand, there was Mum's walnut cake. It was made with ground nuts and whipped egg whites and completed with a dusting of icing sugar. In theory it should have lasted a few days between us, but this was never the case. One sliver with tea would become four throughout the day; this cake was impossible to resist as it sat there in a non-compete with the fruit bowl. This is true for all of Mum's baked treats – her Victoria Sponge, her classic scones or her very popular Christmas cake, made in October and spoon fed Brandy every 2 weeks so it's lovely and moist come December – her English roots permeating every single one of her delicious creations. The smell of Mum's cooking is, for me, on par with the smell of rice; her head was always tucked into another cookbook, where she'd conjure up new finds or old favourites from Delia Smith, Ken Hom or Anissa Helou. After-school lunches were always a surprise, but my favourites were her mushroom risotto, her once-a-year Pancakes (page 36) and a good Bolognese (page 223). Mum, in her self-taught years of practice, would cook from every corner of the world, except for one distinct territory. She would never, for the life of her, cook the food of the Gulf.

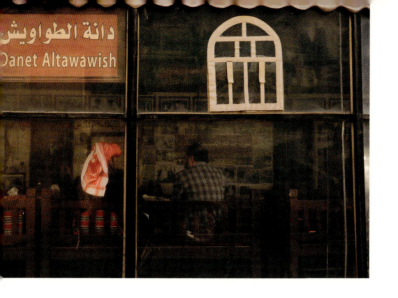

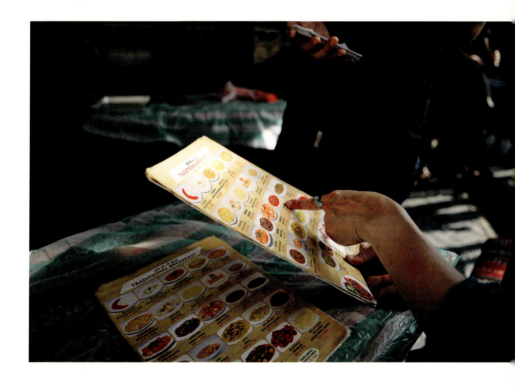

Looking back I suppose this is what fuelled my curiosity. Many Middle Eastern cookbooks back then, and to this day, were centred around the foods of the Levant, which are delicious but also very different. The only way to learn about Gulf food was to eat at other people's houses, learn how so-and-so makes it, which is different from how someone else from another home would make it. It's a battle of the households, a well-kept secret of the families, a word-of-mouth cuisine that is passed over from one generation to the next. It's a measurement of the eye, a seasoning of the tongue, a technique of practice and instinct. Growing up, I felt I was severely lacking in this department, but islanders are very generous (and super-keen) when it comes to feeding others. As I asked around, visited, tasted and conversed, I jotted down all the tales and stories, all the memories and experiences, all the spices and know-how I needed to put these recipes into print.

Lugma is an ode to the food of my childhood, a mash-up of food from Bahrain and the surrounding countries, with a slightly Westernized take, thanks to my English roots. On the food front, Bahrain is unique in that it pulls on different cultural influences: on the abundance of herbs, dried limes and sour flavours from Iran; on the liberal spice and chilli heat from India; on the elaborate rice dishes which the region is so famous for; and on the foods of the Levant that the world is more familiar with. There are therefore lots of recipes that call for cardamom, dates, rice, lamb and legumes. Alongside are plenty of vegetarian dishes, which I feel aren't included enough in the regional diet, as, being an arid desert, historically the options were limited. Nowadays though, you can find all sorts of vegetables in the local supermarkets, and so I'll often take Middle Eastern flavours and use them to amplify vegetarian meals. Dotted throughout all of this are stories: some of them my own and some of women you may never know but may relate to regardless. These are all women who call Bahrain home, despite hailing from different parts of the world. Their voices are a melting pot of nostalgia, emotion, memory and all the warming foods that they have become attached to.

The journey to *Lugma* wasn't always smooth sailing. It took me a year of upheaval, reflection and a proper deep dive into my own relationship with food and cooking to put it all together. I often questioned how to approach tradition, if I should land left or right, if it would be okay to tamper with a classic and, if so, how far could I push it and, when inevitably I did, because I always do, would it still be okay? The questions I asked myself, with every single dish, every resounding success or ultimate disaster were: would I eat/cook this for myself and my friends? And, if so, does this fit into *Lugma*? Two yeses was all it took, but you'd be surprised by how many nos I gave way to. The recipes needed to remain true to who I was, an honest mirror reflection, in a way I haven't had to do with my cooking professionally. In this respect, *Lugma* has been my lifetime in the making, plates upon plates of Middle Eastern foods meeting Western foods and finding their place on the same table. *Lugma* is multiple bites – a great many delicious mouthfuls – of all that I know.

ON RICE

I often try to describe the smell of rice cooking. It smells of vanilla and pandan. Of butter and sweetcorn. Of musk. If comfort had a smell, it would be of steaming, simmering, bubbling rice. If comfort had a look it would be of families sat cross-legged on plastic-lined flooring, a big, glorious rice platter perched proudly in the centre, hungry hands reaching forwards to grab one generous bite – a 2:1 ratio of rice to lamb – scrunched skilfully in the right hand, the perfect *lugma*.

Lugma is Arabic for a bite, or a mouthful. Which seems fitting really, as I feel like my whole career has been centred around taking bites of things and analysing them: more acid here, a pinch of salt there, missing sweetness overall. As a recipe developer, you learn to become decisive, to rely on your tastebuds and your instincts. Inevitably it comes down to whether or not there's a second bite, or a third. If it's a dish you want to keep eating, it's probably really good. If it's a dish you can't wait to make for others, then you know it's a winner. In our brainstorms about food I'd often ask my colleagues to tell me about what they grew up eating, what excited them, what they wanted to eat, really, in that moment. This would always spark a few inspired ideas and inevitably, some very delicious dishes – cooked purposefully and with a lot of heart. Eventually I began to direct those questions inwards.

At the time it seemed nothing really excited me any more. No foods surprised me. No books inspired me. Social media felt like this big, dreadful overwhelming vacuum and I was in free fall.

But it wasn't always this way. Culture wasn't always so divisive. Identity wasn't always so black and white. Boxes weren't always formed to place us. Once upon a time I was just a girl from Bahrain, born to an Arab dad and an English mum. Life was slow and calm, the island was sunny, and the smell of rice cooking wafted all the way up to my bedroom.

ON SAMBOOSAS AND MARMITE

Fridays were my favourite day of the week growing up. Being a Muslim country meant our weekends were on Thursdays and Fridays (it's since changed to Fridays and Saturdays), with Fridays being a holy day of prayer, observance and family time. I didn't come from a particularly religious family and I often found this conflicting, with faith being such an integral part of the Muslim Arab existence. I felt that I wasn't as I should be, but I didn't know what this meant at the time, or what it would continue to mean into my adult years.

But Fridays were the best days because I'd often wake up to the sound of Mum fiddling about in the kitchen, and Dad's car no longer outside – which could only mean one thing: samboosas were en route. If I woke up in time I'd eagerly go with him. We'd drive down to his favourite samboosa spot, which was basically just a haphazardly made shack with a gas burner, a vat of oil and a massive slotted spoon. Come to think of it, the whole setup was a safety hazard, but none of that really mattered because these were next-level samboosas. One *rubya*, the equivalent of 20p, would give you 5 deep-fried triangular pastries filled with spicy potatoes, spicy mung beans, or cheese. Dad was a potato man so that's what we often had, eating them greedily in the car from oil-stained paper bags, burning our mouths and making a mess in the process. We'd get a second bag to take home, just so Mum wouldn't know that we had already eaten, but she always knew. I used to think it was a mum's super-power but, in reality, the grease stains most definitely gave us away.

The day would continue to be food-centred, a lunch out as Mum was 'off-duty' on Fridays, followed by a walk in the desert with our dog, Max. I'd will these days to last forever while driving home into the sunset, nursing an ice-cold lemon and mint juice from a street vendor, the call to prayer filling the streets with beautiful, wondrous sound. Tomorrow would be another day in my school uniform, sitting uncomfortably with a Marmite sandwich and a Ribena, and wishing my lunchbox looked like everyone else's.

Looking back now, I don't really think that a Marmite sandwich should've caused as much of a ruckus as it did, but perhaps Marmite really is more divisive than we care to admit. Kids at school would peer at the thick, dark paste with a mixture of curiosity and slight disgust, whispers of '*omha englaizya*' ('her mum is English'), by way of explanation. I still ate the sandwich, though, because I am and always will be team Marmite.

ON LUGMA

ON VINE LEAVES AND DISCO FRIES

I often say that I grew up in a bubble. The tiny island that is Bahrain I find hard to explain to anyone who wasn't raised in, or at least exposed to, that part of the world. To some it's just another country in the Middle East, landing somewhere between the whispers of Saudi Arabia and the loudness of Dubai. To others it's part of the oil-rich Arabian Gulf, whose people are said to come equipped with a treasure chest of disposable income. These perceptions I cannot change but I do find redundant, and not particularly reflective of the world I grew up in. Bahrain is equal parts arid desert and high-rise city, salty sea and hot tarmac, stifling heat and calm waters. It's loudly opinionated and quietly reserved, extraordinarily traditional and fleetingly modern. It's small islanders with big dreams, transient opportunities with messy realities. It's hard living for most and easy breezing for some. It's big hearts, humorous personalities and unbreakable resilience. It's every shade of complicated and every definition of kind. It's a balancing act of all the above. The island, in its many guises, draws you in and holds you tight and, in your own time, you learn to love each and every one of its perfectly smooth corners and imperfectly sharp edges.

But as is always the case with small-island fever and the fierce independence of a defiant teenager, I was itching to leave. There had to be more to it, I was convinced, than this dichotomy of two cultures. Life felt structured and orderly and ever so planned and – just like every pair of jeans I've ever owned – it simply didn't fit right.

The first time I stepped into a production kitchen I was 16 years old and had landed a summer job in hotel banquets. I remember it all being very loud, messy, unglamorous and unlike any environment I'd ever been in before. Naturally, I had absolutely no clue what I was doing, but something about it – the chaos of it all – stuck. As I went about rolling rows upon rows of vine leaves and being reprimanded for overfilling them, I made the abrupt decision that this was where I was meant to be. From that point on, life just got louder.

Four years spent in America transformed me from shy and reserved to abrasive and terribly opinionated, or, as my mum put it, 'a proper New Yorker'. I went from attending a fast-paced culinary school to working in a fast-paced Manhattan restaurant, operating on little sleep, a sugar-fuelled diet and an absolute coffee addiction. Towards my last year I was exhausted; I yearned for the smell of the sea, the kindness of community and the sense of belonging that I definitely lacked. America helped me find my voice, fed me late-night milkshakes and cheese and bacon-loaded disco fries, but ultimately, America felt too much like West, and too little like East. I missed home.

ON BLACK LIMES

It feels overly simplistic to talk about a 'defining moment' when, in reality, big life events are just a cluster of built-up moments, woven together the way skilful Bahraini hands weave palm leaves to form baskets. My early twenties spent back in Bahrain often felt this way, where each moment built on the next, weaving themselves quietly yet intricately, waiting patiently for that one definitive, catapulting moment.

When I was young I marvelled at the novelty of my name, Noor, which means light. I thought it was pretty fitting considering how much I loved the sun. I loved clear blue skies and the familiar heat scorching my skin. I loved the feel of cool fabrics, free-flowing dresses and slip-on sandals. I despised socks, boots, scarves, hats, snug puffer jackets and anything that constrained me. More than anything I dreaded the night, as it meant my night-owl friends were out and about and I would struggle to keep my heavy, drooping eyelids open. I didn't consider then that with light there must come darkness, that the two go hand in hand like Marmite and fluffy white bread, like potatoes and crisp pastry. But the darkness came anyway: it showed up in missed work opportunities and male-dominated kitchens; it showed up in food restrictions and dreaded mirror reflections; it showed up in the Arab Spring that set the whole island alight with rage. I never thought it would show up in love, though. Love, for me, was indestructible. That was until I met my moment.

No one tells you just how tough divorce is. No one explains that there really is no remedy, no direction, no manual to picking yourself up and dusting yourself off. And as I hadn't seen this coming, hadn't planned for it, hadn't written it on the to-do list of my life, I did what any impulsive being would do in these moments. I fitted my belongings into one case and bought a one-way ticket heading west. Six thousand kilometres should do the trick.

Winter in London felt cold, cruel and larger than I could wrap my little island head around. The dark days dimmed my soul, but a job as a chef de partie at one Ottolenghi deli felt like a distant – but very much attainable – tiny little light. The city's greatest gift was anonymity; in this very loud kitchen, among these very loud chefs, wearing this very striped apron, I could lose myself.

I'd like to say I never looked back, but that would be a lie. I stole moments in the chopping of aubergines and the cooking of shakshukas. I stole moments in cold walk-ins and in crammed dry-stores. I stole every moment there was to look backwards while the days, months, years propelled me forwards. But I never really got a handle on time, and the more time passed the more disconnected I became from a past that once made sense to me. I clung on to the foods I knew and the flavours I loved – the rice dishes, the black limes and spice mixes, the herbs and the lemons and the one bit of identity I felt no one could take away. And in time, just like they said it would, the ache stayed but the pain dulled, the loneliness remained but the emptiness filled, the scar existed but the wound healed. I moved forwards. I took the black limes with me.

ON LUGMA

ON DATES AND OTTOLENGHI

'*Noor, tabeen tamur [do you want dates]?*', my dad always asks, in the days before he flies to London. The answer is always a resounding yes, I'd never say no to Bahraini dates, but especially not ones cared for by my dad, and grown in our home garden. The most delicious dates around, in my humble opinion.

He will also bring other things: *gahwa* (Arabic coffee), *loomi* (black limes) or *oud* (my favourite fragrance). In fact, the longer I stayed away the more I craved these comforts, decorating my meals, my home and myself with things I once overlooked. It took some time, but London had begun to feel like home. To this day I don't feel overly British, but I don't feel overly foreign either. I also know that I'm not alone in this feeling, that so many of us come from multiple cultures, multiple faiths, multiple homes, who belong everywhere but don't belong anywhere at all. In this there is a wonderful world of freedom, of individuality.

Then, of course, there was my career. My intention had always been to bury myself deeply into my work, but I never once thought that running the Ottolenghi test kitchen, or co-authoring Ottolenghi cookbooks, was written in my cards. Self-limiting beliefs had always been my downfall, but this time I decided to have a little faith, and with it came a whole world of opportunity. At the test kitchen, I was given the space to grow, learn and navigate my way through life in London, alongside colleagues who have now become lifelong friends, and are off doing magnificent things in the industry. For my years at Ottolenghi, I will forever be grateful; it was the hand that reached out to me when I needed it most.

ON *BUKHOOR* AT THE VERY END

There's something to be said about Middle Eastern hospitality. A house visit, for example, doesn't really have a set time frame. 'Arrive at midday' means 'We expect you sometime between midday prayer [*salat el duhr*] and afternoon prayer [*salat el asr*]', while 'Stay for lunch' means 'We're not sure what time we're eating, but it'll go on until dark.' Then there's the food and drink, which are only ever served with abundance and generosity, a buffet and never a set menu. There is a time though, towards the end of all this, where your belly is full and your heart content, where conversation has lulled and well wishes are often repeated. With this comes the familiar whiff of *bukhoor*, or Arabic incense, the aroma warm and intense and the message clear: It's time to leave. And with that the visit ends, the guests shake hands and kiss, touch noses and close doors, the smoky scent of *bukhoor* following them all the way back to their own doorsteps.

Author's notes

Language

You'll notice a lot of Arabic thrown into the mix here, starting with the title of this book. If you're an Arabic speaker, you might even notice that the dialect is much different to yours. The reason I use Arabic throughout this book, and I might be terribly biased here, is because I think that Arabic is the most beautiful language in the world. The reason I bring up dialect is because it ties into one of my main purposes behind *Lugma*, in that it showcases the richness in diversity of the Arab world, so much so that even our dialects differ from one country to the other, or from one region to the next. What a beautiful thing to know and celebrate! The dialect here is mostly always Bahraini, except when conversing with Mama Hala on page 216, who's Lebanese and therefore speaks slightly differently. I don't tend to use classical Arabic, as although this is what we are all commonly taught at school, it's simply not the way most Arabs will converse.

Black limes, dried limes and what's the deal with *loomi*

Dried limes are the backbone of cooking throughout the Persian Gulf, Iraq and Iran. They're basically exactly as you'd think: limes that have been dried out until they're hollow. What makes them super special is their intense, slightly bitter citrus flavour that lends well to all sorts of dishes. Black limes are basically regular dried limes that have been heat treated to give them their dramatic black colour. Black limes and regular dried limes can mostly be used interchangeably except in specific dishes, such as traditional Bahraini Tikka, where meat is marinated in a black lime rub and then skewered and grilled over charcoal. You'll often hear different names thrown around for dried limes, such as *noomi basra* in Iraq, *limoo omani* in Oman or *loomi aswad* in Bahrain. Throughout the book I often just call them *loomi*. Dried limes are extremely versatile and, yes, you'll probably have to invest in a bag for *Lugma*, but I assure you that there are myriad ways in which to use them. They can be ground up to be used in a rub, such as with the Loomi Lemon Chicken (page 220), thrown into a dal (page 148) or a stew, made into a tea (page 55) or used as a subtle flavouring in various rice dishes (page 132). They can even make their way into desserts, such as the Labneh and Loomi Flan (page 240).

Using dried limes:

- When using dried limes whole, use a small sharp knife to pierce them two or three times so that they can soften and subtly release their flavour into the dish. When used in a stew, soup or dal, you can squeeze them to extract some of their liquid before discarding them. You could also chop up some of the softened lime and throw it back into the dish once cooked, but this really depends on preference.

- To grind dried limes into a powder, press down firmly on the lime with the palm of your hand to crush it. Open it up and pick out and remove the pips if you can – these are quite bitter so you want to discard them. The best way to grind the dried lime is to use a spice grinder, but you can otherwise use a pestle and mortar and some perseverance. I will usually grind about 3 limes at a time and keep the powder in a small jar. That way I can use it when called for in certain recipes and only have a small enough quantity that it always remains fresh. In the Gulf, you can buy ground black lime in the supermarkets, but I don't recommend anyone do this; as with any whole spice or aromatic, it tends to lose its potency as it sits.

Cumin, coriander and cardamom

Bahrainis are pretty vigilant with their spices. By this I mean, spices are often bought in their whole form, then washed of any dust, grit or sand, before being dried out very well in the sun. At this point they'll be stored individually in their jars, the most commonly used ones are toasted then ground up to quantity. And certain spices are combined to create different homemade spice mixes: one for fried fish, one for meat machboos, one for fish machboos, one for saloona (stew) – but only chicken saloona because the prawn one is different – one for biryani, the spicy kind, and so on. I don't think I'm as vigilant as this, but there's something to be said about using a pestle and mortar to grind your own cumin, coriander and cardamom seeds as and when you need them. Not only is this more economical, but it's also so much more flavourful and potent to do it this way.

What's up with Lebanese cucumbers?

Also known as Persian cucumbers in the US, they are thin-skinned, slightly sweet, crisp, not very watery and have small seeds that can easily be scraped down the centre. They are used throughout the Middle East, mainly in delicious salads, or chopped up alongside a breakfast spread. I urge you to use them, if you can source them, throughout this book as they really are my favourite cucumber variety. You can, however, swap them out with regular English cucumbers if you wish.

There's a whole chapter on rice

And, to be perfectly honest, it only just brushes the surface. Once rice was introduced to the Persian Gulf, it quickly became a staple dietary food alongside other grains like barley or *jareesh,* a type of cracked wheat similar to bulgur. Some say that bread still rivals rice in parts of the Middle East, and this is probably true. In Bahrain, however, rice consumption is high, and my own household is no exception. In my personal favourite carb ranking, rice sits at the very top.

You'll notice that for the majority of the rice dishes, I'll ask you to wash and soak the rice for a minimum of 20 minutes and up to 2 hours. This helps get rid of excess starch, so the rice grains remain nice and separated through the cooking process, and it also aids the digestion and absorption of minerals from the rice. A quick wash and soak while you prepare your other dinner ingredients will quickly pass by, and make your rice dish that much better.

Why Lebanese pita (*khobez Lebnani*)?

Not all pitas are created equally and when it comes to the bread used in *Lugma*, I'll always direct you towards Lebanese pita. Lebanese pita is thin and flat, rather than thick and fluffy like some pita can be, which makes it perfect for frying into thin and crisp pita chips for fattoush (page 71) or using as the crispy base for *tahdig* (page 168). It's also perfect for recipes not included in the book, such as *arayes*, a meat stuffed pita, or shawarma, no explanation needed. You can find them sold in most Middle Eastern supermarkets. If you can't find Lebanese pita, then you can use regular pita for things like pita chips (they won't be as thin and crisp) or other flatbreads like flour tortillas for *tahdig*. As for shawarma, well, there should be a very generous filling-to-bread ratio, so a fluffy pita simply will not do.

Fenugreek seeds, a pestle and mortar and whether you should invest in a spice grinder

Someone once asked me what I think the most underrated spice is, to which I answered 'fenugreek'. I use fenugreek seeds in quite a few recipes and their flavour truly is unmatched – sort of bitter, tangy and very fragrant. Combined with other spices and a little bit of sugar to balance it out, it creates the perfect spiced framework for stews (page 227), slow cooked meats (page 228) and burnt aubergines (page 151). A word of caution though: fenugreek seeds are hard and therefore hard to grind. I don't often recommend specific kitchen equipment but if there's one piece I'd say every keen cook should own, it's a spice grinder. They're small and compact and therefore easy to tuck away into your cupboards, but they're also just perfect to create your own spice mixes, grind your black limes and, if you're a coffee fanatic, grind your own beans as and when you need them. Pestles and mortars are a close second to this, although they require some might and, of course, a little bit of patience.

Tamarind pulp

I use tamarind pulp (from a block) as opposed to jarred paste or purée as it is basically the tamarind fruit pulp, stripped of its outer husk and then compressed with more pulp to create a block. It is ideal to use when you need to create your own paste or tamarind liquid, as you can control how concentrated or not you want it based on how much liquid is added. It also lasts for a long time in your cupboards if well sealed.

Wheat vermicelli

Not to be confused with rice vermicelli, which is more commonly found but also very different. Wheat vermicelli is often broken and toasted, to be used in soups (page 58), rice dishes (page 128) and the iconic breakfast dish of sweet vermicelli and salty eggs, aka Balaleet (page 30). You can find it in most Turkish, Middle Eastern or Southeast Asian grocery stores, but if you can't find it, then you can just as easily use broken-up pieces of angel hair pasta. It's not exactly the same in terms of thickness, but it will do.

The lack of hummus, and how dare there not be any shawarma

Yes, it is a Middle Eastern cookbook without hummus, a shawarma, a falafel or even a shakshuka in sight. And yes, I absolutely have done this on purpose. It's not that I don't enjoy all of the above, or that I don't have strong opinions on hummus or how random vegetables don't belong in shawarma (they really don't). It's simply because these foods are well-known, abundant and have a really great PR team. But there's more, so much more, and I'd love to push the more obscure dishes and ingredients forwards, so that Tomato Achar (page 269) becomes your favourite condiment or that Machboos (page 132) makes it onto your family dinner table, or that black limes become as familiar as za'atar or sumac.

Why I think *lugma* is the ultimate form of love

Someone you know goes to make you a sandwich. But it's not just any sandwich. They tear off a piece of bread from their plate, fold it in half and stuff it with a small piece of kofta, a slither of raw onion, some garlic yoghurt, a dash of hot sauce and then they hand it to you. It's one bite, one mouthful, delivered to you from their heart to their hand, from their hand to your soul. This is *lugma*, and it's the ultimate form of love.

BREAKFAST AND BRUNCH

Baith oo Tamat: Eggs and Tomatoes

I used to think that, with so many variations of eggs and tomatoes – Tunisian shakshuka, Turkish menemen, Chinese tomato egg stir-fry – there can't possibly be room for much more. But there is. There always is. In Bahrain we literally call this breakfast dish what it is: *baith* (egg) and *tamat* (tomato). But even within this very simple scope there isn't one actual way to make it: some people add spices, others simply refuse, some like more egg than tomato or vice versa, some are saucier, some drier. Pretty much everyone will agree that the eggs should be scrambled into the tomatoes at some point. I hope I'll be forgiven for not adhering to any of these rules. I'm reintroducing my favourite turmeric-fried eggs, and this easy, buttery tomato sauce for them to sit on. Serve with your bread of choice.

Serves 2

20g (¾oz) unsalted butter
300g (10½oz) Datterini or large cherry tomatoes
¾ tsp cumin seeds, roughly crushed using a pestle and mortar
2½ tbsp olive oil
⅓ tsp ground turmeric
4 large eggs
8 fresh curry leaves
1 tbsp roughly chopped coriander (cilantro) leaves, to serve
fine sea salt and freshly ground black pepper

Add the butter, tomatoes, cumin, 3 tablespoons of water, ½ teaspoon salt and a generous grind of black pepper to a medium, lidded sauté pan. Top with the lid, then place over a medium-low heat and leave to cook undisturbed for 10 minutes, to soften the tomatoes. Remove the lid, turn up the heat to medium-high and cook for 4 minutes more, or until the tomatoes have burst and collapsed very slightly and the sauce has homogenized. Keep warm over a very low heat while you fry the eggs.

Add the oil and turmeric to a large frying pan (skillet), stirring to combine and place over a medium-high heat. Once hot, but not smoking, crack in the eggs and sprinkle with a pinch each of salt and pepper. Use a spatula to separate the whites so the eggs are not joined together and fry for 3–4 minutes, spooning some of the oil over the whites. You want the eggs to be crispy around the edges and the yolk to be runny – fry them for longer if you like your eggs more cooked.

When ready, spoon the tomato mixture onto a medium serving platter, then use a spatula to transfer the fried eggs on top, leaving the oil in the pan. Quickly return the pan to a medium-high heat and add the curry leaves, frying for just 30–60 seconds, until translucent. Spoon these over the eggs (plus any of the oil, if you wish), and sprinkle with the coriander. Serve right away.

Arabic Baked Beans

Quick dinners as a kid were often baked beans on toast, smothered in cheddar and stuck under a hot grill until all melty. I could never be patient enough to wait either, and would burn my tongue on hot cheese lava and tomato sauce (worth it). It's not uncommon to find some kind of white bean at a Middle Eastern breakfast table, stewed in a tomato-based sauce. This recipe is a happy amalgamation of the two. You can scoop it right out of the pan with warm pitas, or spoon it onto sourdough or baked potatoes and serve it for breakfast, lunch or even dinner.

Serves 4

3 plum tomatoes (350g/12oz)
3 tbsp olive oil
1 onion, very finely chopped (180g/6¼oz)
4 garlic cloves, finely grated
25g (1oz) fresh ginger, peeled and finely grated
1 green chilli, finely chopped, seeds and all
2 tsp cumin seeds, finely crushed using a pestle and mortar
2 tsp coriander seeds, finely crushed using a pestle and mortar
1 tsp paprika
3 tbsp tomato paste (purée)
1 tsp sugar
2 x 400g (14oz) cans cannellini beans, rinsed and drained (480g/1lb 10oz)
25g (1oz) fresh coriander (cilantro), finely chopped
120g (4½oz) labneh, bought or homemade (see page 101, made without the garlic), or cream cheese
120g (4½oz) mature cheddar, roughly grated (shredded)
fine sea salt and freshly ground black pepper

For the topping
3 tbsp olive oil
3 garlic cloves, finely chopped
15g (½oz) fresh ginger, peeled and finely chopped
3 spring onions (scallions), green parts only, finely chopped

Use a small knife to cut around and remove the tomato stems then make a small 'X' incision on the opposite end. Place in a medium heatproof bowl and pour over enough boiling water to cover by a couple of centimetres (an inch). Leave for about 2–3 minutes, or just until the tomato skins visibly start to peel off. Drain, then carefully remove and discard the skins. Cut the tomatoes into quarters and set aside.

Preheat the oven to its highest setting, placing a rack on the top shelf.

In a large, cast-iron pan (or ovenproof sauté pan), heat the oil over a medium-high heat. Add the onion and ⅛ teaspoon of salt, turn down the heat to medium and cook for 10 minutes, stirring occasionally, until softened and very lightly coloured. Add the garlic, ginger, green chilli, spices and tomato paste and cook for 2–3 minutes more, stirring often, until deeply red. Pour in 450ml (16fl oz) of water, then stir in the sugar, beans, tomatoes, ¾ teaspoon salt and a good grind of pepper. Bring to a simmer and cook for about 12 minutes, stirring occasionally, or until the tomatoes are only just starting to lose their shape and the sauce has thickened just slightly. Stir in the coriander and remove from the heat. Top evenly with spoonfuls of the labneh (or cream cheese) then sprinkle with the cheddar. Bake for 12–15 minutes, or until browned and bubbling.

Meanwhile, make the topping. Add all the ingredients plus a tiny pinch of salt to a small frying pan (skillet) and place over a medium-low heat. Cook gently for about 12–15 minutes, stirring occasionally, or until softened and fragrant. You don't want it to colour at all, so if it starts to bubble too much, turn down the heat to low. Transfer to a bowl.

When the beans are ready, spoon the topping all over the beans and serve warm.

Balaleet: Sweet Noodles and Salty Eggs

Balaleet is ingrained into the breakfast offering throughout many of the Gulf countries. I've often felt like this dish needs to come with its own caveat, something along the lines of: 'I know it sounds odd but I promise it's really, really delicious', but with a much punchier tagline. It's not a combo you'd often think of, but it works, if you're open to straddling that line between slightly sweet but also savoury. I'd serve this on weekends or special occasions, where there's plenty of time for a cup of tea afterwards. If you can't get hold of wheat vermicelli noodles, you can use angel hair pasta instead – less traditional, but still okay.

Serves 4

180g (6¼oz) wheat vermicelli noodles, broken into 4–5cm (about 2in) pieces
40g (1½oz) unsalted butter
seeds from 12 cardamom pods, finely crushed using a pestle and mortar
¼ tsp tightly packed saffron threads, finely crushed, soaked in 2 tbsp hot water
1 tsp rosewater
45g (1½oz) caster (granulated) sugar
4 large eggs
¼ tsp ground turmeric
4 tsp olive oil
2 tbsp finely sliced spring onions (scallions)
fine sea salt and freshly ground black pepper

Place a large, lidded sauté pan over a medium heat. Once hot, add half the vermicelli noodles and toast, stirring occasionally at first then more frequently until deeply browned, about 6–7 minutes. Transfer to a plate, then repeat with the remaining noodles. Don't worry if some are more coloured than others – this is the desired effect. Return all the noodles to the pan, increasing the heat to medium-high, and pour over enough water to cover by a couple of centimetres (an inch). Top with the lid and cook for just 4 minutes, or until the noodles are just cooked through but not overly soft. Drain through a sieve (strainer). Return the pan to a medium-high heat (don't worry if some of the noodles are stuck to the base), add the butter and cardamom and cook until the butter has melted. Add back the noodles with the saffron mixture, rosewater and sugar and cook, stirring occasionally with a spatula, until the sugar has dissolved and the noodles begin to caramelize in places, about 5–7 minutes. Transfer to a large platter while you quickly make the eggs.

In a jug beat together the eggs, turmeric, ½ teaspoon of salt and a very generous grind of pepper.

Heat a medium, non-stick frying pan (skillet) with 1 teaspoon of the oil over a medium-high heat. Once the oil is hot, add a quarter of the beaten egg mixture, swirling to cover the base and cook for just 30 seconds, or until nicely browned on the bottom and starting to dry around the centre. Use a spatula to flip the omelette over and cook for about 20 seconds more. Transfer to a plate and continue with the remaining oil and egg mixture to make 4 omelettes in total. Loosely scrunch each omelette as you would a tissue and place them over the noodles. Sprinkle with the spring onions followed by another good grind of pepper and serve warm.

BREAKFAST AND BRUNCH

'Cheese and Olives': Halloumi with Spicy Olives and Walnuts

This works really well for brunch, alongside soft-boiled eggs, but can just as easily be eaten as a light lunch or dinner. Feel free to make this vegan, by swapping out the halloumi for fried and salted tofu.

Serves 4

For the salsa
4 tbsp olive oil
3 garlic cloves, finely chopped
2 tsp coriander seeds, roughly crushed using a pestle and mortar
1 tsp Aleppo chilli flakes
70g (2½oz) jarred red (bell) peppers, very finely chopped
1 tbsp rose harissa
2 tbsp apple cider vinegar
2 tsp maple syrup
50g (1¾oz) walnuts, well toasted and roughly chopped into 1cm (½in) pieces
70g (2½oz) pitted Nocellara olives, roughly chopped
5g (⅛oz) mint leaves, roughly chopped
10g (¼oz) parsley leaves, roughly chopped
2 tsp pomegranate molasses

For the halloumi
2 x 225g (8oz) blocks of halloumi, drained
2 tbsp olive oil
2 tsp maple syrup

Make the salsa by adding the oil and garlic to a small frying pan (skillet) and placing it over a medium heat. Cook until beginning to bubble and smell fragrant, about 1½ minutes, then add the coriander seeds and chilli and cook for about 30 seconds more. Stir in the peppers, harissa, vinegar and maple syrup and cook for 5 minutes. Set aside to cool to room temperature, then transfer to a large bowl, add the remaining ingredients and mix to combine.

Preheat the oven to 180°C fan/200°C/400°F/Gas mark 6.

Halve each of the halloumi blocks lengthways (so they are the same shape, but thinner now) to give you four rectangular pieces. Pat them well dry. Use a small sharp knife to make a criss-cross pattern across one side of each piece, with incisions about 1.5cm (⅝in) deep.

Heat the oil in a medium frying pan over a medium-high heat. Add the halloumi pieces and fry until nicely golden on both sides, about 4–5 minutes in total. Transfer to a small tray, criss-cross side up, and pour over the excess oil left in the pan, followed by the maple syrup. Bake for 7 minutes, or until really nicely softened through the centre.

Transfer to a plate, pouring over any juices left in the tray, then spoon over the salsa. Serve right away, while the halloumi is still warm.

Pancakes on Tuesday

I've watched Jayne make her pancakes more times than I can count: 125g of plain flour, 1 medium egg, 300 millilitres of milk, 1 tablespoon of melted butter, *oh, and a tiny pinch of salt*, she nods. She makes them lacy thin, more like a French crêpe than an American pancake, stacking them between pieces of baking paper before moving on to make another. She moves fast, so they stay warm, and as she finishes she'll douse them in fresh lemon juice and a sprinkling of sugar. We eat them quickly, the sugar still maintaining its crunch and the lemon juice sour but only just enough. It's two per person, a sensible portion really, but I always wish it was three. Just like that, pancake Tuesday is over and I'll marvel at the idea of having to wait another year.

Jayne says that her love of pancakes stems from a week spent in France when she was little, a school trip to Brittany and Normandy. She begged her parents to let her go even though she knew it would make things tight for them at home, her curiosity for the world too overwhelming to keep her put. She loved that trip and the food memories she came back with, the silkiest *purée de pommes* and the crêpes! I'd often listen to Jayne talk about her childhood, her years growing up in rural England, being born in a farmhouse with secret passageways and grand fireplaces. She'd talk about riding her bike in the countryside, playing cricket and netball, going blackberry-picking or holidaying in Scotland, all things that were so unfamiliar to my own experiences, exotic almost. But, as destiny had it, Jayne ended up in Bahrain, and this is the story I'll often set my heart on.

Jayne met her husband in a small-town college in Buckinghamshire. At the time, he had a full head of thick, black messy curls, an 80s moustache, bushy eyebrows and big, brown kind eyes. His English was, for want of a better word, questionable. She later went on to find out that he was from Bahrain and somehow, in all their differences, this unlikely pair had found common ground. Jayne never looked back.

Her transition wasn't always smooth sailing. Bahrain was exciting but she also approached it with a little trepidation: a new culture, new language, new way of life. Not to mention, it was awfully hot. But it was also kind, welcoming, very cosmopolitan and, more than anything, it had a slow, island-pace of life. This last part she could relate to: moving from one small community in the Midlands, to another equally small community in the Persian Gulf. Eventually she settled, had her two girls, learnt some Arabic and made friends just like her, many of them also European and married to Middle Eastern men. Their kids they call 'halfies' and, yes, there are quite a few of us around.

The pancakes, though, are an important part to this story. If Bahraini food and English food were placed on a spectrum, there would be very little overlap, if any at all. Jayne learnt this the hard way, some flavours she couldn't automatically warm to, specifically dishes such as *ghoozi*, a whole lamb served over rice, or *harees*, a porridge of beaten cracked wheat, mutton and ghee. But then there were things that she really enjoyed, like *mehyawa* (page 270), a type of fermented fish condiment, and *mana'eesh* (page 47), baked flatbreads with various toppings. She began teaching herself how to cook: Madhur Jaffrey's chicken curry with cardamom, Ken Hom's beef stir-fry, Anissa Helou's fattoush and tabbouleh. As the years went by, her cookbook collection steadily grew, as did her pantry, her spice rack brimming with more jars than she had room for. She set herself challenges, like mastering how to cook rice or learning how to get the crispy bits at the bottom of the pot (*tahdig*). Among all of this though, she held on to who she was, what she knew, the reliable comforts she could always turn to: scones with jam and butter, proper cauliflower cheese, baked beans on toast, foolproof Victoria sponges and, most importantly, pancakes. Always with lemon and sugar.

This is a story about Vanessa Jayne Murad, my mum, who, without really intending to, instilled in me a love of pancakes, a love of travel and, to no surprise, a love of food. Here's to taking big, blind, 6,000-kilometre leaps of faith, from one side of the world to the other, our journeys in reverse.

Cardamom Pancakes with Honey Lime Syrup

I wouldn't say I had a particularly English upbringing, but there were two things my mum held on to fiercely when it came to her children celebrating cultural holidays. Of the utmost importance was Christmas, of course, but Pancake Day came a close second. I'm not really sure why this day mattered so much, but I have a sneaking suspicion it's to do with eating pancakes for dinner, lovingly doused in lemon and sugar. Yeasted pancakes mixed with saffron and cardamom (called *chebab*) are typical of Gulf countries, but I must confess I much prefer these lacy thin crêpes. So here's an ode to Mum's pancakes, with a bit of a twist.

Serves 4

110g (3¾oz) plain (all-purpose) flour
⅛ tsp fine sea salt
seeds from 15 cardamom pods, finely crushed using a pestle and mortar
2 large eggs
280ml (9¾fl oz) whole milk
20g (¾oz) unsalted butter, melted, plus an extra 30g (1oz) for frying
25g (1oz) pistachios, toasted
1½ tsp caster (granulated) sugar
1½ tsp finely grated lime zest (the limes are used for the syrup)

For the honey lime syrup
100g (3½oz) runny honey
30g (1oz) unsalted butter, cut into cubes
5 tbsp lime juice (from about 3 limes)
1 tsp orange blossom water

Sift the flour into a medium bowl, then whisk with the salt and two-thirds of the crushed cardamom. Make a well in the centre, crack in the eggs, then pour in the milk. Whisk for a couple of minutes until smooth and lump-free, then whisk in the melted butter to incorporate. Leave to rest for 20 minutes.

Meanwhile, roughly crush the pistachios using a pestle and mortar. Add the sugar, lime zest and remaining cardamom and crush just to combine. Set aside.

Heat a 24cm (9½in) crêpe pan or similar non-stick pan over a medium-high heat. Add a small dot of butter, swirling to spread it around the pan, then add about 3 tablespoons of the batter (two-thirds of a ladle) to the centre of the pan and swirl to fill the dimensions of the pan. Cook for about 1–1½ minutes, until nicely browned in places, then flip over and cook for 30 seconds more. Transfer to a large tray or plate, and gently fold in half and then in half again to form a triangle. Continue this way with all the batter (give the batter a little mix), adding a dot of butter to the pan each time, to make 8 pancakes in total.

To make the syrup, add the honey to a large, lidded sauté pan and place it over a medium heat. Cook for 10–12 minutes, stirring occasionally with a spatula, or until bubbling and a deep amber caramel. Carefully add the butter cubes, stirring to melt. Pour in the lime juice and 2 tablespoons of water and cook for 3 minutes more, or until the sauce is nice and glossy. Stir in the orange blossom water, then slide in the pancakes (don't worry if they're overlapping or not fully submerged), top with the lid and cook for 2 minutes, just to heat through. Transfer the pancakes to a large platter, pouring over any syrup left in the pan. Sprinkle with the pistachio mixture and serve warm.

Fried Eggs with Mehyawa and Crispy Sage

This is my favourite way to use *mehyawa*, a fermented fish condiment made with dried sardines and plenty of spices, which you can read about on page 270. Mehyawa is hard to come by unless, like me, you frequently smuggle some into your suitcase and hope, more than anything, that this bottle of fish sauce doesn't smash to pieces on the flight back from Bahrain. Luckily for you, and me really, I've come up with a cheat's mehyawa that you can make in 15 minutes from start to finish (see page 270) and, having put it to the test in front of a panel of very honest Bahrainis, I'm happy to report that it passed with flying colours. For these eggs I've added fried sage, inspired by the sage plant that was going a bit mad in my garden. Although untraditional, the leaves really complement the salty mehyawa.

Serves 1–2

1½ tbsp olive oil
2 large eggs
A small handful of fresh sage leaves
1 tbsp Mehyawa (page 270)
freshly ground black pepper

Heat the oil in a medium non-stick frying pan (skillet) over a medium-high heat. Once hot, crack in the eggs, one at a time, and season generously with pepper (but no salt). Fry for about 3 minutes, using a spoon to baste the tops with oil, or until the egg whites are cooked through and browned around the edges, and the yolks are nice and runny (or cook for longer, depending on how you like your eggs). Towards the last 30 seconds, sprinkle the sage leaves into the oil and fry until translucent. When ready, transfer the eggs and sage leaves to a plate with a slotted spoon, leaving behind the oil in the pan. Quickly mix the mehyawa into the hot oil and then spoon this all over the eggs. Serve right away.

Ful with Chickpeas and Tahini

You'll find variations of *ful* on most breakfast menus in all corners of the Middle East. It's a dish made with fava beans and is perfectly filling and completely vegan; all you need is some pita bread to scoop it all up. This variation includes chickpeas and various toppings, which I think make it all the more special, but you can easily play around with toppings and spices to suit your own palate. I usually recommend using canned fava beans as opposed to cooking dried ones from scratch, as they can be quite a faff and cook unevenly. Allow some extra time to remove all the skins, as they are tough and hard to digest. If you can't find broad beans, then feel free to use a couple of cans of unpeeled pinto beans (320g/11¼oz drained weight) instead.

Serves 4–6

5 tbsp olive oil, plus extra to serve (optional)
4 garlic cloves, crushed
1 green chilli, finely chopped, seeds and all (10g/¼oz)
2 tsp cumin seeds, finely ground using a pestle and mortar
1½ tsp coriander seeds, finely ground using a pestle and mortar
2 x 400g (14oz) cans broad beans (fava beans), drained and skins removed
½ jar or 1 x 400g/14oz can good-quality chickpeas (garbanzo beans) (240g/8½oz drained)
2½ tbsp lemon juice
70g (2½oz) tahini
2 plum tomatoes, roughly grated (shredded) and skins discarded (180g/6¼oz)
10g (¼oz) coriander (cilantro), roughly chopped
10g (¼oz) parsley, roughly chopped
½ tsp Aleppo chilli flakes, to serve
fine sea salt and freshly ground black pepper

Add 2 tablespoons of the oil, three-quarters of the garlic, all the green chilli and the spices to a medium saucepan then place it over a medium-high heat. Cook for about 3 minutes, stirring often, until fragrant and the garlic is just beginning to colour. Add the beans and chickpeas, 300ml (10½fl oz) of water, ¾ teaspoon of salt and a good grind of pepper and bring to a simmer. Once simmering, turn down the heat to medium and cook gently for 10 minutes, stirring occasionally. The mixture will thicken slightly; use a spoon to gently mash some of the beans to help this along. You don't want the mixture to be too thick – still easily spoonable – so, if necessary, add a splash more water. Off the heat, stir in 1 tablespoon of the lemon juice.

Meanwhile, add the tahini to a medium bowl with the remaining garlic and lemon juice, 4 tablespoons of water and ⅛ teaspoon of salt, then whisk together until you have a smooth and pourable sauce.

Place the grated tomatoes into a sieve to drain them of their liquid. Transfer the pulp to a small bowl and season with ¼ teaspoon salt and a good grind of pepper.

Add the herbs and remaining 3 tablespoons of oil to the bowl of a small food processor and blitz until smooth.

When cooked, transfer the ful mixture to a large shallow bowl. Drizzle over the tahini sauce, followed by the grated tomato, herb oil and Aleppo chilli. Drizzle over some extra olive oil if you like. Serve warm.

Liver and Charred Onions in a Squishy Bun

When I was little I'd eat liver sandwiches with my dad, from a hole-in-the-wall type shop, and gobble them up greedily in the car. Dad kept it to himself that it was in fact liver that I was eating. In hindsight, this was probably for the best as I was a bit of a picky eater once upon a time, and perhaps I would've never appreciated how good liver can taste when done right. I don't eat liver that often nowadays but when I do, it's this way and this way only. We typically eat this for breakfast, but you can have it any time of the day.

Serves 2 · Soaking time: 1–2 hours

250ml (9fl oz) whole milk
200g (7oz) calf's liver
1¼ tsp ground black lime
1 tsp cumin seeds, finely crushed using a pestle and mortar
⅓ tsp ground cinnamon
1¼ tsp soft light brown sugar
1 small onion, halved and cut into 1.5cm (⅝in) thick half-moons (150g/5½oz)
1½ tbsp olive oil, plus extra to dress
1½ tbsp lemon juice
20g (¾oz) unsalted butter
fine sea salt and freshly ground black pepper

To serve
30g (1oz) rocket (arugula) leaves
2 squishy bread buns, lightly toasted

Add the milk and liver to a medium bowl, cover and leave in the refrigerator to soak for 1–2 hours. Drain the liver (discard the milk) and pat with paper towels to dry. Use a sharp knife to cut into 1.5–2cm (⅝–¾in) strips, trimming off and discarding any sinew.

In a medium bowl combine the black lime, spices, sugar and ½ teaspoon salt. Add the liver and toss to coat.

Heat a medium frying pan (skillet) over a medium-high heat. Once very hot, add the onion slices, keeping them intact for ease, and cook to char, about 2½ minutes per side. Once nicely browned in places, add ½ tablespoon of the oil and ⅛ teaspoon of salt, cook for another minute, then transfer to a plate. You want the onion to be just cooked with a slight bite.

Add the remaining tablespoon of oil to the pan and return to a medium-high heat (you want the pan very hot at this point). Add the liver and cook for 45 seconds, turning quickly to brown on all sides. Working quickly, stir back in the onion with the lemon juice and butter and cook for just 20 seconds, then remove from the heat and immediately transfer to a serving plate.

Lightly dress the rocket with a drizzle of oil and season with a pinch each of salt and pepper, then pile this to one side of the plate. Serve right away, with the squishy buns to form your own sandwich.

Onion and Potato Frittata with Charred Pepper Salsa

This makes for a really delicious brunch dish, on a day when you have a little more time and are craving a substantial start to your morning. The salad is optional, but I do like to serve this with something fresh, so feel free to rustle up a quick salad with whatever you might have to hand to eat alongside.

Serves 4

For the salsa
50g (1¾oz) jalapeño chillies, pierced a couple times with a knife
1 green (bell) pepper, stem and seeds removed, quartered (150g/5½oz)
4 tbsp olive oil, plus 1 tsp for roasting
2 tsp coriander seeds, toasted and roughly crushed using a pestle and mortar
1 tbsp lime juice
10g (¼oz) fresh coriander (cilantro) leaves, finely chopped

For the frittata
350g (12oz) baking potato (about 1 large)
5 tbsp olive oil
2 large onions, halved, then cut into 0.5cm (¼in) half-moons (480g/1lb 10oz)
4 garlic cloves, crushed
½ tsp ground turmeric
2 tsp cumin seeds, finely crushed using a pestle and mortar
6 large eggs
75g (2½oz) thick Greek yoghurt
fine sea salt and freshly ground black pepper

For the salad (optional)
500g (1lb 2oz) ripe heirloom tomatoes, or other in-season tomatoes, cut into bite-sized chunks
½ red onion, thinly sliced (75g/2½oz)
2 tsp sumac
1 tbsp olive oil

Preheat the oven to 220°C fan/240°C/475°F/Gas mark 9.

For the salsa, place the jalapeños and green pepper on a baking tray and toss with the teaspoon of oil. Roast for 10 minutes, or until the jalapeños have browned slightly. Remove them from the tray and return the pepper to the oven for 10 minutes, or until charred and softened. Once cool enough to handle, peel the pepper and finely chop the flesh. Remove the stem and seeds from the chillies and finely chop the flesh and skins until almost paste-like. Add both to a bowl with the remaining salsa ingredients and ¼ teaspoon salt. Stir, then set aside.

Meanwhile, place the potato into a lidded saucepan and pour over enough water to cover by about 5cm (2in). Bring to the boil, then turn down the heat to medium, cover and boil for about 25–30 minutes, or until a knife is easily inserted into the centre. Drain and, when cool enough to handle, peel, then roughly chop into 3cm (1¼in) cubes.

Heat 3 tablespoons of the oil in a lidded, non-stick sauté pan (about 20cm/8in diameter) over a medium-high heat. Stir in the onions and ¼ teaspoon salt, turn down to medium heat and cook for 22 minutes, stirring occasionally, or until softened but not browned – adjust the heat if necessary. Add the garlic and spices and cook for 3 minutes, then set aside to cool slightly, about 15 minutes.

In a large bowl beat together the eggs, yoghurt, ¾ teaspoon salt and a very generous grind of pepper until smooth. Stir in the cooled onion mixture and the potato. Add the remaining 2 tablespoons of oil to the wiped-out sauté pan and heat over a medium heat. Pour in the egg mixture, using a spatula to distribute everything evenly. Cover, turn down the heat to medium-low and cook for 10 minutes, rotating the pan a few times to ensure even browning. Remove the lid, turn the heat back up to medium, and cook for 7 minutes more, rotating the pan once, or until the edges look brown and the middle is starting to set. Run a spatula around the sides of the frittata (it should easily release) and then, very gently, slide the frittata onto a plate, browned side down. Place a similar-sized plate on top and flip it so the browned side is now facing upwards. Gently slide the frittata back into your pan and cook for about 6 minutes more, or just until the bottom takes on a little colour and the centre is cooked through.

At this point, make the salad by tossing together all the ingredients with a good pinch of salt (taste for seasoning) and transfer to a serving bowl. Slide the frittata out onto a large serving plate and spoon the salsa all over the top. Serve warm or at room temperature, with the salad to eat alongside.

BREAKFAST AND BRUNCH

MANA'EESH – TWO WAYS

Cheesy Leek and Za'atar Fatayer

These *fatayer* are similar to the Arabic pizza (see overleaf), except that they're a folded-over flatbread and stuffed, like calzone. You can make the dough in the morning for more of a brunch affair, or leave the dough to prove overnight in the refrigerator. If you love za'atar as much as I do, then make a quick za'atar oil by mixing together a spoonful of za'atar with a generous amount of good-quality extra virgin olive oil and use this to dip your fatayer into.

Makes 4 · Proving time: 2 hours 20 minutes, or overnight

For the fatayer
190ml (6½fl oz) lukewarm water
¾ tsp fast-action dried yeast
2 tsp olive oil, plus extra for greasing
2 tsp sugar
300g (10½oz) plain (all-purpose) flour, plus extra for shaping
½ tsp salt

For the filling
3 leeks, white and light green parts only, halved, cleaned and thinly sliced (320g/11¼oz)
1 tbsp olive oil
20g (¾oz) za'atar, plus 4 tsp for baking
150g (5½oz) labneh, bought or homemade (see page 101)
100g (3½oz) feta, roughly crumbled
125g (4¼oz) buffalo mozzarella, patted dry and thinly sliced
1 egg yolk, beaten with 1 tsp water
fine sea salt

Add all the fatayer ingredients to a stand mixer, fitted with the dough hook, and mix on medium-low speed for about 1½ minutes or until the dough comes together into a shaggy ball. Increase the speed to medium-high and continue to mix for 6 minutes or until the dough comes away from the sides of the bowl and is nice and soft. Lightly grease a medium bowl with some oil, then use well-greased hands to tip the dough into it. Lightly grease the top as well. Cover with a clean tea towel and leave in a warm place (like on top of the fridge) to prove for 2 hours; it will double in size. Alternatively, put in the refrigerator and leave to prove overnight (and allow to come to room temperature before working the dough again).

Meanwhile, put the leeks, oil and ½ teaspoon salt in a medium saucepan and top with a lid. Place over a medium heat and cook for about 15 minutes, stirring 2–3 times throughout, until the leeks are completely softened but not at all coloured. Off the heat, stir in the 20g (¾oz) of za'atar and set aside to cool.

Preheat the oven to 230°C fan/250°C/500°F/Gas mark 9. Once the dough has risen, dust a clean work surface with flour and divide the dough into 4 equal pieces, shaping each into a ball. Cover with a tea towel and let rest for 15 minutes. Meanwhile, place a large tray in the oven to heat up.

Liberally dust your work surface and rolling pin with flour and, working one ball at a time, roll out the dough into roughly a 20cm (8in) disc. Spread with a quarter of the labneh, leaving a 1.5cm (⅝in) border. Top one half of the labneh with a quarter of the feta, a quarter of the leek mixture and a quarter of the mozzarella. Fold over the other half so the filling is now encased. Pinch together the ends and either roll them up slightly or crimp with your fingers by pulling small sections of dough and then folding them up (this isn't necessary, but looks nice). Repeat to make a second (you'll bake two at a time).

When ready to bake, dust the hot tray with flour. Very carefully use a spatula to lift the two doughs onto the tray, spacing them nicely apart. Brush the beaten egg yolk all over and then sprinkle each with 1 teaspoon of za'atar. Finally, use kitchen scissors or a small sharp knife to make two small snips into the top, to let some steam escape when baking. Bake for 10–12 minutes, rotating the pan or tray halfway, until deeply golden. Carefully transfer to a wire rack to cool while you assemble and bake the remaining two.

MANA'EESH – TWO WAYS

Arabic Pizza: Mana'eesh with Red Pepper, Onions and Akkawi

Arabic pizza is actually *mana'eesh*, a flatbread with various toppings, but as a kid I was convinced that this meant I was eating pizza for breakfast, especially when we had this version. Akkawi hasn't had its debut moment in the food world yet, for reasons I can't quite wrap my head around. It's a salty Palestinian cheese soaked in brine, from the city of Akka. It has a mild taste and melts really nicely, which is why it works so well on mana'eesh or the very popular Arabic dessert *knafeh*. You find akkawi in most Middle Eastern supermarkets and it's well worth sourcing for this recipe, as it really is what makes it stand out. (You can still make this using mozzarella and a sprinkle of grated halloumi, but the result won't be quite the same.) I like to serve it with marinated olives and chopped cucumber and tomatoes.

Makes 4 · Proving time: 2 hours 15 minutes, or overnight · Soaking time: 2 hours

For the dough
190ml (6½fl oz) lukewarm water
¾ tsp fast-action dried yeast
2 tsp olive oil, plus extra for greasing
2 tsp caster (granulated) sugar
300g (10½oz) plain (all-purpose) flour, plus extra for dusting
½ tsp fine sea salt
2 tbsp olive oil, plus extra for greasing

For the marinated olives
3 tbsp olive oil
2 garlic cloves, finely chopped
4 strips of finely shaved unwaxed lemon zest
1 tsp Aleppo chilli flakes
1 tsp coriander seeds, roughly crushed using a pestle and mortar
1 tsp dried oregano
200g (7oz) pitted black and green olives (I like Kalamata and Nocellara)
1½ tbsp parsley leaves, finely chopped

Continued ingredients overleaf

First, soak the akkawi. Place the akkawi in a bowl and cover with cold water. Leave to soak for about 2 hours, changing the water 2–3 times, which will help to remove the excess salt. When ready, drain and pat dry, then finely chop.

Meanwhile, add all the dough ingredients to a stand mixer, with the dough hook in place, and mix on medium-low speed for about 90 seconds or until the dough comes together into a shaggy ball. Increase the speed to medium-high and continue to mix for 6 minutes or until the dough comes away from the sides of the bowl and is nice and soft. Lightly grease a medium bowl with some oil, then use well-greased hands to tip the dough into it, lightly greasing the top as well. Cover with a tea towel and leave in a warm place in your kitchen (like on top of the fridge) to rise for 1–1½ hours – it will double in size. Alternatively, refrigerate and let rise in the fridge overnight. If refrigerating, allow to come to room temperature before working with the dough again.

For the olives, add the oil, garlic, lemon strips, spices and oregano to a small frying pan (skillet) and place it over a medium-low heat. Leave to gently cook for about 10 minutes, or until the garlic has softened and the mixture is fragrant. If it starts to bubble at all, turn down the heat to low. Transfer to a bowl, stir in the olives and set aside to cool completely. Once cool, stir in the parsley.

Continued overleaf

For the topping
150g (5½oz) akkawi
2½ tbsp olive oil
2 small onions, finely chopped (300g/10½oz)
3 garlic cloves, crushed
1½ tbsp mild Turkish red pepper paste (biber salçası)
1 tsp cumin seeds, roughly crushed using a pestle and mortar
1 tsp caraway seeds, roughly crushed using a pestle and mortar
1 large plum tomato, roughly grated (shredded) and skins discarded
80g (2¾oz) buffalo mozzarella, thinly sliced
fine sea salt

For the topping, heat the oil in a medium sauté pan over a medium-high heat. Add the onions and ⅛ teaspoon of salt, then turn down the heat to medium and cook for about 20–25 minutes, stirring occasionally, or until very soft but only lightly coloured (lower the heat if necessary). Turn up the heat to medium-high then add the garlic, red pepper paste and spices and cook for 2 minutes more, until fragrant. Stir in the tomato and cook for 5 minutes, stirring occasionally, or until thickened. Set aside to cool.

Preheat the oven to 230°C fan/250°C/500°F/Gas mark 9.

Once the dough has risen, dust a clean work surface with flour and divide the dough into 4 equal pieces, shaping each into a ball. Cover with a tea towel and let rest for 15 minutes. Meanwhile, place 2 large trays in the oven to heat up.

Roll out each dough ball into a disc around 20cm (8in) in diameter – don't worry if the rounds aren't perfect; I actually prefer them this way. Working quickly, remove the trays from the oven and dust them with flour. Carefully place two of the discs onto each tray (or, if they won't fit, then bake two at a time), making sure they don't touch. Spread the onion mixture onto each, leaving a 1.5cm (⅝in) border, then top evenly with the akkawi and mozzarella. Bake for 8–10 minutes, or until the dough is cooked through and the cheese is bubbling and nicely browned. Serve warm, with the marinated olives spooned on top or to eat alongside.

Chai Culture

Chai o gahwa? (Tea or coffee?), is the typical question asked after breakfast, lunch, mid-morning, late afternoon and sometimes also dinner. As lunch is typically the main meal for many Bahraini households, you'll see two large flasks placed on the coffee table, one to be poured into an *istikana*, a little glass tea cup, and the other to be poured into a *finyal*, a small coffee cup. Both are an important part of the culture and social interaction, but coffee, or *gahwa* – particularly Bahraini coffee – is a bit more complicated to make at home. Also, since my tea obsession might also stem from my English roots, it only feels appropriate to include a little ode to tea here. It's not quite builder's tea, but these are my three favourite types of chai.

CHAI KARAK

Makes 2 mugs

600ml (21fl oz) water
5g (⅛oz) fresh, unpeeled ginger, thinly sliced
8 cardamom pods, bashed open
4 cloves
½ cinnamon stick
4 tsp loose-leaf Assam tea
300g (10½oz) evaporated milk
sugar, to taste

Chai karak came to the Gulf countries via India and took this part of the world by storm. You'll find karak and chapati shops pretty much everywhere, small takeaway shops selling those two very things – and they really do go hand in hand. I like to add lots of different spices but some swear by only adding cardamom. I also use evaporated milk, as I feel it has the edge here over whole milk. Chai karak will be frothed up by pouring it from a height several times – this is when you know you're in safe hands, and the chai guys know what they're doing.

―――――――

Add the water, ginger and whole spices to a small saucepan and bring to the boil over a medium-high heat. Once boiling, add the tea leaves and boil for 4 minutes. Turn down the heat to medium-low and add the evaporated milk. Cook gently for 20 minutes, stirring occasionally so the bottom doesn't catch. Strain into a separate pan, pushing down on the solids to extract as much flavourful liquid as possible. Add sugar to taste.

To get that signature frothy *chai karak* appearance, pour the tea into a cup then into the pan back and forth a few times until you get nice bubbles. Divide between two cups and drink right away.

BREAKFAST AND BRUNCH 53

CHAI HAMAR

Makes 4 small cups

Steeping time: 20 minutes

2 tbsp sugar
1 tbsp loose-leaf Assam tea
1/8 tsp loosely packed saffron threads, finely ground
1 tsp rosewater

This tea occupies a special place in my heart, as we always had it every year on National Day, when, as a family, we'd go watch the fireworks together. My dad would make his *dellat chai*, or flask of tea, and since National Day is just nine days before Christmas, my mum would always bake her gingerbread men. We'd park the car nearby, sit on the bonnet and dunk gingerbread into chai hamar while the fireworks sparkled in the sky above us. These days are still some of my fondest memories. Some will not add saffron to their chai hamar but this is the way I grew up drinking it. If you prefer your tea weaker, then start with 2 teaspoons of leaves, and adjust the amount of saffron and rosewater to your liking.

Add 1 litre (35fl oz) of water and the sugar to a medium saucepan and bring to the boil over a medium-high heat, stirring to dissolve the sugar. Once boiling, turn down the heat to medium and add the tea leaves. Simmer gently for 5 minutes, then strain through a sieve (strainer) into a separate saucepan, pressing down on the tea leaves, and then add the saffron and rosewater. Discard the leaves. If you have a tea flask or Thermos, then transfer it to the flask, seal tightly and let sit for 20 minutes before serving. If not, then let sit for 20 minutes in the pan and reheat very gently to serve. You want to give the chai this steeping time, so the saffron and rosewater infuse nicely.

CHAI LOOMI

Makes 2 mugs, or 4 small cups

1½ tbsp sugar
2–3 black limes, or regular dried limes (15g/½oz), washed and dried
2 tsp fresh lemon juice

I adore this tea. It's so simple yet so unique and delicious and is said to aid digestion (unconfirmed; I just really like the taste of black limes). Add more or less sugar to taste, but it does need it here, as it helps with the bitterness. You can always swap it out for honey if you'd prefer.

Add 700ml (24fl oz) water and the sugar to a small saucepan and bring to the boil over a medium-high heat. While it comes to the boil, press down on the limes to open them up and pick out and discard the seeds. Roughly break apart the limes into random pieces and, once the water is boiling, add them to the pan and turn down the heat to medium. Simmer for just 5 minutes (any longer and it will become bitter), then add the lemon juice. Strain through a sieve (strainer) set over a jug. Don't push down on the limes – they'll only release more bitterness – discard these. Drink right away.

MEZZE, SALADS AND SOUPS

Vermicelli Chicken Soup

Heat in Bahrain is variable, sort of like a Scoville scale of mildly hot to intolerable. There's a winter, yes, but it's often short lived and doesn't require the many layers, the many socks and the many boots that I acquired later on in my adult life, once I'd moved to the UK. But whether it's summer or not, much of our food is quite warming – slow-cooked meats, stewed beans, steamy rice. I'm not sure how this came to be but I am sure that I'll have soup any time of year, regardless of where I am in the world. Chicken soup is one which I think every household should have in its rotation. This is mine, and I'd love for you to adopt it too.

Serves 4–6

For the chicken stock
800g (1lb 12oz) chicken wings
1 onion, quartered (180g/6¼oz)
1 head of garlic, halved widthways
2 cinnamon sticks
½ tsp black peppercorns
1 tbsp apple cider vinegar
herb stems and carrot peel (see below)
fine sea salt

For the soup
4 tbsp olive oil
2 medium carrots, peeled and cut into 2.5cm (1in) cubes (280g/10oz)
1 large red potato, or other waxy variety, peeled and cut into 2.5cm (1in) cubes (250g/9oz)
2 fresh bay leaves
2 plum tomatoes, roughly grated (shredded) and skins discarded
1 tsp tomato paste (purée)
½ tsp ground turmeric
80g (2¾oz) wheat vermicelli noodles, broken into 3–4cm (1¼–1½in) lengths
100g (3½oz) kefir, at room temperature
1 tbsp lemon juice
4 garlic cloves, finely chopped
20g (¾oz) coriander (cilantro) leaves, finely chopped
2½ tsp cumin seeds, finely crushed using a pestle and mortar

Make the stock by adding the wings to a large, lidded saucepan and pouring over enough water to cover by about 3cm (1¼in). Bring to the boil over a medium-high heat and then, once boiling, pour the wings into a colander set over the sink, discarding the water and any impurities. Wipe out the pan, then add back the wings along with the remaining stock ingredients, 1¾ teaspoons of salt and 1.7 litres (60fl oz) of water. Bring to the boil over a medium-high heat, then reduce the heat to medium-low, cover with the lid and leave to simmer gently for 1 hour 20 minutes. Once ready, pour the broth through a large colander into a separate bowl and set aside. Once cool enough to handle, pick out the meat from the chicken wings, discarding the skin and bones. Set aside.

To make the soup, wipe out the pan and return to a medium-high heat with 1 tablespoon of the oil. Once hot, add the carrots, potato and bay leaves and cook for about 3 minutes, stirring occasionally, to soften. Add the grated tomato, tomato paste, turmeric and 1 teaspoon of salt and cook for about 3 minutes, stirring occasionally, until thickened. Pour in all of the broth and bring to a simmer over a medium-high heat. Turn down the heat to medium and simmer for 15 minutes, or until the vegetables have softened.

While the soup is simmering, add the noodles to a dry frying pan (skillet) and place over a medium-low heat. Toast, stirring often, for 8–10 minutes, or until deeply browned. Set aside.

Use a ladle to remove about 300g (10½oz) of the soup, of equal parts solids to liquids, avoiding the bay leaves, and transfer to a blender (or use a jug and a hand-held blender). Blitz until smooth, then stir this back into the soup, along with the kefir, noodles and chicken meat. Don't worry if it looks a little split after adding the kefir – this will even out as it cooks. Cook over a medium heat for another 15 minutes, or until the noodles are soft. Off the heat, stir in the lemon juice.

Lastly, add the remaining 3 tablespoons of oil and the garlic to a small frying pan over a medium heat. Cook for 1½–2 minutes, stirring often, or until the garlic starts to lightly colour, then stir in the coriander and cumin and cook for 30 seconds more. Immediately pour this into the soup, stirring to incorporate. Divide the soup between bowls and serve warm.

Chickpea and Bread Soup with Roasted Garlic and Coriander

It's not uncommon to buy steaming hot chickpeas from local Bahraini bakeries, served up in double-bagged plastic baggies (I'll admit it's not the wisest of packaging). The broth contains nothing more than salt and a few dried chillies, and we'll have this with tannour bread and, if feeling fancy, a squeeze of lemon or a dash of hot sauce. This soup is a nod to that, although the recipe is a complete divergence from tradition. Be sure to plan ahead by soaking the chickpeas the night before. Since it's really all about the chickpea broth, I would not advise using canned or jarred chickpeas here.

Serves 4

For the soup
7 tbsp olive oil
1 large onion, finely chopped (220g/7¾oz)
2 fresh bay leaves
3 garlic cloves, crushed
1 tbsp white miso
250g (9oz) dried chickpeas (garbanzo beans), soaked overnight in plenty of cold water and ¼ tsp bicarbonate of soda (baking soda), then drained
150g (5½oz) sourdough, crusts on, cut into 3–4cm (1¼–1½in) cubes
2 egg yolks
100g (3½oz) thick Greek yoghurt
3 tbsp lemon juice (from 1½–2 lemons)
fine sea salt

For the topping
2 heads of garlic, top eighth trimmed
1 tbsp coriander seeds, well toasted and roughly crushed using a pestle and mortar
10g (¼oz) coriander (cilantro) leaves, roughly chopped
3 tbsp olive oil

Heat 4 tablespoons of the oil in a large, lidded saucepan over a medium-high heat. Add the onion, bay leaves and ¼ teaspoon salt and cook for about 5 minutes, stirring occasionally, until softened and only lightly coloured. Add the garlic and miso and cook for 30 seconds, then stir in the drained chickpeas and 800ml (28fl oz) of water. Bring to the boil, skimming off any scum from the surface, cover, turn down the heat to medium-low and cook gently for 30 minutes. Season with 1½ teaspoons of salt, replace the lid and leave to cook for 35–40 minutes, or until the chickpeas are nice and soft.

Meanwhile, make the topping. Preheat the oven to 200°C fan/220°C/425°F/Gas mark 7. Drizzle the exposed tops of the garlic bulbs with a little oil and then wrap each individually in foil. Place on an oven rack and roast for 35–40 minutes, or until softened. Remove and allow to cool. Turn down the oven temperature to 165°C fan/180°C/350°F/Gas mark 4.

Once cool enough to handle, squeeze the roasted garlic out of their papery skins into a medium bowl (discarding the skins). Use a fork to roughly mash, then stir in the coriander seeds, chopped leaves, oil and ⅛ teaspoon salt. Set aside.

Add the bread to a tray and toss with ¼ teaspoon salt and the remaining 3 tablespoons of olive oil. Bake on the top shelf of the oven for about 8 minutes, or until golden in places.

When the chickpeas are ready, discard the bay leaves. Remove 100g (3½oz) of the solids (minus any liquid) and transfer to a blender along with the egg yolks, yoghurt and lemon juice, and blitz until very smooth. Temper this mixture by stirring a couple of ladlefuls of the hot soup directly into the blender, then pour it all back into the saucepan. If not serving right away, keep over low heat, but do not allow to boil (it might split).

Divide the croûtons between bowls, then ladle in the soup. Spoon over the garlic topping and serve warm.

Nourishing Herb and Barley Soup

This soup is inspired by a traditional Bahraini dish called *shillah*, in which six or seven different types of pulses and grains are cooked together with loads of herbs and meat. The result is very wholesome, and is usually served up during the month of Muharram, when the Shi'a Muslim communities will typically gather. As with quite a few Bahraini dishes, the Persian influences really shine through thanks to the plethora of herbs that form the bulk of this meal (use a food processor to help you chop them). I've significantly dialled down the ingredient list here, with far fewer pulses and no meat at all. I do like to use bone broth for the base, though, which you can easily swap out for veggie stock if you like.

Serves 4–6 · Soaking time: 2 hours

- 4 tbsp olive oil
- 2 onions, finely chopped (360g/12¾oz)
- 4 garlic cloves, crushed
- 1½ tsp cumin seeds, finely ground using a pestle and mortar
- 1 tsp ground turmeric
- 90g (3¼oz) barley, soaked in plenty of water for 2 hours, then drained
- 1 litre (35fl oz) chicken or beef bone broth, or vegetable stock
- 90g (3¼oz) Puy (French) lentils, washed well
- 3 tbsp red split lentils, washed well
- 130g (4¾oz) parsley leaves, finely chopped
- 130g (4¾oz) coriander (cilantro), leaves and soft stems finely chopped
- 90g (3¼oz) dill fronds, finely chopped
- 90g (3¼oz) spring onions (scallions), finely chopped
- 2½ tbsp lemon juice
- fine sea salt and freshly ground black pepper
- 150g (5½oz) natural (plain) yoghurt, or a non-dairy alternative, to serve

For the topping
- 4 tbsp olive oil
- 2 red chillies, stem and seeds removed, finely chopped
- 4 garlic cloves, finely chopped

Heat the oil in a very large, lidded stockpot over a medium-high heat. Add the onions and cook for 8–10 minutes, stirring occasionally, or until softened and golden. Stir in the garlic and spices and cook for another minute, until fragrant. Add the barley, broth and 400ml (14fl oz) of water and bring to a simmer. Once simmering, top with the lid and turn down the heat to medium-low. Leave to cook for 30 minutes, then stir in both types of lentils, the herbs, spring onions, 1½ teaspoons of salt and a generous grind of pepper. Replace the lid and leave to cook for a further 40 minutes, or until the Puy lentils have completely softened. At this point, add a splash more water or stock if you prefer a thinner soup. Off the heat, stir in the lemon juice.

Meanwhile, make the topping by adding the oil, chillies, garlic and tiny pinch of salt to a small frying pan (skillet) and then placing it over a low heat. Leave to cook and bubble very gently, stirring occasionally, for 10–12 minutes, or until softened and fragrant but not at all coloured.

Divide the soup between bowls and top each one with a spoonful of yoghurt, followed by the chilli and garlic topping. Serve warm.

MEZZE, SALADS AND SOUPS

Steamed Carrots with Harissa Onions and Herbs

This is a perfect dish to serve alongside a larger spread, as it can happily sit at room temperature while the carrots marinate and take in all the flavour of the harissa onions. Feel free to get creative and add in some pistachios, chopped dates or feta.

Serves 4, as a side · Marinating time: 1 hour

1kg (2lb 4oz) carrots, peeled and cut into 1.5–2cm (⅝–¾in) thick rounds
4 tbsp olive oil
1 red onion, finely chopped (150g/5½oz)
4 garlic cloves, crushed
1 tsp cumin seeds, roughly crushed using a pestle and mortar
2 tsp coriander seeds, roughly crushed using a pestle and mortar
1 tsp caraway seeds, roughly crushed using a pestle and mortar
2 tbsp rose harissa
2 tsp runny honey
2½ tbsp apple cider vinegar
10g (¼oz) parsley leaves, roughly chopped
10g (¼oz) mint leaves, roughly chopped
30g/1oz preserved lemon, flesh and seeds removed, skin finely sliced (15g/½oz)
fine sea salt

Prepare a steamer over a medium-high heat. Add the carrots to the steamer basket, top with the lid and steam for 10 minutes, or until cooked but with a slight bite (add more time if your carrots need it). Transfer to a large bowl.

Meanwhile, heat the oil in a medium frying pan (skillet) over a medium-high heat. Add the onion and fry for about 4 minutes, stirring occasionally, until softened and lightly browned. Add the garlic and spices and cook for a minute, until fragrant, then stir in the harissa, honey, vinegar and ¾ teaspoon of salt. Cook for a minute more, then remove from the heat. Pour this over the carrots in the bowl and toss to coat. Set aside to marinate for at least 1 hour. Before serving, stir through the herbs and preserved lemon and transfer to a serving bowl.

Cauliflower Mutabal

The word *mutabal* in Arabic actually means savoury, spiced and well seasoned, but it has also become synonymous with the mezze of burnt aubergines and tahini. Here I use roasted cauliflower in place of aubergines, and I love how easily this dish comes together. Be sure to roast and mix only on the day you want to serve it, and to have it at room temperature, as I've always found cauliflower to develop a bit of a funk when prepared a day or two ahead.

Serves 4, as a mezze

1 medium cauliflower (700g/1lb 9oz), trimmed and cut into bite-sized florets (550g/1lb 4oz)
1 tbsp olive oil, plus extra to serve
90g (3¼oz) Greek yoghurt
150g (5½oz) tahini
2 garlic cloves, crushed
1 tsp cumin seeds, toasted and finely crushed using a pestle and mortar
2–3 unwaxed lemons, to yield 5 tbsp juice and 1 tsp finely grated zest
5g (⅛oz) mint leaves, finely chopped
5g (⅛oz) parsley leaves, finely chopped
1 tsp Aleppo chilli flakes
fine sea salt and freshly ground black pepper

Preheat the oven to its highest setting. Line a large baking tray with baking paper.

Add the cauliflower, 1 tablespoon of oil and ¼ teaspoon of salt to the lined tray, toss to combine and spread out evenly. Roast for 20 minutes, or until nicely coloured and cooked through. Leave to cool, then set aside 3–4 florets (about 60g/2¼oz) for later. Finely chop the rest until it resembles rice. Don't worry if it's not perfect – texture is good.

In a large bowl, whisk together the yoghurt, tahini, garlic, cumin, lemon juice and ¼ teaspoon salt until well combined. Pour in about 160ml (5½fl oz) water and whisk until smooth – it should be easily pourable. (Tahini brands can differ, so add a little more water if needed.) Mix in the finely chopped cauliflower and let it sit for 20 minutes, for the flavours to meld together. Check the consistency of the mutabal at this point – it should have thickened significantly – so add a splash more water so that it's still easily spoonable and not super thick. Adjust salt and lemon levels to taste here too. Transfer to a large, shallow bowl, using a spatula to create a well in the centre.

Roughly chop the reserved florets and add these to a small bowl with the herbs, chilli and lemon zest and spoon this into the well. Drizzle with a good glug of oil and serve.

Photos from a Bahraini farm where natural spring water is used to harvest local greens, herbs and vegetables.

A Herby Leafy Salad

Almost all Middle Eastern households will know about the elusive herb basket. It's not so talked about – not really the main event – but it's there, existing on our tables, as necessary a component as salt and pepper. It's mostly just a basket (aka a plastic colander) of picked herbs – parsley, basil, tarragon, mint etc – or greens like romaine or rocket and *ba-gill*, a type of wild leek. They're always washed well, dried well, undressed and abundant, waiting to be picked up and eaten with the main meal – rice or fried fish or whatever might be served that day. As much as I can't really write a recipe for a herb basket, or even get you on board with this trend, I do think any meal can benefit from a simple, herby, leafy salad. Feel free to play around with the herb dressing here. You'll notice I ask you to succumb to a wild amount of herbs throughout this book, so here's a great way to use them up.

Serves 2–4, as a side

2 heads of Little Gem (Boston) lettuce, leaves picked, washed and dried well

½ tsp Daqoos, the spice mix (page 272), or ½ tsp Aleppo chilli flakes, to serve (optional)

For the dressing

10g (¼oz) parsley leaves and soft stems, picked

5g (⅛oz) basil leaves, picked

5g (⅛oz) mint leaves, picked

1 spring onion (scallion), trimmed and sliced

1 small garlic clove, finely chopped

¾ tsp Dijon mustard

1½ tbsp lemon juice

4 tbsp olive oil

fine sea salt and freshly ground black pepper

First make the dressing. Add the herbs, spring onion, garlic, mustard, lemon, oil and ⅛ teaspoon salt and a good grind of pepper to the bowl of a small food processor and blitz until smooth, scraping down the sides of the bowl as you go. Transfer the mixture to a medium mixing bowl, add the leaves and a pinch of salt and mix until nicely coated. Transfer to a serving bowl and, if using, sprinkle with the daqoos or Aleppo chilli.

Springtime Fattoush

Feel free to bake the pita here instead of frying, if you prefer – just make sure you open the pita pockets up first, for thin crisp pieces. If you can't find Lebanese pitas (*khobez Lebnani*), which are thin and flat, then flour tortillas will work just as well. I love to turn this salad into a full meal by adding some crumbled feta, jarred chickpeas or some seared prawns.

Serves 2–4, as a side

150g (5½oz) red round radishes, trimmed and thinly sliced into rounds
2 celery sticks, trimmed, stringy bits peeled, then thinly sliced at a slight angle (120g/4¼oz)
150g (5½oz) fresh or frozen broad beans (fava beans), soaked in boiling water for 5 minutes, skins removed (100g/3½oz)
½ small red onion, thinly sliced into half-moons (50g/1¾oz)
90g (3¼oz) pomegranate seeds (about ½ large pomegranate)
10g (¼oz) mint leaves, roughly torn
10g (¼oz) parsley leaves, picked
1 tbsp olive oil, plus an extra 2 tsp to serve
2 tsp lemon juice
¾ tsp sumac, plus an extra ½ tsp to serve
2 tsp pomegranate molasses

For the fried pita
500ml (17fl oz) vegetable oil, for deep frying
2 Lebanese pitas, opened up, then cut into 2.5–3cm (1–1¼in) cubes
fine sea salt

First fry the pitas. Line a tray with paper towels. Add the vegetable oil to a small, high-sided saucepan and place it over a medium-high heat. Test the oil is hot enough by dropping in a cube of pita – it should start to sizzle but not brown immediately. Working in two batches, fry the pita cubes for 3–4 minutes, stirring frequently with a slotted spoon, until golden. Transfer to the lined tray and sprinkle with a little salt. Repeat with the second batch. Set aside to cool and crisp up completely (save the oil for another use).

In a large mixing bowl combine the radishes, celery, broad beans, onion, pomegranate and herbs.

In a small bowl whisk together the tablespoon of olive oil, the lemon juice, ¾ teaspoon of sumac and ¼ teaspoon of salt.

Just before serving, pour the dressing over the radish mixture and season with another ¼ teaspoon salt. Toss everything together, then transfer to a shallow bowl and pile as much of the pita in the centre as you like, serving any extra in a bowl alongside. Sprinkle over the extra sumac, then drizzle with the pomegranate molasses and extra oil.

Ginger Peaches

This is a wonderfully easy way to bring summer to your table. Serve this salad al fresco – it goes really well alongside anything you throw on the barbecue. I personally like it with grilled halloumi.

Serves 4, as a side

35g (1¼oz) fresh ginger, peeled and julienned
4 tbsp olive oil
1 tsp black mustard seeds
1 tsp Aleppo chilli flakes
3 semi-ripe peaches or nectarines, halved, stoned and cut into 0.5cm (¼in) slices (475g/1lb 10z)
15g (½oz) coriander (cilantro), leaves and soft stems picked
1½ tbsp lime juice
1½ tsp maple syrup
fine sea salt

Add the ginger and oil to a small frying pan (skillet) and place over a medium heat. Cook, stirring occasionally, for about 10 minutes or until the ginger starts to turn lightly golden and crisp. Add the mustard seeds and chilli and cook for just 45 seconds more, until the ginger is nicely golden and the seeds begin to pop. Immediately strain the solids through a sieve (strainer) set over a bowl. Set both the oil and solids aside to cool, separately.

Just before serving, add the peaches, coriander, lime juice, maple syrup, half the cooled ginger oil and ¼ teaspoon salt to a large bowl and toss everything together. Transfer to a serving plate and pour over the remaining ginger oil. Top with the fried aromatics and serve right away.

Cheesy Filo Rolls with Burnt Honey, Chilli and Mint

These cheesy filo rolls are guaranteed to please a crowd and are perfect to serve at a party or when you have multiple mouths to feed. You can make the rolls up to a day ahead and keep them well covered and refrigerated – just allow a few more minutes in the oven if baking from cold.

Makes 21 rolls

200g (7oz) feta, finely crumbled
120g/4¼oz cream cheese
10g (¼oz) fresh mint leaves, finely chopped, plus optional extra roughly torn leaves to serve
5g (⅛oz) parsley leaves, finely chopped
1 large egg
65g (2¼oz) unsalted butter
2 tbsp olive oil
7 sheets good-quality filo (phyllo), defrosted if frozen
fine sea salt

For the toppings
75g (2½oz) runny honey
1½ tbsp lemon juice
2 tbsp olive oil
1¼ tsp Aleppo chilli flakes
1½ tsp white and black sesame seeds, toasted

Preheat the oven to 180°C fan/200°C/400°F/Gas mark 6 and line a large baking tray with baking paper. Have a pastry brush at the ready.

Make the filling by adding the feta, cream cheese, chopped mint, parsley, egg and ⅛ teaspoon of salt to a small bowl. Mix well to combine.

Add the butter to a small pan and place over a medium heat. Once melted, remove from the heat and add the oil. Leave to cool slightly.

Place the filo sheets under a slightly damp tea towel to stop them from drying out. Lay one sheet of filo on a clean work surface and, using a small sharp knife, cut it lengthways into three strips, roughly 10cm (4in) wide. With the shorter ends facing you, spoon roughly 2 teaspoons of the cheese mixture along the shorter end of one of the strips, leaving a 2cm (¾in) gap either side. Lightly brush the exposed pastry with the butter mixture. Fold the exposed ends over the cheese mixture and then roll upwards into a tight cigar-shaped roll. Continue in this way with all the filling and filo until you have made 21 rolls.

Arrange the rolls, seam-side down, on the lined tray so they're not touching. Brush the tops with any remaining butter mixture. Bake for 25 minutes, or until golden.

Meanwhile, add the honey to a small frying pan (skillet) and place over a medium-high heat. Cook for 3–4 minutes, stirring occasionally with a spatula, until the honey turns a dark amber. Off the heat, quickly mix in the lemon juice (careful, it might spit) and transfer to a small bowl. Rinse and dry out the pan, then return to a medium-low heat with the oil and chilli. Cook gently for just 4 minutes, or until heated through but not bubbling. Set aside.

When the rolls are ready, arrange them on a large plate with some overlapping. Pour over the honey mixture followed by the chilli oil and the toasted sesame seeds. Sprinkle with the extra mint, if you like, and serve warm.

Cucumber Yoghurt

This is the simplest of mezze, also known as *mast-o-khiar*, *tzatziki*, *laban bil khiar* and more, depending on where you are in the world. It's not that I think it needs a recipe, or that yours will be similar to mine, but I say 'serve with cucumber yoghurt' so many times throughout this book that I feel it'd be rude not to include it. This goes with just about any of the rice dishes in the rice chapter, and is a welcome side for well-spiced stews, dals or curries.

Serves 4, as a side

2 small Lebanese cucumbers, seeds removed, diced into 1cm (½in) cubes (180g/6¼oz)
10g (¼oz) parsley leaves, picked
3 tbsp olive oil
½ tsp dried mint
300g (10½oz) Greek-style yoghurt
1 garlic clove, crushed
1 tbsp lemon juice
1½ tsp dried rose petals
fine sea salt

Place the cucumbers in a medium bowl and toss with ½ teaspoon salt. Leave for 15 minutes, then strain through a sieve (strainer) and discard the liquid. Wipe out the bowl and add the cucumbers back in.

Meanwhile add the parsley and oil to the bowl of a small food processor and blitz until finely chopped. Stir in the dried mint, then mix with the drained cucumbers to coat nicely.

In a separate bowl mix the yoghurt, garlic, lemon juice and ¼ teaspoon salt. Add half the cucumber, mixing only a couple of times to swirl through, then transfer to a plate or shallow bowl. Top with the remaining cucumber cubes and sprinkle with the rose petals.

Batata Harra oo Helwa: Hot and Sweet Potatoes

You'll find *batata harra* (hot potatoes) on most menus in the Middle East. It's such a simple dish and is lovely to have alongside a bunch of other mezze, or as a side to your protein of choice. Here I've used sweet potatoes, as I like how their sweetness balances the hot acidic sauce. If you prefer things spicier, feel free to adjust this by upping the chilli.

Serves 4

1kg (2lb 4oz) sweet potatoes (about 3 medium), skin on, cut into 5–6cm (2–2½in) chunks at different angles
5 tbsp olive oil
1 mild red chilli, finely chopped, seeds and all
4 garlic cloves, finely chopped
1 tbsp coriander seeds, finely crushed using a pestle and mortar
1½ tsp hot Turkish red pepper paste (biber salçası)
½ tsp smoked paprika
2½ tbsp lime juice
10g (¼oz) coriander (cilantro), roughly chopped, plus extra leaves to serve
fine sea salt

Preheat the oven to 220°C fan/240°C/475°F/Gas mark 9. Line a large baking tray with baking paper.

In a large bowl, toss the sweet potatoes with 1 tablespoon of the oil and ¾ teaspoon salt. Arrange on the tray, spaced nicely apart, and bake for 30–35 minutes, until cooked through and browned in places.

Towards the last 10 minutes of baking, add the remaining 4 tablespoons of oil and the chilli, garlic and coriander seeds to a medium high-sided sauté pan and place over a medium-low heat. Cook gently, stirring occasionally, until fragrant and softened but not at all browned, about 4 minutes. Stir in the red pepper paste, paprika and ⅛ teaspoon of salt and cook gently for 4 minutes more, until deeply red and the garlic is very lightly coloured. Turn down the heat if it starts to bubble too much. Stir in the lime juice, fresh coriander and the still-warm sweet potatoes. Stir everything gently to coat.

Transfer to a large plate and sprinkle with the extra coriander. Serve warm or at room temperature if you prefer.

Savoury Trifle Salad with Aubergines, Yoghurt and Pita

Like any good trifle, this salad is all about the layering: yoghurt for creaminess, pita for crunch, aubergines and chickpeas for substance; not too much of any, not too little of all. This is a bit epic for a salad, but you can prepare all the elements the day before, leaving you with just the layering on the day you want to serve it. Plus, it's a pretty impressive-looking dish to serve at the table. You will find Lebanese pita bread in Middle Eastern stores, sometimes sold as *khobez Lebnani*.

Serves 4–6

For the vegetables
3 aubergines (eggplants), cut into 3–4cm (1¼–1½in) cubes (750g/1lb 10oz)
2½ tbsp olive oil
1 head of Cos (Romaine) lettuce, halved lengthways, cored, then thinly shredded
10g (¼oz) mint leaves, picked
10g (¼oz) parsley leaves, picked
1 tbsp lemon juice
250g (9oz) drained jarred chickpeas (garbanzo beans)
90g (3¼oz) pomegranate seeds (about ½ large pomegranate)
fine sea salt and freshly ground black pepper

For the fried pita
400ml (14fl oz) sunflower or vegetable oil
2 Lebanese pitas, opened up then cut into 2.5cm (1in) cubes

For the yoghurt
400g (14oz) Greek yoghurt
1½ tsp dried mint
1 garlic clove, crushed
2 tbsp lemon juice

For the smoky oil
4 tbsp olive oil
30g (1oz) pine nuts
1½ tsp sesame seeds
½ tsp smoked paprika
1 tsp urfa chilli

Preheat the oven to 210°C fan/230°C/450°F/Gas mark 8 and line a large baking tray with baking paper.

Spread out the aubergines on the lined tray and toss with the olive oil, ½ teaspoon salt and a good grind of pepper. Roast for 30–35 minutes, stirring halfway through, until nicely browned and softened. Set aside to cool.

Meanwhile, line a tray with paper towels. Fry the pitas by adding the sunflower oil to a small, high-sided saucepan and placing it over a medium-high heat. Test the oil is hot enough by dropping in a cube of pita – it should start to sizzle but not brown immediately. Working in two batches, fry the pita cubes for 3–4 minutes, stirring frequently with a slotted spoon, until golden. Transfer to the lined tray and sprinkle with a little salt. Repeat with the second batch. Set aside to cool and crisp up completely (save the oil for another use).

For the yoghurt, add all the ingredients to a bowl with 6 tablespoons of water and ½ teaspoon salt. Whisk until smooth.

To make the smoky oil, add the olive oil and pine nuts to a small frying pan and place it over a medium-high heat. Cook for about 1½ minutes, until the pine nuts begin to colour, then stir in the sesame seeds and fry for 30 seconds. Off the heat, stir in the paprika, chilli and a tiny pinch of salt. Pour into a heatproof bowl to stop it from browning any further.

In a large bowl toss together the lettuce, herbs, lemon juice, ¼ teaspoon of salt and a good grind of pepper.

To layer the trifle, add half the lettuce mixture to the base of a 20cm (8in) trifle bowl and top with half the aubergine and half the chickpeas. Spoon over half the yoghurt and, using a spatula, gently spread it evenly over the top. Drizzle over half the smoky oil then sprinkle with half the pomegranate seeds and half the pita. Repeat the layers. Serve within an hour, to keep the pitas nice and crisp.

Charred Courgettes with Saffron, Kefir and Sticky Onions

This is inspired by one of my favourite dips, *kashk-e-bademjan*, an Iranian dish of mashed aubergines topped with fermented whey (aka *kashk*), that is just perfect in its own right. Here courgettes take centre stage, and I could easily eat this whole thing with a spoon, but some warm fluffy pitas would do just as well.

Serves 4, as a mezze

⅛ tsp loosely packed saffron threads, crushed
¼ tsp rosewater
1kg (2lb 4oz) courgettes (zucchini)
3 tbsp olive oil, plus extra 1 tsp to drizzle
1 small onion, finely chopped (150g/5½oz)
3 garlic cloves, crushed
½ tsp ground turmeric
1 tsp cumin seeds, finely crushed using a pestle and mortar
1½ tsp dried mint
15g (½oz) walnuts, toasted and roughly chopped
2½ tbsp kefir
1 tbsp fresh mint leaves, picked
fine sea salt and freshly ground black pepper

For the sticky onions
1 tbsp olive oil
1 small onion, halved and cut into 0.5cm (¼in) slices (150g/5½oz)
1½ tbsp maple syrup

Add the saffron to a small bowl with the rosewater and 1 tablespoon hot water. Set aside.

Preheat the oven to its highest setting. Line a medium baking tray with foil.

Place the courgettes on the lined tray, drizzle with the teaspoon of oil and use your hands to coat. Roast for 40–45 minutes, turning halfway, until nicely charred and softened through the centre. Set aside to cool and, once cool enough to handle, make a slit down the middle and spoon out the flesh, discarding the skin and stems. Place the flesh into a sieve (strainer) set over a bowl, mix with ½ teaspoon of salt and leave to drain for about 30 minutes. Press down with the back of a spoon to extract as much liquid as possible (discard the liquid).

Meanwhile, make the sticky onions by heating the oil in a medium non-stick frying pan (skillet) over a medium heat. Add the sliced onion and a tiny pinch of salt and cook for 12 minutes, stirring occasionally, until lightly browned and softened. Add the maple syrup and cook for 5 minutes more, stirring often, until deeply browned and caramelized. Set aside.

Rinse and wipe out the pan and return to a medium-high heat with the 3 tablespoons of oil. Add the finely chopped onion and fry for 6–7 minutes, stirring occasionally, until softened and browned. Add the garlic, turmeric and cumin and cook for another 1½ minutes, stirring, until fragrant. Add the dried mint, the courgette flesh and ¼ teaspoon salt and cook for 2 minutes, stirring to combine. Set aside to cool to room temperature.

Spread the courgette mixture on a lipped plate. Sprinkle all over with the walnuts, followed by the kefir, saffron water, sticky onions and mint leaves.

Kebab Nekh-y: Chickpea and Veg Fritters with Mango Pickle

There's kebab and then there's kebab. In Bahrain they both exist, which makes things very confusing indeed. Unlike the meaty kebab you're more familiar with, this type of kebab is completely vegan – very similar to an Indian bhaji. It's filled with lots of herbs and vegetables; I add tomatoes and onions, but others will also add grated carrots and different spices. You can expect to find them at any Bahraini gathering, as they're the perfect finger food. They are pretty loose-form – you might make more or less depending on your size preference – so don't worry about making them look uniform or perfect! I like to serve them with this quick mango pickle, but you can just as easily enjoy these fritters with a squeeze of lime. Save any extra to stuff into a pita with tahini and chopped veggies.

Makes about 20–25 kebabs

For the fritters
200g (7oz) gram flour
1½ tbsp cornflour (cornstarch)
1¼ tsp baking powder
½ tsp ground turmeric
1 tsp ground cumin
1 tsp Kashmiri chilli powder, or paprika
1 tsp garam masala
1 small red onion, finely chopped (100g/3½oz)
1 large tomato, seeds and insides discarded, then chopped into ½ cm cubes (100g/3½oz)
30g (1oz) ginger, peeled and finely grated
1 green chilli, finely chopped, seeds and all
3 spring onions (scallions), finely chopped
25g (1oz) coriander (cilantro), finely chopped
25g (1oz) dill fronds, finely chopped
fine sea salt
700ml (24fl oz) sunflower oil, for deep frying

For the mango pickle
3 tbsp olive oil
10 fresh curry leaves
¾ tsp black mustard seeds
½ tsp Kashmiri chilli powder
1 plum tomato, blitzed into a purée (120g/4¼oz)
2 garlic cloves, crushed
2 tbsp apple cider vinegar
1 large ripe mango, cut into 1cm (½in) cubes
200g (7oz) Greek yoghurt or non-dairy alternative

Combine the flours, baking powder, spices and 1 teaspoon of salt in a large bowl and whisk well to get rid of any lumps.

Add the red onion, tomato, ginger, chilli, spring onions and herbs to a separate bowl and mix to combine.

Add the vegetable mixture to the dry ingredients and stir to combine. Pour in 170–190ml (5½–6½fl oz) water and whisk to a fairly thick batter. Leave at room temperature for 20 minutes.

Meanwhile make the mango pickle. Add the olive oil to a medium frying pan (skillet) over a medium-high heat. Once hot add the curry leaves and fry, stirring constantly, until they start to turn translucent, about 30–60 seconds. Add the mustard seeds and chilli powder and cook for 30 seconds more, until the seeds just start to pop. Stir in the blitzed tomato, garlic, vinegar and ½ teaspoon salt and turn down the heat to medium. Cook for about 6 minutes, stirring occasionally, until thickened and the tomato visibly separates from the oil. Set aside to cool to room temperature, then stir in the mango.

Heat the sunflower oil in a medium, high-sided saucepan over a medium-high heat, and line a tray with paper towels. Test the oil is hot enough by dropping a small spoonful of the batter into the oil – it should sizzle immediately but not colour right away. When ready, use two dessertspoons to carefully drop a large spoonful of the batter into the oil. Try to spread the mixture as you drop the batter, so you get maximum surface area and more crispy bits. The fritter will rise to the surface and puff up right away. Fry 5–6 at a time, for about 4–5 minutes, or until nicely browned and cooked through, adjusting the heat if the fritters get too brown too soon. Transfer to the lined tray and continue with the rest. Don't worry about them being different sizes and shapes; this only adds to their charm.

Add the yoghurt to a bowl and spoon over the mango pickle. Arrange the fritters on a large platter or shallow bowl and serve warm, or at room temperature if you prefer.

Pan-fried Tomatoes with Za'atar, Pine Nuts and Halloumi

This is an impressive side dish to serve as part of a summer spread, or alongside the Loomi Lemon Chicken (page 220) as an easy lunch or dinner. Make sure your tomatoes are not overly ripe here, you want them to keep their shape when pan-frying.

Serves 4–6, as a side

4 tbsp olive oil
4 tsp maple syrup
6 medium-large vine tomatoes, cored and halved widthways
35g (1¼oz) pine nuts
4 garlic cloves, finely chopped
2 tbsp oregano leaves, picked
2½ tsp za'atar
60g (2¼oz) halloumi, finely grated (shredded)
50g (1¾oz) ricotta
fine sea salt and freshly ground black pepper

Add 1 tablespoon of the oil and 2 teaspoons of the maple syrup to a large, non-stick frying pan (skillet) over a medium heat. Sprinkle the cut side of half the tomatoes with ¼ teaspoon salt and a generous grind of black pepper. Once hot, arrange the seasoned tomatoes, cut-side down in a single layer, in the pan. Sprinkle the tops with a pinch of salt and pepper and fry for 10–12 minutes, until they're nice and caramelized at the bottom. Turn up the temperature to medium-high if needed. Use a spatula to gently flip them over and fry the other side for 2 minutes more. You want the tomatoes to be softened and cooked but still retain their shape – some tomatoes might soften faster than others. Gently remove them as they're ready and arrange them, cut-side up, on a serving plate. Pour any remaining oil or juices left in the pan over the tomatoes, then rinse and dry the pan. Replace over a medium to medium-high heat with another tablespoon of oil and the remaining 2 teaspoons of maple syrup. Sprinkle the remaining half of the tomatoes with ¼ teaspoon salt and a generous grind of pepper and, once hot, continue frying in the same way.

Once all the tomatoes are fried, rinse and dry the pan again, then place over a medium heat with the remaining 2 tablespoons of oil, the pine nuts and a tiny pinch of salt. Cook for 1½–2 minutes, stirring constantly, or until the pine nuts just begin to colour. Add the garlic and oregano and cook for a minute more, stirring all the while, until the pine nuts are golden and the garlic fragrant and lightly coloured. Off the heat, stir in 2 teaspoons of the za'atar and pour into a bowl to stop the cooking.

Combine the halloumi and ricotta in a small bowl and spoon this all over the tomatoes. Spoon over the pine nut and oil mixture and sprinkle with the last ½ teaspoon of za'atar.

Roasted Broccoli Salad with Lime and Chilli Dressing and Bombay Mix

I love all the textures that come through in this salad, which make for a very fun eating experience. Feel free to use your favourite Bombay mix – some come with nuts, others don't – just be sure not to add it until right before you intend to serve, as you want it to stay nice and crisp. I've given you the option of one or two chillies here, depending on your heat preferences.

Serves 4, as a side

2 medium heads of broccoli (900g/2lb), heads cut into bite-sized florets (650g/1lb 7oz), stems reserved

7 tbsp olive oil

8 spring onions (scallions), trimmed, left whole

1–2 mild red chillies, thinly sliced at a slight angle, seeds and all

20 fresh curry leaves

10g (¼oz) coriander (cilantro) leaves and soft stems, picked

10g (¼oz) basil leaves, picked

1–2 unwaxed limes, to yield 2 tsp finely grated zest and 2½ tbsp juice

¾ tsp poppy seeds

30g (1oz) Bombay mix, store-bought, roughly crushed

fine sea salt

Preheat the oven to its highest setting. Line a large and a medium baking tray with baking paper. Add the broccoli florets to the large tray and toss with 2½ tablespoons of the oil and ½ teaspoon salt. Add the spring onions to the medium tray and toss with 1½ teaspoons of oil. Transfer both trays to the oven and roast for 15 minutes, stirring halfway, or until cooked through and nicely charred in places. Set aside to cool to room temperature.

Meanwhile, add the remaining 4 tablespoons of oil and the chilli to a small frying pan (skillet) and place it over a medium heat. Fry gently for 5–6 minutes, stirring occasionally, or until the chilli begins to turn translucent but is not coloured, then add the curry leaves and cook for 2 minutes more, or until the leaves start to become shiny and deep green. Drain through a sieve (strainer) set over a bowl, reserving the oil, then transfer the solids to a small plate lined with paper towels to cool and crisp up.

Trim the reserved broccoli stems so they are roughly rectangular – they don't need to be perfect. Shave the stems lengthways into thin strips, ideally using a mandoline. Stacking a few on top of each other at a time, cut the strips into fine julienne, then add to a large mixing bowl with the herbs. Roughly chop the charred spring onions into 3cm (1¼in) lengths, then add these and the broccoli to the bowl.

Add the lime zest and juice, the poppy seeds and ¼ teaspoon salt to the now-cooled chilli oil and whisk to combine (alternatively, add them to a jar, secure with a lid and give everything a good shake). Pour this all over the broccoli mixture and give it a taste, adjusting the seasoning as you like. Transfer to a large serving platter and top with the fried chillies, curry leaves and the Bombay mix.

Samboosa Tikka with Green Yoghurt

Two truths you might not know: the Arabic word for samosa is actually *samboosa* or *sambousek*; in Bahrain we call it *samboosa*. The second is that the Indian flavours associated with the word 'tikka' don't actually apply here. Bahraini tikka is any meat marinated in ground black lime and lots of lemon. Some will add other spices, such as cumin or cinnamon, and others will also add yoghurt. The main thing is to make sure they have that sour, bitter, intense taste offered via the black lime. Tikka is often sold on skewers cooked on charcoal, served with tannour bread, raw onion, rocket and a green chutney. Here I've used the tikka flavouring for the filling of these samboosas, which make a great finger food to share with friends.

Makes 20 samboosas

For the filling
2 tbsp olive oil
1 large onion, finely chopped (220g/8oz)
400g (14oz) minced (ground) lamb (15–20% fat)
4 garlic cloves, crushed
1¾ tbsp ground black lime
2 tsp ground cumin
½ tsp sugar
2 tbsp lemon juice
10g (¼oz) coriander (cilantro) leaves, roughly chopped
fine sea salt and freshly ground black pepper

For the samboosas
4 tsp cornflour (cornstarch)
5 sheets good-quality filo (phyllo), defrosted if frozen
1½ tbsp olive oil
½ tsp ground black lime

For the green yoghurt
20g (¾oz) coriander (cilantro), leaves and soft stems, roughly chopped
10g (¼oz) mint leaves, picked
1 jalapeño, roughly chopped, seeds and all
1 garlic clove, roughly chopped
1 tbsp olive oil
130g (4¾oz) Greek-style yoghurt

Make the filling by heating the oil in a large sauté pan over a medium-high heat. Add the onion and cook, stirring occasionally, for about 5 minutes, until softened and lightly coloured. Add the minced lamb and use a spoon to break the clumps into a fine crumble. Season with 1 teaspoon of salt and a very generous grind of pepper and fry for about 8 minutes, stirring occasionally, until nicely browned. Stir in the garlic, black lime, cumin and sugar and cook for 1½ minutes more, until fragrant. Pour in 200ml (7fl oz) of water and cook for another 3 minutes, or until most of the water is absorbed but not completely dry. Off the heat, stir in the lemon juice and coriander and set aside to cool completely.

Preheat the oven to 200°C fan/220°C/425°F/Gas mark 7 and line two large baking trays with baking paper.

To make the samboosas, whisk together the cornflour and 1 tablespoon of water in a small bowl and set aside. Place the filo sheets under a slightly damp tea towel to stop them from drying out. Lay one sheet of filo on a clean work surface and, using a small sharp knife, cut it lengthways into four strips roughly 8cm (3¼in) wide. Place a little over 1 tablespoon of filling at the bottom of each strip, then (very lightly) brush the exposed part with the cornflour mixture – a few dabs will do. Fold a corner of the pastry over the filling, to make a triangle, then fold again in the opposite direction. Continue folding in alternate directions all along the strip, until you have made a triangular parcel. Use a little more of the cornflour mixture to seal the ends if needed. Place, seam-side down, on the lined tray then continue until all the filling and sheets are used up. You should make 20 samboosas. Brush the tops and bottoms of the samboosas with the oil, then sprinkle the tops with the black lime. Bake for 18–20 minutes, or until deeply golden and crisp.

Meanwhile, make the green yoghurt by adding all the ingredients and ⅛ teaspoon salt to the bowl of a small food processor and blitzing until smooth. Transfer to a small bowl.

Arrange the samboosas on a platter and serve warm with the yoghurt alongside.

BABY AUBERGINES – TWO WAYS

These make the perfect food for entertaining, as you don't have to worry about serving them warm and they're versatile enough to eat as an appetizer, a mezze, or as part of the main meal. Try to find the longer, thinner baby aubergines rather than the rounder, fatter ones, as they are the perfect type to fill. If you can't find these, then you can also roast thick slices of regular aubergines and top them with the fillings instead.

Baby Aubergines with Walnuts, Ricotta and Herbs

Feel free to get creative with the filling here – swap out the walnuts for smoked almonds, for example, or the basil for whatever herbs might need using up in your fridge. The main aim here is crunch from the nuts, creaminess from the ricotta and freshness from the herbs and lemon.

Makes 12

12 baby aubergines (eggplants) – the longer, thinner ones
2 tbsp olive oil, plus an extra tbsp to serve
fine sea salt and freshly ground black pepper
1 tsp sumac, to serve

For the stuffing
55g (2oz) walnuts, well toasted and finely chopped
15g (½oz) basil leaves, finely shredded
2 spring onions (scallions), trimmed and finely sliced
30g (1oz) preserved lemon, seeds removed, skin and pulp finely chopped (25g/1oz)
½ green (bell) pepper, stem and seeds removed, diced into 1cm (½in) cubes
1 tbsp coriander seeds, toasted and roughly crushed using a pestle and mortar
120g/4¼oz whole-milk ricotta
1 tbsp olive oil
1½ tbsp lemon juice

Preheat the oven to 200°C fan/220°C/425°F/Gas mark 7 and line a baking tray with baking paper.

Trim off the stems of the aubergines, then, using a small, sharp knife, make a slit lengthways through the centre, but don't cut all the way through. Use your fingers to open them up slightly (still keeping them whole), then toss them in a bowl with the oil, ¼ teaspoon of salt and a good grind of pepper, using your fingers to push the seasoning into the insides. Place the aubergines, slit-side up, on the lined tray and bake for 25 minutes, or until softened and cooked through. Set aside to cool to room temperature.

Meanwhile, make the stuffing by combining all the ingredients together in a bowl with ⅓ teaspoon salt and a generous grind of black pepper.

Once the aubergines have cooled, stuff them with the ricotta mixture. Transfer to a large platter, drizzle with the extra oil then sprinkle with the sumac.

Baby Aubergines with Tomato and Pepper Salsa

The salsa is super fresh and versatile and works really well spooned onto grilled fish or other grilled vegetables. You can use store-bought fried onions or shallots as the crunchy topping, but I do recommend making your own – be sure to make extra though, as they're very moreish and you'll want to sprinkle them onto everything.

Makes 12

12 baby aubergines (eggplants) – the longer thin ones
2 tbsp olive oil
fine sea salt and freshly ground black pepper
2 tbsp fried onion or shallots, store-bought or homemade (see Note on page 151), to serve

For the salsa
2 ripe plum tomatoes, finely chopped (220g/8oz)
½ large red (bell) pepper, finely diced into 1cm (½in) cubes (100g/3½oz)
1 green chilli, finely chopped, seeds and all
1 garlic clove, finely chopped
1½ tbsp apple cider vinegar
2 tsp pomegranate molasses
1½ tbsp olive oil
5g (⅛oz) mint leaves, roughly chopped
10g (¼oz) coriander (cilantro), leaves and soft stems, roughly chopped

Follow the recipe on the left for preparing and baking the aubergines.

Meanwhile, make the salsa by mixing the tomatoes, red pepper, chilli, garlic, vinegar, molasses, oil, ½ teaspoon of salt and a good grind of pepper together in a medium bowl. Just before you are ready to serve, stir in the herbs.

Once the aubergines have cooled, stuff them with the salsa, reserving the liquid in the bowl. Arrange on a large serving platter, then pour over the salsa liquid. Sprinkle with the fried onions and serve.

Labneh with Slow-cooked Leeks and Peas

I've probably eaten more labneh in my time than I have hummus, and if I had to choose between the two, then I must confess that labneh would always win. Mainly that's because it slots into menus so easily, both as a side or as a starter, and is often the welcome, creamy, tangy addition to an otherwise heavy meal. Opt for thicker leeks here, rather than the super-thin ones, as they'll look the prettiest. Serve with fluffy pita bread.

Serves 4, as a mezze · Draining time: overnight

For the labneh
500g (1lb 2oz) natural (plain) yoghurt
1 garlic clove, crushed
fine sea salt

For the veg
2 chunky leeks, trimmed, white and light green parts only, and cut into 2cm (¾in) rounds (320g/11¼oz)
6 thyme sprigs, plus an extra ½ tbsp of picked leaves to serve
8 garlic cloves, unpeeled, lightly bashed with the side of a knife
6 tbsp olive oil
150g (5½oz) frozen peas, defrosted
20g (¾oz) chives, finely chopped
1 lemon

First make the labneh. Mix together the yoghurt and ½ teaspoon salt. Line a sieve (strainer) with cheesecloth or a clean tea towel with plenty of overhang and place over a clean bowl. Transfer the yoghurt to the lined sieve and fold over the overhang to encase the yoghurt. Top with a weight (a couple of tins will do) and place the whole thing in the refrigerator overnight. The next day, unwrap the mixture, discarding the collected liquid – you now have labneh. Mix in the garlic and set aside at room temperature.

Wash the leek rounds very well by soaking them in water to get rid of any grit, then dry thoroughly. Add the leeks to a medium, lidded sauté pan with the thyme, garlic, oil and ¼ teaspoon salt. Arrange the leeks so they're lying on their round cut sides. Top with the lid and place over a low heat. Cook for 15 minutes, undisturbed, then remove the lid and use a fork to carefully flip over each leek round, keeping them intact. Replace the lid and cook for 15 minutes more, or until they're completely soft. Remove from the heat and leave to cool for 20 minutes. Discard the thyme sprigs and peel off and discard the garlic skins, stirring the peeled garlic flesh back into the pan, along with the peas, chives and another ¼ teaspoon of salt.

Meanwhile, top and tail the lemon using a small sharp knife, then cut around its edges to remove the skin and pith. Release each lemon segment by cutting between the membranes. Roughly chop the segments into 3–4 pieces, then stir them into the cooled leek and pea mixture.

Spread the labneh onto a shallow bowl. Top with the leek and pea mixture, sprinkle with the thyme leaves and serve at room temperature.

MEZZE, SALADS AND SOUPS

The Disappearing Island

There's something quite magical about the disappearing island. Named Jarada, the disappearing island is actually a sandbank in the middle of the Persian Gulf. At low tide you'll find this beautiful stretch of white sand, surrounded by water and brought to life with sea creatures, birds and the odd human and their anchored boat. At high tide, you'd never know it exists. It's impossible to write about Jarada, though, without first addressing the sea.

Bahrainis have a strong affinity with the water. Pearl-diving runs in our bloodline, but the sea... well the sea runs in our hearts. Not many people know that Bahrain is in fact an archipelago of more than 30 islands. When I was little my grandfather would often sit me on his lap and talk to me about subjects far too advanced for my young mind, but certain conversations stood out to me, like how fish was good for my brain, that eating with our hands makes everything taste much better and that, when he was younger, he would wade from village to village through shallow waters. This last one stood out to me the most, the image of my grandfather wading through waters when, at the time, we drove everywhere, not a single thought of how 'things used to be'. I often contemplate how he must have felt in his old age, watching his landscape change so drastically from endless stretches of desert and shallow coastal waters to skyscrapers and flyovers, from a sea brimming with marine life to hardly brimming at all; the realities of land reclamation so very damaging to our already delicate waters.

This affinity never escaped my dad either. When I was little he'd set off fishing early on a Friday morning and return home sometime before sunset, the smell of the salt, sea and sweat permeating his T-shirt, his fingers covered in small cuts from the fishing wire and his smile wide, from ear to ear, as he presented his catch of the day, a couple of *safi* (rabbitfish), maybe a *chen'ad* (kingfish) or if we were very lucky, a *hamour* (grouper). He'd quickly set to work in our kitchen and I'd watch him, fascinated, as he scraped away at the fish scales, unabashedly gutting and cleaning their insides and portioning the fish into steaks or fillets, ready to be frozen or cooked up that week. I'd eagerly listen to his adventures that day, what surprises the water had in store for him, as he recalled time and time again that you can never predict what the sea is willing to give you, that you must always be open to receive. As the years went on he would often come home empty-handed, the bounties from our waters gradually becoming more scarce by the day.

And then there is Jarada. Dad would take us out on his little fishing boat, timing it just right so we got there at low tide. He'd anchor the boat and we'd excitedly jump into the water and get lost in the sand, sun and sea. I'd run up and down that sandbank, following a seagull's footprints or searching for the prettiest shell to add to my collection. I never thought of the heat of the sun back then, was never conscious of the passing of time or the worries of tomorrow. All that mattered was that the island had appeared, that the tide had worked with us that day, that the sea was alive. There was one thing, however, that managed to snap me out of my island trance and, to no surprise, it was Mum's call for food. We'd quickly scramble back onto the boat as she unpacked the icebox and lay out a selection of sandwiches, veggie sticks and cold juices. I'd sit cross-legged and ravenous, suddenly aware of my hunger, and devour whatever Mum put in front of me. The sandwiches were simple, but ever so welcome: tuna mayo, chicken mayo, turkey and lettuce or cheese and tomato. In those moments, they were the best sandwiches known to man.

For this book I sent my friend and photographer Matt Wardle out to Jarada with my dad. It was Matt's very first time. 'What do you mean you haven't been?' I had screamed down the phone. 'You've been living in Bahrain for over 12 years!' I was semi-appalled but also quite pleased that this man from Liverpool would now get to experience a place so dear to my heart. My instructions to my dad were quite clear at the time: give him beer, give him food, and for God's sake Dad don't embarrass me. My dad chuckled, he was excited too, having not been to Jarada in years. Matt called me later that day, slightly buzzing, his voice excitable and happy. I sat down on a cold, rainy November day in London and listened to him chat cheerfully about Jarada, about how the skies had smiled down on him that day and how his favourite photos might not even be of the island, but of my dad, the sea spraying him playfully as the boat crashed up and down against the waves. 'What a legend your dad is,' he'd said, 'Oh and we had the most delicious sandwiches!' I smiled knowingly; Jarada sandwiches just hit differently.

As I struggled to attach a recipe to this piece, I knew then that it had to be one of my favourites: Salad Olivieh stuffed into a soft bun, with plenty of crunchy vegetables and pickles. It's my small nod to the magic of the disappearing island, the wonders of the sea and the memories I know will always be attached to them.

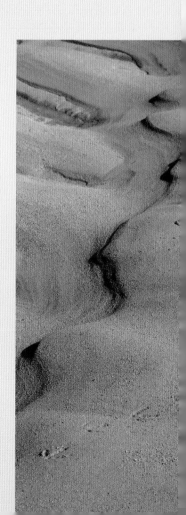

MEZZE, SALADS AND SOUPS

The Disappearing Island's Salad Olivieh

This recipe is dedicated to the disappearing island, otherwise known as Jarada (see pages 102–105). As I replay my childhood memories of time spent there, I think of how apt this Salad Olivieh would've been, or that perhaps one day I'll go back and this would be my meal. Disappearing island aside, this is a perfect thing to pack for a picnic, or just to enjoy outside on a warm summer's day. I've diverged ever so slightly from tradition with this classic Persian potato salad, but you'll find the flavours are generally the same.

Serves 4

For the base
2 large chicken legs, skin on, bone in (500g/1lb 2oz)
1 small onion, quartered
2 fresh bay leaves
¼ tsp black peppercorns
1 tbsp apple cider vinegar
300g (10½oz) red potato (about 1 large or 2 small), left whole, poked a couple times with a fork
3 large eggs
90g (3¼oz) mayonnaise
100g (3½oz) Greek yoghurt
1½ tbsp lemon juice
½ tsp ground white pepper
fine sea salt

To serve
1 small carrot, peeled, halved widthways and cut into julienne strips (90g/3¼oz)
100g (3½oz) breakfast radishes, trimmed and cut into julienne strips
1 Lebanese cucumber, seeds removed, halved widthways and cut into julienne strips (100g/3½oz)
100g (3½oz) gherkins, cut into julienne strips
10g (¼oz) tarragon leaves, roughly chopped
10g (¼oz) basil leaves, roughly torn
2 tsp lemon juice
1 tbsp olive oil
2 tsp coriander seeds, toasted and crushed using a pestle and mortar
1 tsp nigella seeds
½ tsp Aleppo chilli flakes
1 small head of Baby Gem (Boston lettuce), leaves separated
½ small head of radicchio
1 small red Belgian chicory (endive)
4 crusty bread rolls

Add the chicken legs, onion, bay leaves, peppercorns, vinegar, 700ml (24fl oz) of water and ¾ teaspoon of salt to a medium, lidded saucepan and bring to the boil over a medium-high heat. Skim off any scum that rises to the surface, then top with the lid, turn down the heat to medium-low and leave to cook gently for 1 hour 20 minutes, until very tender. Remove the legs (saving the broth) and, once cool enough to handle, discard the skin and bones and finely shred the meat using your hands or two forks. Place in a large bowl.

Meanwhile, add the potato to a small, lidded saucepan and pour over enough water to cover by about 4cm (1½in). Bring to the boil, then loosely cover with the lid, turn down the heat to medium and cook for 25–30 minutes, or until cooked through and a knife is easily inserted into the centre. Drain and, once cool enough to handle, peel and discard the skin and cut the flesh into roughly 1.5cm (⅝in) cubes. Add these to the bowl with the chicken.

Hard-boil the eggs – cook for about 9–10 minutes if starting from cold. Plunge into cold water then peel, finely chop and add to the same bowl.

Make a dressing by whisking together the mayonnaise, yoghurt, lemon juice, 3 tablespoons of the reserved stock (save the rest to use in multiple recipes throughout the book!), 1 teaspoon of salt and the white pepper. Pour over the chicken and potato mixture, stir to combine and set aside to marinate for at least 20 minutes. Don't worry if it seems a bit wet – the potato cubes will drink this all in as it sits.

When ready to serve, in a bowl combine the carrot, radishes, cucumber, gherkins, herbs, lemon juice, olive oil and a small pinch of salt.

Spread the chicken mixture over two-thirds of a large rimmed platter. Top with the vegetable mixture, then sprinkle with the coriander and nigella seeds and the chilli flakes. Arrange the salad leaves on the remaining third of the plate. Serve with the crusty rolls to build your own sandwich.

Watermelon Salad with Cucumber, Red Onion and Ricotta Salata

Growing up, watermelons were a much-loved treat to sink my teeth into during the peak of the summer heat when I needed something refreshing and hydrating. It seems almost wrong of me not to include a recipe for watermelon in this book, as it's such a unifying ingredient across the Middle East, for reasons both cultural and political. So here is a very simple salad, which I instruct you to devour on the hottest day of the year with reckless abandon.

Serves 4 · Draining time: 20 minutes

½ red onion, finely chopped (60g/2¼oz)
1 tsp sumac, plus an extra ½ tsp to serve
1 tbsp lemon juice
2 Lebanese cucumbers (240g/8½oz), seeds removed, cut into 1cm (½in) cubes (180g/6¼oz)
10g (¼oz) parsley, roughly chopped
10g (¼oz) basil leaves, picked
4 tbsp olive oil
¼ large or ½ small ripe watermelon, seeds removed, cut into 2–3cm (1–1¼in) cubes to give 700g (1lb 9oz); snack on any left over
70g (2½oz) ricotta salata (or use feta), finely crumbled
fine sea salt

Add the onion, sumac, lemon juice and ¼ teaspoon salt to a small bowl and toss to combine. Set aside to pickle gently while you get on with the rest.

Mix the cucumbers with ½ teaspoon salt, then place in a sieve (strainer) set over a bowl. Leave for about 20 minutes, then discard any liquid in the bowl.

Add the parsley, basil and 3 tablespoons of the oil to the bowl of a small food processor and blitz until very smooth. Add this to the drained cucumbers and mix to combine.

To serve, arrange the watermelon and ricotta salata on a large plate and evenly spoon over the onion and cucumber mixtures. Drizzle with the remaining tablespoon of oil, sprinkle with the extra sumac and serve right away.

Yoghurty Butter Beans with Middle Eastern Chilli Crisp

This recipe is all about the Middle Eastern Chilli Crisp (page 264), where the yoghurty beans provide a creamy, subtle platform for the condiment to take centre stage. You can make the chilli crisp well in advance, ready to be used in this way whenever you're craving a quick lunch or snack. If you've got some fluffy pita, then I would use it here; it's the perfect vehicle to scoop up the beans and their yoghurty, oily sauce.

Serves 4

120g/4¼oz natural (plain) yoghurt
1½ tbsp lime juice
1 small garlic clove, crushed
1 jar good-quality butter beans (lima beans), rinsed and drained (500g/1lb 2oz)
1½ tbsp coriander (cilantro) leaves, roughly chopped (optional)
1 x quantity of Middle Eastern Chilli Crisp (page 264)
fine sea salt

In a large bowl, whisk together the yoghurt, lime juice, garlic and ¼ teaspoon salt. Add the butter beans and use a spatula to gently mix until nicely coated. Transfer to a large platter, spreading out the beans, and sprinkle with the coriander, if using. Spoon over about half of the chilli crisp, or as much as your heart desires (jar up the rest if not using), and serve at room temperature.

MEZZE, SALADS AND SOUPS 111

Sesame Beets with Charred Spring Onions

This is a very simple dish to serve alongside a mezze spread, or to accompany grilled meats or veggies.

Serves 4–6, as a mezze

500g (1lb 2oz) cooked beetroot (beet), cut into 2cm (¾in) cubes
4 spring onions (scallions), trimmed (60g/2¼oz)
2 tsp olive oil
1 tsp black and white sesame seeds, toasted, to serve
fine sea salt

For the dressing
40g (1¼oz) natural (plain) yoghurt
30g (1oz) tahini
1 garlic clove, crushed
1½ tsp lime juice
1 tsp maple syrup
1 tsp toasted sesame oil, plus ½ tsp extra to serve
1 tbsp water

First make the dressing by whisking all the ingredients together in a medium bowl with ½ teaspoon of salt. Stir in the cooked beetroot and set aside to marinate while you char the spring onions.

Heat a large frying pan (skillet) over a high heat. Toss the spring onions with 1 teaspoon of the oil and a tiny pinch of salt and add them to the hot pan, then weigh them down with a saucepan that has a base slightly smaller than the frying pan. Char for 2 minutes, then remove the saucepan, flip the spring onions over and repeat to char the other side for 1–2 minutes more; you want them softened and browned in places. Set aside to cool.

Transfer the beetroot mixture to a serving bowl, drizzle with the extra sesame oil and sprinkle over the sesame seeds. Toss the spring onions with the remaining teaspoon of olive oil, then pile these on top and serve at room temperature.

Note: I like to cook my beetroot by placing them in a baking dish half-filled with water. Cover the dish well with foil and bake at 200°C fan/220°C/425°F/Gas mark 7 until they are easily pierced with a knife. This takes about 1 hour – longer if your beets are particularly large. Peel while they're still warm and continue with the recipe.

RICE

Tomato, Potato and Saffron Rice

The Gulf countries are known for their elaborate rice dishes, of which there are many. Some of the best and most traditional are cooked in deep underground fire pits over charcoal and palm wood, the smokiness taking over every grain. Practically this isn't feasible in most homes, but I like to think that we can still produce the most wonderful rice dishes with just a few simple ingredients and a lot of love. This one can be a side or a main dish. I like to eat this with pan-fried fish, a fresh chopped salad and a spicy pickle.

Serves 4–6 · Soaking time: 20 minutes–2 hours

⅓ tsp loosely packed saffron threads, finely crushed
1 tsp rosewater
4 tbsp olive oil
1 large onion, thinly sliced (220g/7½oz)
400g (14oz) floury potatoes like Maris Pipers (about 2 medium ones), peeled and cut into rough 2.5cm (1in) cubes
350g (12oz) basmati rice, washed until the water runs clear and soaked for at least 20 minutes and up to 2 hours, then drained
3 fresh bay leaves
5 cloves
5 cardamom pods
50g (1¾oz) unsalted butter, cut into small cubes
4 large ripe plum tomatoes, halved lengthways (600g/1lb 5oz)
2 green chillies, left whole
1½ tbsp parsley, roughly chopped (optional)
fine sea salt and freshly ground black pepper

Add the saffron, 1½ tablespoons hot water and the rosewater to a small bowl and set aside to infuse for at least 20 minutes, or up to overnight if getting ahead.

Add 2 tablespoons of the oil, the onion and ½ teaspoon salt to a lidded non-stick sauté pan and place over a medium-high heat. Cook for 10 minutes, stirring occasionally, until the onions are nicely golden. Add the potatoes, 2 tablespoons of water and another ¼ teaspoon salt, give everything a good stir, cover with the lid and turn down the heat to medium-low. Cook for 15 minutes, stirring halfway, until the potatoes are cooked through and have taken on some colour.

Meanwhile, fill a large, lidded, non-stick saucepan (roughly 26cm/10in in diameter) with water. Add 2 teaspoons of salt and bring to the boil over a medium-high heat. Add the rice, bay leaves and spices and boil for just 5 minutes, until half cooked. Strain through a sieve (strainer) set over the sink.

Rinse out and dry the pan. Add the remaining 2 tablespoons of oil and half the butter. Sprinkle the cut side of the tomatoes with ¾ teaspoon salt and a good grind of pepper and arrange them cut-side down with the chillies in the bottom of the pan. Top evenly with half the rice (including the aromatics), spoon over half the saffron water and half the potato mixture, then repeat with the remaining rice, saffron water and potatoes. Use the handle of a wooden spoon to poke three or four holes into the rice mixture and dot with the remaining butter. Cover the pan with a clean tea towel, followed by the lid, bringing the ends of the towel up and over the lid and securing them together with a rubber band or by tying the ends together. Place over a medium-high heat for 10 minutes, then turn down the heat to low and steam the rice for 45 minutes, undisturbed.

Remove the lid and the towel and set aside for 5 minutes or so. Place a very large plate over the pan and, in one swift movement, invert the whole thing onto it. If some of the tomatoes stick to the bottom of the pan just remove these and arrange them on top of the rice. Shake the plate a little to spread things out and then sprinkle with the parsley.

Baked Mushroom Rice with Cinnamon and Allspice

This dish is for all the mushroom lovers out there. Typically this type of rice is made with lamb mince and can be eaten as is or used to stuff a whole chicken or vegetables. I'm quite partial to this veggie alternative, especially in the cooler months as a meatless main to an autumn spread. The sweet spices and the mushrooms marry really well together, and the whole thing will have your kitchen smelling fantastic.

Serves 6 · Soaking time: 20 minutes–2 hours

450g (1lb) portobello mushrooms, stems discarded, roughly broken into 5cm (2in) chunks
450g (1lb) oyster mushrooms, left whole, or halved if they're larger
1 large onion, halved and cut into 1cm (½in) slices (220g/7¾oz)
6 garlic cloves, halved lengthways
2½ tsp ground cinnamon
2 tsp ground allspice
105ml (3¾fl oz) olive oil
500ml (18fl oz) chicken or vegetable stock
1½ tbsp white miso
350g (12oz) basmati rice, washed until the water runs clear, then soaked for at least 20 minutes or up to 2 hours, then drained

For the topping
3 tbsp olive oil
4 garlic cloves, thinly sliced
30g (1oz) blanched almonds, roughly chopped
30g (1oz) pine nuts
1 tsp Aleppo chilli flakes
½ tsp sweet smoked paprika
2 tbsp roughly chopped parsley, to serve
fine sea salt and freshly ground black pepper

Preheat the oven to 220°C fan/240°C/475°F/Gas mark 9.

Put the mushrooms, onion, halved garlic, spices, olive oil, 1¼ teaspoons salt and a good grind of pepper into a large roasting tin (pan) – about 26 x 34cm (10½ x 13½in). Give everything a good stir, then bake for 40–45 minutes, stirring twice throughout, until well browned.

Meanwhile, pour the stock and 350ml (12fl oz) of water into a medium saucepan and bring to a gentle simmer over a medium heat. Whisk in the miso and 1 teaspoon of salt and keep warm on a low heat.

When the mushrooms are roasted, stir the rice into the tin until evenly distributed. Pour over the warm stock mixture and use a spoon to push down on any exposed rice grains so they're fully submerged, resisting the urge to mix everything together. Wrap the tin tightly in foil and bake for 25 minutes. Remove from the oven, leaving the foil on, and let steam for a further 10 minutes.

Meanwhile, for the topping, add the oil and sliced garlic to a small frying pan (skillet) and place over a medium heat. Fry for about 3 minutes, stirring occasionally, or until the garlic just starts to turn lightly golden (turn down the heat if it gets too coloured too soon). Add the almonds and fry for another minute, then add the pine nuts and fry for a minute more, or until everything is golden. Stir in the spices and a pinch of salt and immediately pour the whole thing into a heatproof bowl to stop it from cooking further.

When ready, transfer the rice to a large platter, spoon over the fried garlic and nut mixture and sprinkle with the parsley.

Emmawash: Spiced Rice with Mung Beans and Prawns

The name *emmawash* comes from the word *maash*, which means mung beans in Arabic. Traditionally, this rice is made with dried salted shrimp, which you soak and wash very well. I've opted to use fresh prawns instead, which some also prefer for their milder taste. If you happen to get shell-on prawns, do save the shells to make a prawn stock and use this to cook the base – it'll only make it even tastier. Be sure to use split green mung beans here as they cook much faster – you can find them in most Middle Eastern or South Asian grocery stores. Don't skip out on serving this with plenty of crispy fried onions and the *daqoos* sauce, for the whole authentic experience.

Serves 4–6 · Soaking time: 20 minutes–2 hours

8 cardamom pods, left whole
½ cinnamon stick
5 cloves
2 tsp cumin seeds
2 tsp coriander seeds
½ tsp chilli flakes (optional)
6 black peppercorns
1½ black limes
1½ tsp ground turmeric
2 red onions, finely chopped
110g (3¾oz) ghee
5 garlic cloves, finely grated
35g (1¼oz) fresh ginger, peeled and finely grated
350g (12oz) vine tomatoes (about 3), finely chopped
500g (1lb 2oz) peeled and deveined extra-large raw king prawns (jumbo shrimp), patted dry
30g (1oz) fresh coriander (cilantro), finely chopped, plus an extra 2 tbsp, to serve
30g (1oz) dill fronds, finely chopped, plus an extra 1 tbsp, to serve
150g (5½oz) green split mung beans, soaked for at least 2 hours in boiling water, then drained
225g (9oz) basmati rice, washed until the water runs clear, then soaked for at least 20 minutes and up to 2 hours, then drained
2 green chillies, left whole
1 red chilli, left whole
fine sea salt and freshly ground black pepper

To serve
50g (1¾oz) crispy fried onions, bought or homemade (see Note on page 151)
1 lemon, cut into wedges
Daqoos, the sauce (see page 272)

Add the cardamom, cinnamon, cloves, cumin and coriander seeds, chilli flakes and peppercorns to a small frying pan (skillet) and toast over a medium heat until fragrant, about 3–4 minutes. Transfer to a spice grinder with the ½ black lime and blitz until completely smooth. Stir in the turmeric and set aside.

Heat a large (about 26cm/10½in), lidded, deep-sided pan over a medium-high heat. Once hot, add the red onions, and cook, stirring often, until browned, about 7 minutes. Don't add any fat just yet – if the onions start to catch, then add a tablespoon of water. When ready, add 60g (2oz) of the ghee to melt, then stir in the whole black lime, garlic, ginger and spice mix and cook for a minute until fragrant. Add the tomatoes and cook, stirring occasionally, for 4–5 minutes, or until nicely broken down. Stir in the prawns, herbs and 1 teaspoon salt. Cook for about 1½ minutes, until the prawns have mostly turned pink (they won't be cooked all the way through). Spoon slightly more than half the mixture into a bowl and set aside.

Add the mung beans to the pan with 600ml (21fl oz) of boiling water. Bring to a boil, cover, and cook for 7 minutes. Remove the lid and stir in the rice, whole chillies and 1½ teaspoons of salt. Boil for 2 minutes, for the rice grains to soak up some of the liquid, then, without stirring, dot all over with the remaining 50g (1¾oz) of ghee and spoon over the reserved prawn mixture. Top with a clean tea towel, followed by the lid, securing the ends of the towel up and over the lid with a rubber band or by tying the ends together. Turn down the heat to low and leave to cook, undisturbed, for 30 minutes. Without removing the lid, set aside to steam gently for 20 minutes more.

To serve, remove the towel and invert the emmawash onto a large, wide platter and spread it out nicely. Sprinkle with the fried onions and the extra herbs. Serve with the lemon wedges to squeeze over the top and the daqoos sauce in a bowl alongside.

Fega'ata: Bottom of the Pot Chicken and Rice

Fega'ata refers to the very bottom of something, with *ga'a* meaning 'bottom' and *fe* meaning 'in'. Fishermen will often talk about *ga'aet el bahar*, meaning bottom of the sea, and in this uniquely Bahraini recipe it means 'bottom of the pot', where all the good stuff happens. The meat (or fish or vegetables) is left to steam and cook gently without any liquid, and the rice is piled on top. As with many of our dishes, it is inverted so that bottom is top and top is bottom. Don't skimp on the onions as their moisture is what helps move things along. The chicken skin doesn't get crispy here; it acts as a shield, keeping the meat nice and tender.

Serves 6–8 · Soaking time: 20 minutes – 2 hours

½ tsp loosely packed saffron threads
2 tsp rosewater
2 tsp cumin seeds, finely crushed using a pestle and mortar
2 tsp coriander seeds, finely crushed using a pestle and mortar
1 tsp mild curry powder
1 tsp ground turmeric
1 tsp paprika
½ tsp ground cinnamon
2 black limes: 1 finely ground to yield 1 tsp; the other broken in half, pips removed
1kg (2lb 4oz) chicken thighs, bone in, skin on (about 8 thighs), patted dry
100g (3½oz) yellow split peas, soaked in boiling water for at least 1 hour
3 onions, halved, and each half cut into 4 wedges (540g/1lb 3oz)
400g (14oz) floury potatoes like Maris Piper (2–3), peeled and cut into 5cm (2in) chunks
1 large plum tomato (130g/4¾oz), cut into 8 pieces
3 green chillies, left whole
35g (1¼oz) fresh ginger, peeled and finely grated
5 garlic cloves, finely grated
4 tbsp melted ghee
4 cloves
3 fresh bay leaves
6 cardamom pods
375g (13oz) basmati rice, washed until the water runs clear, then soaked for at least 20 minutes or up to 2 hours, then drained
2 tbsp coriander (cilantro), roughly chopped, to serve
fine sea salt and freshly ground black pepper

Add the saffron, rosewater and 1½ tablespoons of hot water to a small bowl and set aside. Mix together all the ground spices and ground black lime in a small bowl. Marinate the chicken thighs by adding them to a medium bowl with half the spice mixture, 1½ teaspoons salt and a generous grind of pepper. Mix well and set aside while you continue with the rest.

Bring a medium saucepan of water to the boil. Drain the split peas, add them to the boiling water and cook for 15 minutes, until two-thirds cooked. Drain and add to a large bowl, with the onions, potatoes, tomato, green chillies, ginger, garlic, the halved black lime, remaining spice mixture, 2 tablespoons of the ghee, 1 teaspoon salt and a generous grind of pepper, and mix together with your hands.

Half-fill a large (around 28cm/11¼in), deep-sided, non-stick saucepan with water. Bring to the boil with 2½ teaspoons of salt, then add the cloves, bay leaves, cardamom and rice. Boil for just 4 minutes, then drain through a large sieve (strainer) set over the sink. Rinse and dry out the pan.

To assemble, spread 1 tablespoon of ghee around the base of the clean pan. Spread with half the potato mixture, then top with all the chicken thighs, skin-side down. Top evenly with the remaining potato mixture, then spoon over half the saffron water. Now top with the rice and aromatics, without compressing, and spread it carefully so as not to break apart the grains. Pour over the remaining saffron water and the final tablespoon of ghee. Top with a clean tea towel, followed by the lid, bringing the ends of the towel up and over the lid and securing them with a rubber band or by tying them together. Place over a medium-high heat for exactly 15 minutes, rotating the pan halfway. Then, turn down the heat to low and leave to cook, undisturbed, for 1 hour and 45 minutes.

Remove the lid and towel and let settle for 10 minutes. Place your largest platter over the pan and, in one swift movement, invert the whole thing onto the platter. Lift off the pan and shake the platter to distribute everything nicely. Don't worry if a few bits stick to the base of the saucepan, spoon these onto the rice. Sprinkle with the coriander and serve.

Herby Meatball Rice with Kohlrabi and Pistachio Slaw

This is loosely inspired by a Shirazi rice dish called *kalam polo* of herby rice layered with fried onions and kohlrabi and tiny little meatballs. The traditional dish is truly spectacular and well worth giving a go if time allows. Here, however, I hope I'll be forgiven for making a major divergence; I've kept the meatballs a little larger, and transformed the kohlrabi into a fresh slaw to eat alongside, which I feel the rice really begs for. I recommend using a non-stick pan for this, as it'll help you easily achieve a wonderfully crispy *tahdig* – that bottom-of-the-pot layer of crispy rice. If your large pan isn't non-stick, I recommend lining the base with baking paper. Another tip is to use a food processor to chop all the herbs – this will massively save on time. As always, the only thing that's needed here is some yoghurt to serve it with and, if you're anything like me, mixed pickles (page 267) to have alongside.

Serves 6 · Soaking time: 20 minutes–2 hours

For the meatballs

400g (14oz) minced (ground) lamb (15–20% fat), or beef, or a mixture of both
½ large onion, roughly grated (shredded) on a box grater, then squeezed of its water (55g/2oz)
1 tsp ground turmeric
1 tsp ground cinnamon
1 tbsp cumin seeds, roughly crushed using a pestle and mortar
2 tbsp olive oil, plus extra for shaping

For the rice

350g (12oz) basmati rice, washed until the water runs clear then soaked for at least 20 minutes and up to 2 hours, then drained
25g (1oz) chives, finely chopped
25g (1oz) tarragon leaves, finely chopped
25g (1oz) basil leaves, finely chopped
25g (1oz) dill fronds, finely chopped
40g (1½oz) unsalted butter
2 tbsp olive oil
½ tsp loosely packed saffron threads, then crushed and soaked in 3 tbsp hot water for at least 20 minutes

Continued ingredients overleaf

First make the meatballs. Add the lamb, onion, spices, 1 tablespoon of the oil, ¾ teaspoon salt and about 50 grinds of pepper to a medium bowl. Use your hands to knead very well for about 4 minutes. Using lightly oiled hands, roll the mixture into compact balls, each weighing 20g (¾oz) – you should make 24. Heat the remaining tablespoon of oil in a large frying pan (skillet) over a medium-high heat. Once very hot, working in batches if necessary, add the meatballs and fry until browned all over, turning as necessary, about 4 minutes. Transfer to a plate, draining off any excess fat.

Three-quarters fill a large (about 26cm/10½in), lidded, non-stick saucepan with water. Bring to the boil over a medium-high heat, then season with 2½ teaspoons of salt. Taste the water at this point, it should be nicely salty but not as salty as pasta water. If necessary, add a little more salt. Add the rice and set a timer for 4 minutes, until the grains have plumped up but the rice isn't fully cooked. Stir in the herbs, cook for 30 seconds more, then drain through a large, fine-mesh sieve (strainer) set over the sink. Very gently stir a couple times with a silicone spatula to evenly distribute the herbs, without breaking the grains.

Rinse out and dry the pan, then return to a medium-high heat with 25g (1oz) of the butter, all the oil and half the saffron water. Swirl to melt and combine, then spoon a thin layer of rice over the melted butter mixture in the base of the pan, compacting it with the back of the spoon. Set a timer for 12 minutes. Working quickly, sprinkle over half the remaining rice mixture, spooning it lightly and so it starts to form a mound (do not press or compact it). Evenly top with half the meatballs, then sprinkle over the rest of the rice in the same way. Top with the remaining meatballs, then spoon over the remaining saffron water and dot with the last 15g (½oz) of butter.

Continued overleaf

For the slaw

10g (¼oz) basil leaves, roughly torn

10g (¼oz) chives, roughly chopped

5g (⅛oz) tarragon leaves

5g (⅛oz) dill fronds

3 tbsp olive oil

1 tbsp lemon juice

40g (1½oz) pistachios, toasted and roughly chopped

2 tsp coriander seeds, toasted and roughly crushed using a pestle and mortar

2 medium kohlrabi (500g/1lb 2oz), peeled and cut into thin matchsticks (380g/13oz)

1 tsp sumac

fine sea salt and freshly ground black pepper

Using the spoon's handle, make six holes in the rice, all the way to the bottom of the pan. Sprinkle all over with 4 tablespoons of water, then cover with a clean tea towel, followed by a lid, bringing the ends of the towel up and over the lid and securing them together with a rubber band or by tying the ends together. Rotate the pan at this point, to ensure even browning. Once 12 minutes is up, turn down the heat to medium-low and leave to cook gently for 45 minutes. When ready, take off the heat and, without removing the lid, let steam gently for 15 minutes more.

Meanwhile, make the slaw by adding the herbs and oil to a food processor and blitzing until smooth, scraping the bowl a few times as you go. Empty into a medium bowl and stir in the lemon juice, pistachios, coriander seeds, ¼ teaspoon salt and a good grind of pepper. Immediately before serving, stir in the kohlrabi to nicely coat (it will get watery if it sits for too long). Transfer to a serving bowl and sprinkle with the sumac.

Remove the lid and the towel from the rice pan, then place a large, round platter over it. In one swift movement, invert the whole thing onto the platter – it should easily slide out. Use your hands to break apart the *tahdig* into random pieces, then shake the platter to spread everything nicely and expose the meatballs. Serve with the slaw alongside.

Plain Buttery Saffron Rice

This is a simple method for a rice pilaf that can easily slot in as a side to any dish you please. If you're not into saffron, then leave this out – you'll still have a simple and delicious plain buttery rice. Alternatively, swap out the saffron for some cumin or black mustard seeds, or a small pinch of turmeric for colour. Once you get the base right, you can play around with the flavourings as you please.

Serves 4 · Soaking time: 20 minutes–2 hours

30g (1oz) unsalted butter

⅛ tsp tightly packed saffron threads, very finely crushed

250g (9oz) basmati rice, washed until the water runs clear, then soaked for at least 20 minutes and up to 2 hours, then drained

fine sea salt

Add 20g (¾oz) of the butter and all the saffron to a medium, lidded saucepan and place over a medium-high heat. Once melted, stir in the rice until nicely coated in the fat then pour over 400ml (14fl oz) of hot water. Season with 1 teaspoon of salt, bring to the boil, then top with a tight-fitting lid and turn down the heat to low. Leave to cook, undisturbed, for 18 minutes then, without removing the lid, remove from the heat and leave to steam for a further 15 minutes.

Serve topped with the remaining 10g (¼oz) of butter to melt through.

Vermicelli Chicken and Rice with Cardamom and Cinnamon

This one-pot chicken and rice is a dinner-time winner, and a go-to meal I'll make when I'm not sure of what to cook. It gives you everything you need really: protein power, carb comfort, and joy in the form of crispy edges.

Serves 4 · Soaking time: 20 minutes–2 hours

seeds from 20 cardamom pods, finely crushed using a pestle and mortar
1½ tsp paprika
1½ tsp dried oregano
1½ tsp ground cinnamon
4 tbsp olive oil
6 large chicken thighs (or 8 smaller ones), bone in, skin on
150g (5½oz) wheat vermicelli noodles, broken into roughly 3–4cm (about 1½in) lengths
1 onion, finely chopped (180g/6¼oz)
2 cinnamon sticks
3 fresh bay leaves
250g (9oz) basmati rice, washed until the water runs clear, then soaked for at least 20 minutes and up to 2 hours, then drained
20g (¾oz) unsalted butter, cut into 6–8 cubes
fine sea salt and freshly ground black pepper

To serve
5g (⅛oz) parsley, roughly chopped
½ lemon

In a large bowl combine the cardamom, paprika, oregano, ground cinnamon, 2 tablespoons of the oil, 1 teaspoon salt and a generous grind of pepper. Add the chicken, coat well and set aside to marinate for at least 20 minutes, or refrigerate for longer if getting ahead. If the latter, remove the chicken from the refrigerator at least 30 minutes before you start cooking.

Preheat the oven to 180°C fan/200°C/400°F/Gas mark 6.

Place a large, lidded, non-stick, ovenproof sauté pan over a medium heat. Once hot, add the noodles and toast, stirring often, until deeply brown, about 10–12 minutes. Transfer the toasted noodles to a plate, then return the pan to a medium-high heat. Add half the chicken thighs, skin-side down, and cook for about 5 minutes or until nicely coloured. Turn the pieces over and cook on the other side for 2 minutes more. Transfer to a tray or plate and repeat with the other half.

Add the remaining 2 tablespoons of oil, the onion, cinnamon sticks, bay leaves and a tiny pinch of salt and cook for about 4–5 minutes, stirring often, until softened and lightly browned. Add the rice, toasted vermicelli and 1 teaspoon of salt and cook for a minute more, stirring continuously. Pour in 720ml (25fl oz) of hot water, give everything a stir, then top with the chicken thighs (don't push them into the rice), skin-side up, along with any of their juices. Cover and transfer to the oven for 40 minutes.

Remove from the oven and turn up the temperature to 220°C fan/240°C/475°F/Gas mark 9. Top each chicken thigh with a cube of butter, then bake, lid off, for 10 minutes more, or until the chicken is nice and crisp and the edges of the pan are browned. Take out of the oven and let it settle for 5–10 minutes, then transfer the chicken thighs onto a tray or plate. Use a slotted spoon to gently loosen the rice, then place a very large platter on top of the pan. In one swift movement, and using a tea towel to help you, carefully invert the whole thing onto it. You should have some nice, crisped-up rice around the top and edges. Use a small serrated knife to break apart the crispy rice (the *tahdig*) into random chunks, then top with the chicken thighs. Sprinkle over the parsley, squeeze over the lemon half and serve warm.

RICE

Lemony Vine Leaf Rice

I love the unique, sour taste of this rice, which gives you the flavour of stuffed vine leaves without having to go through the whole process of stuffing and rolling them. You can eat this as is, with a spoonful of yoghurt and some roasted veggies if you like, but it also works really well as part of a mezze spread. If you can't find Egyptian rice, then arborio is a good substitute.

Serves 4

120ml (4fl oz) olive oil
1 red onion, finely chopped (150g/5½oz)
4 garlic cloves, crushed
1 tsp ground allspice
1 tsp Lebanese seven-spice
1 tsp cumin seeds, finely ground using a pestle and mortar
2 tsp paprika
3 tbsp tomato purée (paste)
2 ripe tomatoes (250g/9oz), very finely chopped
160g (5¾oz) vine leaves in brine, washed to remove any salt, stems removed, squeezed dry then finely chopped
30g (1oz) parsley, finely chopped, plus an extra 1 tbsp, to serve
30g (1oz) coriander (cilantro), finely chopped
200g (7oz) Egyptian rice, washed until the water runs clear, then drained
30g (1oz) mint leaves, finely chopped
1 tbsp pomegranate molasses
2½ tbsp lemon juice
35g (1¼oz) flaked almonds
1 tsp urfa or Aleppo chilli flakes
1 tsp dried mint
60g (2¼oz) pomegranate seeds, to serve
fine sea salt and freshly ground black pepper

Heat 4 tablespoons of the oil in a large, lidded sauté pan over a medium-high heat. Add the onion and fry, stirring occasionally, for about 4 minutes or until softened and lightly coloured. Add the garlic, spices and tomato purée and cook for 1½ minutes more, until fragrant and dark red. Stir in the tomatoes and vine leaves and cook for another 3 minutes, until the tomatoes have broken down nicely. Stir in the parsley, coriander, rice, 1½ teaspoons salt and a good grind of pepper, then pour in 900ml (31fl oz) of hot water. Bring to a simmer, top with the lid, then turn down the heat to its lowest setting and leave to cook gently for 30 minutes. Give everything a stir – the rice should be nice and soft and the mixture slightly wet (add a splash more water if necessary). Stir in the fresh mint, molasses and lemon juice, then transfer to a wide shallow bowl.

Heat the remaining 4 tablespoons of oil in a small frying pan (skillet) over a medium heat. Once hot, add the flaked almonds and fry for about 1½ minutes, stirring a couple of times, until lightly golden. Add the chilli and dried mint and cook for just 30 seconds, then immediately pour this all over the rice mixture. Sprinkle with the pomegranate seeds and the extra parsley and serve warm.

Machboos

Machboos is Bahrain's national dish, a spiced rice that will often contain chicken, meat, fish or prawns. This 'base' recipe can be made with any protein you choose, but I also like to have it as is and instead take liberties with the toppings. The split pea and onion topping is often seen at special occasions, for instance during Eid, when you'll have a whole lamb over rice (called *ghouzi*). This would go really well with the Slow-cooked Fenugreek Lamb (page 228) and the Cucumber Yoghurt (page 78).

Serves 4–6 · Soaking time: 20 minutes–2 hours

For the rice

55g (2oz) ghee (use olive oil if vegan)
1 onion, finely chopped (180g/6¼oz)
1 cinnamon stick
1 dried lime (black or regular), pierced a couple of times with a sharp knife (optional)
1 green (bell) pepper, cut into 3–4cm (about 1½in) cubes
4 garlic cloves, finely grated
30g (1oz) fresh ginger, peeled and finely grated
1–2 green chillies, finely chopped, seeds and all
1½ tsp cumin seeds, finely crushed using a pestle and mortar
1½ tsp coriander seeds, finely crushed using a pestle and mortar
4 cloves, finely crushed using a pestle and mortar
8 cardamom pods, roughly bashed open
½ tsp ground turmeric
200g (7oz) tomatoes, finely chopped (about 2 small ones)
10g (¼oz) dill fronds, finely chopped
10g (¼oz) coriander (cilantro) leaves and soft stems, finely chopped
300g (10½oz) basmati rice, washed until the water runs clear, then soaked for at least 20 minutes and up to 2 hours, then drained
fine sea salt and ground black pepper

For the topping

75g (2½oz) yellow split peas, soaked in boiling water for 2 hours
3 medium eggs, boiled to your liking, then peeled (omit if vegan)
25g (1oz) golden raisins
1 tbsp apple cider vinegar
1 large onion, finely chopped
35g (1¼oz) raw cashews
40g (1½oz) ghee (use olive oil if vegan)
½ tsp ground cinnamon
5g (⅛oz) coriander (cilantro), leaves and soft stems picked
5g (⅛oz) dill fronds, picked

Melt 40g (1½oz) of the ghee in a large, lidded saucepan over a medium-high heat. Once hot, add the onion, cinnamon stick and dried lime and fry for 4 minutes, stirring occasionally, until softened and starting to colour. Add the green pepper and continue cooking for 3 minutes, stirring occasionally, then add the garlic, ginger, chillies and spices and fry for a minute more, until fragrant. Stir in the tomatoes and herbs and cook for 5 minutes, stirring occasionally, until the tomatoes have completely broken down. Stir in the rice, 1¼ teaspoons of salt and a generous grind of black pepper, then pour in 500ml (17fl oz) of hot water. Bring to a simmer and dot with the remaining 15g (½oz) of ghee. Cover the pan with a clean tea towel followed by the lid, bringing the ends of the towel up and over the lid and securing them with a rubber band or by tying them together. Turn down the heat to medium-low and leave to cook, undisturbed, for 20 minutes. Once ready, turn off the heat and, without removing the lid, leave to steam for a further 20 minutes.

Meanwhile, prepare the topping. Three-quarters fill a medium saucepan with water and bring to the boil. Add the drained split peas to the pan and boil for 15–20 minutes, or until they are cooked through but still hold their shape. Drain well and set aside. Refill the saucepan with water and use it to boil your eggs at this point. Cool, peel and set aside.

Add the golden raisins and apple cider vinegar to a small bowl and set aside.

Place a medium frying pan (skillet) over a medium-high heat. Once hot, add the onion and the cashews (without any fat at this point) and fry for 6 minutes, stirring occasionally, until nicely browned. Add the ghee and cinnamon, stirring to melt the ghee, then stir in the split peas, ⅓ teaspoon of salt and a good grind of pepper. Fry for a further 4 minutes, stirring occasionally, then add the golden raisins and vinegar and remove from the heat.

Uncover the rice, remove the towel and place a large, round platter over the pan. In one swift movement, invert the whole thing onto the platter, gently shaking the platter and using a spoon to spread everything nicely. Spoon over the split pea mixture, then halve the eggs, seasoning them with a pinch of salt and pepper, and arrange these on the rice too. Lastly, top with the picked herbs.

RICE 133

Um Ahmed's Mathrooba

Her name was Um Ahmed but I never really knew her name. I knew she was a mother, Um, and that her eldest son was called Ahmed. Mother of Ahmed was apparently all I needed to know. I've always imagined her name to be quite powerful in meaning. Something like *Iman*, for faith, or *Amal*, for hope. On this particular day my dad drove me to Muharraq, a part of Bahrain that I feel has retained much of its traditional charm and character. Some of the houses are still kept in the quintessential old style, where there's a *housh*, or open courtyard, running through the centre of the home. In this style the courtyard is the heart of the home; its where kids will play, where chickens will run freely, where gatherings will commence and, most importantly, where spices are laid out to dry under the sun. Um Ahmed's home had this traditional layout, with an outdoor kitchen built under the shade of the courtyard, the light shining just so, and the whole set up a nod to what once was, or what still can be. As my dad drove off that day, Um Ahmed took my hand and guided me into her heart, into the *housh*, not because she knew me but simply because she'd heard that I wanted to learn.

I watched as Um Ahmed leant over her spices, gently distributing them among her baskets made from woven palm leaves. She'd just given them a thorough wash and would be leaving them now to dry in the sun before grinding them into her own special spice mix: Baharat Um Ahmed. I didn't dare tell her at the time that I generally cheated and used conventional spice mixes from the supermarket. I already knew that the recycled jar on the counter was mine to take home, and that it was filled to the brim with her very own spice mix. 'Use it for everything except fish,' she said quite forcefully. 'Fish has its own *khalta siriya* [secret mix].' I nodded emphatically. Fifteen-year-old me was shy of Um Ahmed; shy of asking for the exact proportions of her spice mixes, what the sun had to do with it, could I have the fish spice mix please and, most importantly, what is your name.

Ya benti, my daughter, she beckoned as she walked towards the stove and lifted the lid on the simmering pot we'd put together earlier. I breathed it all in, so many familiar scents in one fantastic inhalation. Ginger and chilli, cardamom and clove, rice and cinnamon, all gently yielding to each other in the most glorious way. My stomach growled, but we weren't quite done yet.

She pushed me down onto a stool and handed me a long wooden paddle. Placing the pot on the floor, she wedged it firmly between my feet and instructed me to beat the mixture. 'How long?' I asked, the sweat trickling down my back. 'Until it's done,' she retorted. The pot was tall and cylindrical, designed especially so the rice grains could be pushed and scraped up and along the sides of the pot with the long paddle, an old-school method for achieving the optimal consistency. (Nowadays I would opt to use a stand mixer with a paddle attachment but, back then, Um Ahmed stuck to her ways and I was none the wiser.) I pushed and scraped and beat that mixture until my shoulders were sore, until the paddle felt like it would slip right out of my clammy little hands. All the while I listened to her delicate prayers, calling onto Allah every time she felt it had become too difficult to beat. 'You can't rush good things,' said Um Ahmed as she grabbed the paddle and took over the reins. Her pace was focused and her beating skilled; she'd done this so many times before.

Mathrooba, the dish we prepared together that day, means 'beaten'. Like most good things, it came to be via a happy accident. The story goes that the dish meant to be cooked on that fateful day was in fact Machboos (page 132), a dish of spiced chicken and rice (sometimes also lamb or fish), cooked in one pot until the rice grains are beautifully separated and the meat tender. The not-so-skilled cook at hand added a disproportionate amount of water to rice, resulting in a big pot of mush. The mixture was then beaten and beaten until it resembled porridge, almost unrecognizable from its original form. And so, the quite literally named *mathrooba* was born and is now one of the most loved dishes in Bahrain, as well as other parts of the Gulf.

Once Um Ahmed was satisfied with her work, she divided the mixture between two large platters, using her spoon to make a well in the centre, nestling in loads of fried onions and drizzling over a good amount of olive oil. She wrapped one platter snugly in foil and placed it firmly in my arms. 'For your family,' she insisted. This was non-negotiable. I'd had *mathrooba* plenty of times before that day but with Um Ahmed's *mathrooba*, I think I loved the dish just that little bit more.

I often think of Um Ahmed, the mother of four sons, leaning over her cylindrical pot, looking focused and purposeful while preparing her family's supper. I think of the sun burning into her back and the sweat trickling down from her forehead and back into her headscarf. I think of her kind eyes and her gentle mannerisms, of her yearning for a daughter that never came and of companionship few and far between. I often think of her name. Perhaps it is *Anoud*, for strong-willed.

This is a story about the traditions I wish would always remain, and the elder voices that make sure they keep living.

Mathrooba: Beaten Chicken and Rice

In testing recipes for this book I'd give away food to friends, neighbours and anyone willing to give the dishes a home. My dear friend Anosha, who eagerly claimed the mathrooba, said that I needed a better description than the one I had given her: 'Hey, it's me again, do you fancy a savoury porridge for dinner?' 'You're massively underselling it,' she fed back to me later that night, 'Even my 2-year-old loved it.' And she's right: this is comforting, delicious and truly unique. *Mathrooba*, meaning 'beaten' in Arabic, is typically served during Ramadan, where it's easy to digest but also satiating. The rice, chicken and spiced tomato base is cooked low and slow until the meat is tender and the rice grains barely discernible. Then, staying true to its name, the mixture is beaten by hand into a consistency similar to a congee, but more heavily spiced and a little thicker. Call it nostalgia but it's one of my all-time favourite dishes that I'll happily eat throughout the year, but especially in the winter months.

Serves 6

For the mathrooba
4 tbsp olive oil
2 red onions, finely chopped
1kg (2lb 4oz) chicken legs (about 4 large ones), skin on, bone in
6 garlic cloves, finely grated
40g (1½oz) fresh ginger, peeled and finely grated
1 tsp ground turmeric
1 tbsp cumin seeds, finely ground using a pestle and mortar
1 tbsp coriander seeds, finely ground using a pestle and mortar
1 tsp garam masala
½ tsp chilli flakes
¾ tsp ground cinnamon
1 dried lime (black or regular), pierced a couple of times with a sharp knife
600g (1lb 5oz) plum tomatoes, roughly grated (shredded) and skins discarded (500g/1lb 3oz)
3 tbsp tomato purée (paste)
40g (1½oz) coriander (cilantro), roughly chopped, plus an extra 1 tbsp, to serve
20g (¾oz) dill fronds, roughly chopped, plus an extra 1 tbsp, to serve
200g (7oz) basmati rice, washed until the water runs clear, then drained
3 tbsp lemon juice
fine sea salt and black pepper

For the topping
3 tbsp olive oil
3 onions, halved and thinly sliced
3 mild fresh chillies, a mixture of green and red, left whole
40g (1½oz) unsalted butter

Heat the oil in a large, lidded, deep-sided, heavy-based pan over a medium-high heat. Add the red onions and cook for 3 minutes, stirring occasionally, just to soften. Add the chicken legs and cook for 6 minutes, turning to seal on both sides (they won't be totally browned). Stir in the garlic, ginger, spices and dried lime and cook for 2 minutes, until fragrant. Add the tomatoes, tomato purée and herbs and cook for 2 minutes more. Pour in 1 litre (35fl oz) of water, then stir in the rice, 2 teaspoons of salt and a generous grind of pepper. Bring to a simmer, cover, turn down the heat to its lowest setting and leave to cook for 80 minutes, stirring every 20 minutes or so to prevent the bottom from catching.

Meanwhile, make the topping. Add the oil to a large frying pan (skillet) over a medium-high heat. Once hot, add the onions, chillies and ¼ teaspoon salt, stirring to coat in the fat, then turn down the heat to medium and cook, stirring occasionally, until the onions are deeply caramelized and the chillies have softened, about 30 minutes. Transfer into a bowl, then return the pan to a medium heat with the butter. Cook for about 7 minutes, stirring occasionally, until browned and smelling nutty. Empty into a small heatproof bowl to stop it cooking further.

Once the mathrooba is ready, turn off the heat and then use tongs to remove the chicken legs and transfer them into a bowl. When cool enough to handle, discard the skin and bones (or save them to make a stock) then use two forks to roughly shred the meat. Stir the shredded chicken and lemon juice back into the pan. Using a whisk or a potato masher, beat the mixture for 5–10 minutes, until the rice grains are no longer discernible and the mixture resembles a spoonable porridge. If you'd like it a little looser, add another 100ml (3½fl oz) of hot water or so until you get your desired consistency. Taste and adjust salt and lemon levels at this point too (you might want to add more of either).

When ready to serve, spread the mathrooba out in a large shallow bowl and top with the onions and chillies. Pour over the browned butter, sprinkle over the extra herbs and serve warm.

Muhammar oo Samak: Date Molasses Rice with Fish

Sweet rice, salty fish. This recipe is dedicated wholeheartedly to my two late grandfathers, one very English, Donald Mckie, one very Arab, Jassim Murad. Donald was a very fussy eater: he liked his veg boiled, his meat well done, his fish battered and all three seasoned in varying degrees of salt. Jassim, the polar opposite, was excited to have Donald over for lunch and made sure that his favourite dish was on the table: *muhammar*, date molasses rice, and *safi*, fried local rabbitfish. The two went hand in hand, as far as he was concerned. Donald, being polite and ever so English and therefore unable to express his absolute dread, forced himself to take a bite. But then he took another, and another. In fact, he went for seconds. Suffice to say everyone was shocked, except for Jassim, who never once doubted his ability to please. I've taken a few liberties here, replacing the fried *safi* with firm white fish pieces and serving a date pickle alongside, which is just a bit of my own touch. I like to add salted and chopped cucumbers to my plate as well.

Serves 4 · Soaking time: 20 minutes–2 hours

For the fish
½ tsp ground turmeric
½ tsp paprika
2 tsp cumin seeds, finely crushed using a pestle and mortar
seeds from 15 cardamom pods, finely crushed using a pestle and mortar
600g (1lb 5oz) skinless hake fillet, cut into 6cm (2½in) pieces (or halibut)
1½ tbsp melted ghee
½ lemon

For the muhammar
2 tbsp melted ghee
5 cardamom pods
5 cloves
1 cinnamon stick
3 fresh bay leaves
150g (5½oz) date molasses
½ tsp loosely packed saffron threads, roughly crushed
300g (10½oz) basmati rice, washed until the water runs clear, then soaked for at least 20 minutes and up to 2 hours, then drained well
fine sea salt and ground black pepper

For the date pickle
2 tbsp olive oil
1 tsp fennel seeds
1 tsp Aleppo chilli flakes
120g (4¼oz) Medjool dates (about 6), pitted and thinly sliced
3 tbsp apple cider vinegar
30g (1oz) red onion (about ¼ of an onion), thinly sliced
10g (¼oz) coriander (cilantro), leaves and soft stems picked

Mix all the ground spices for the fish in a large bowl with ½ teaspoon salt and a generous grind of black pepper. Add the fish and mix well to coat. Refrigerate until needed.

For the muhammar, add the ghee, whole spices and bay leaves to a medium, lidded saucepan and place over a medium heat. Cook for 3 minutes, stirring occasionally, until fragrant. Stir in the molasses (careful, it might spit!) then pour in 620ml (20¾fl oz) of hot water, the saffron and ¾ teaspoon salt. Bring to the boil over a medium-high heat, then stir in the rice. Bring up to a vigorous boil and boil for exactly 5 minutes, without stirring, until the rice grains have started to plump up and have absorbed at least half the water. Top with a clean tea towel followed by a lid, securing the ends of the towel up and over the lid with a rubber band or by tying them together. Turn down the heat to low and cook, undisturbed, for 30 minutes.

Meanwhile, make the pickle by adding the oil and fennel seeds to a small frying pan (skillet) over a medium heat. Cook for just 2 minutes, until fragrant, then stir in the chilli and a tiny pinch of salt and pour into a medium heatproof bowl. Let cool for 5 minutes, then stir in the dates, vinegar and onion. Set aside to lightly pickle.

Once the rice is ready, remove the lid and the towel. Set aside to cool slightly while you fry the fish. Heat the ghee in a large frying pan over a medium-high heat. Add the fish and cook for 2–3 minutes on each side, or until nicely browned and cooked through. Allow more time if your fish pieces are thicker. Squeeze over the lemon juice.

Transfer the rice to a large platter and top with the fish and any fat left in the pan. Stir the coriander into the pickle and serve in a bowl alongside.

For the Love of Rice

Stood outside of this particular restaurant feeling slightly underwhelmed, were myself, my dad, my friend and photographer Matt, and our driver, who had promised he would take us to the most popular rice restaurant in Al-Hufuf. It wasn't often that I'd cross the border into Saudi Arabia, a 30-minute journey down one singular causeway, traffic allowing. Although very close, Saudi often felt like a completely different world to me – a neighbouring country with its own personality, its own culture different to my own – there was a lot I didn't know. What I did know though, what we all knew, was that some of the best rice dishes were made there, different to the ones I grew up with, and arguably more delicious. And if there's one thing you must know about me, is that I will climb mountains, cross borders even, for rice.

We arrived early, around midday, but even then the queue was long, the kitchen visibly bustling. It was less a dine-in restaurant, and more of a cafeteria/take-out vibe. We sat cross-legged on plastic lined flooring, and asked for a selection of rice. It arrived within minutes, topped with a slow-cooked lamb big enough to feed a dozen mouths. There were paper napkins and plastic spoons, if we needed them, and a big basin nearby to wash our hands. I wasn't particularly hungry, but within a few bites I was suddenly ravenous. There was a depth to it, a rich smokiness I couldn't quite pin point. 'I must find out what they did to this rice', I said.

After much imploring and many smiles, the manager let us into the kitchen at the end of service. My heart sank as I realized that the staff were cleaning down, and I wouldn't get to witness the good stuff. Luckily, I was wrong. He led us into this back room with high ventilated ceilings and massive fire pits dug deep into the ground. He showed us the palm wood that they used to burn their fires, and the large pots of rice, covered in broth, fresh tomatoes and chillies, that they'd lower into the scorching ground using long steel rods. He explained how the whole chickens would sit on racks above the rice, followed by the lamb they'd wrap and lay on top of these, both their juices dripping into the rice pots underground. They'd then cover the pits with heavy lids and empty bags of rice, leaving the fire to work its magic. The resulting rice would cook and expand gently in its liquid, becoming smoky, rich, savoury, the tomatoes collapsing into it and the chillies permeating the grains with a subtle heat. The cooks would walk away at this point, their hard work done and dusted, safe in the knowledge that some traditions really can't be beat. Needless to say I have no recipe for this, only a deep appreciation for what we witnessed that day, and for the kindness we were shown during our short visit.

I always knew that I'd include an ode to rice within *Lugma*. Many of the recipes in this chapter showcase rice in its grandest attire: steamed low and slow, perfumed with liquid-gold saffron, cooked from the top down, served from the bottom up, herb heavy, spice bold. But there's something to be said about a steaming bowl of plain white rice, a pat of butter nestled neatly on top, it's edges melting slowly into the grains, coating them in unctuous fat and flavour. In these moments, I often feel like buttered rice could heal the world.

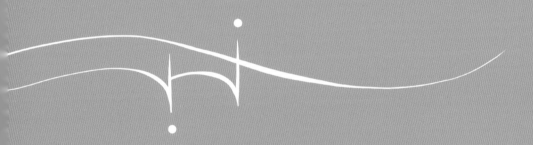

VEGETARIAN

A Very Green Lasagne with Fresh Chilli Sauce

This is my Middle Eastern take on lasagne, which has been lightened a little with the addition of tangy yoghurt, feta, lemon juice and a hefty amount of herbs (300g/10½oz, to be exact). The fresh chilli sauce amplifies the whole dish in a very lovely, spicy way.

I always find making lasagne quite an epic ordeal and, while this one is no exception, it is my go-to when feeding a crowd, because I can focus on one hearty dish, and just serve a couple of simple salads alongside. The best part is: you can assemble the whole thing the day before, then just take it out the refrigerator about an hour before baking.

Serves 6

For the greens
120g (4¼oz) parsley leaves and soft stems
120g (4¼oz) coriander (cilantro) leaves and soft stems
60g (2¼oz) dill fronds
2 tbsp olive oil
2 onions, halved and finely chopped (360g/12½oz)
6 garlic cloves, finely chopped
1 tbsp cumin seeds, finely crushed using a pestle and mortar
1 tbsp coriander seeds, finely crushed using a pestle and mortar
1½ tsp ground cinnamon
2 tsp ground turmeric
500g (1lb 2oz) Swiss chard, leaves roughly shredded (350g/12oz) – save the stems for another use
500g (1lb 2oz) large leaf spinach, leaves roughly shredded (400g/14oz) – save the stems for another use
2 tbsp lemon juice
fine sea salt and freshly ground black pepper

For the yoghurt béchamel
60g (2¼oz) unsalted butter
70g (2½oz) plain (all-purpose) flour
750ml (26fl oz) whole milk
2 garlic cloves, crushed
200g (7oz) Greek yoghurt
1 egg yolk

Continued ingredients overleaf

Start with the greens. Add about a third of the herbs to a food processor and pulse to finely chop. Empty into a medium bowl and repeat with the remaining two batches. Heat the oil in a large, deep-sided pan over a medium-high heat. Add the onions and cook for about 5 minutes, stirring occasionally, until softened and lightly coloured. Turn down the heat to medium, add the garlic and herbs and cook, stirring often to prevent catching, for about 12 minutes, until deeply green and fragrant. Add the spices and cook for a couple of minutes more, then turn the heat back up to medium-high. Add the chard and spinach in five or six batches, stirring well with each addition until wilted, along with ¾ teaspoon of salt and a generous grind of pepper. Continue until all the greens have wilted down, about 5–6 minutes in total. Take off the heat and stir in the lemon juice.

Make the béchamel by melting the butter in a medium saucepan over a medium-high heat. Whisk in the flour and cook for a couple of minutes, until it starts to smell like popcorn, then slowly add the milk in increments, whisking well with each addition to avoid any lumps. Season with ½ teaspoon of salt, then turn down the heat to medium. Cook for 5 minutes, stirring occasionally, until thick. Take off the heat and whisk in the garlic, yoghurt and egg yolk.

Preheat the oven to 200°C fan/220°C/425°F/Gas mark 7.

Start building the lasagne. Add a thin layer of béchamel to the base of a baking dish that measures 20 x 30cm (8 x 12in) with sides at least 7cm (2¾in) deep. Spread it around evenly, then top with three sheets of lasagne, trimming them if they're a little too large. Next, spread with a quarter of the béchamel followed by a quarter of the greens mixture and a quarter each of the feta, mozzarella and halloumi. Continue in this way, until you've used up all the lasagne sheets and end with a layer of béchamel, greens and cheeses. Lightly grease a piece of foil large enough to cover the lasagne and place it over the dish, greased-side down, securing the sides tightly.

Continued overleaf

For building
12 fresh lasagne sheets (320g/11oz)
200g (7oz) feta, finely crumbled
250g (9oz) buffalo mozzarella, drained, cut into 1.5cm (5/8in) cubes
225g (9oz) halloumi, finely grated

For the fresh chilli sauce (optional)
80g (2¾oz) mild red chillies, roughly chopped, seeds and all
1 small tomato, quartered (90g/3¼oz)
1½ tbsp apple cider vinegar
3 tbsp olive oil

Set the dish on a large tray and bake for 30 minutes, then remove the foil and bake for 30 minutes more, or until golden and bubbling. Leave to settle for about 30 minutes (this is the hardest part!).

Meanwhile, make the chilli sauce by adding the chillies and ¾ teaspoon of salt to a food processor and pulsing a few times until finely chopped. Add the tomato and blitz until the tomato is puréed and the chillies very fine. Empty into a bowl and stir in the vinegar and oil.

Serve the lasagne with the chilli sauce to spoon alongside.

Bahraini Dal

Dal is one of the first things that I learnt to make when I started getting into cooking as a teenager. It's also the one dish I never tired of throughout my university years, when I needed something cheap, quick, nourishing and relatively easy. It's the dish that has graced every new home I've lived in, every new country, every new walk of life. It's my 'big feelings and little feelings' dish, the one thing I'll turn to when I'm not really sure where to turn at all. That said, I was a bit hesitant about putting a dal recipe in the book, considering how many already exist in the recipe sphere, but it's such a staple in any Bahraini household. I always serve this with buttery white rice, but you can opt for naan bread or just have it as is with a spoon. I encourage you to play around with this recipe until you get it just how you like it – with more chilli for example, or bulked out with a few handfuls of spinach or other vegetables that might need using up.

Serves 6

300g (10½oz) red split lentils, picked over for any stones, washed and drained very well
1 dried lime, black or regular, pierced a couple times with a sharp knife
2 large plum tomatoes (250g/9oz)
1 chicken or veggie stock (bouillon) cube
½ red onion, finely chopped
250g (9oz) floury potatoes such as Maris Piper (about 1–2), peeled and cut into 3–4cm (about 1½in) chunks
1 tsp cumin seeds, toasted and very finely crushed using a pestle and mortar
2 tsp coriander seeds, toasted and very finely crushed using a pestle and mortar
¾ tsp garam masala
1 tsp ground turmeric
3 tbsp lime juice
20g (¾oz) coriander (cilantro) leaves, roughly chopped
fine sea salt and freshly ground black pepper

For the onion topping
150ml (5fl oz) olive oil
2 onions, finely chopped
30g (1oz) fresh ginger, peeled and finely grated
5 garlic cloves, finely grated
1 green chilli, finely chopped, seeds and all
4 dried mild red chillies
20 fresh curry leaves (from 2 stems)
1½ tsp black mustard seeds
1 tsp cumin seeds

Add the lentils, dried lime and 1.6 litres (54fl oz) of water to a large, lidded saucepan over a medium-high heat. Bring to the boil, skimming any scum from the surface, and cook for 15 minutes with the lid off, or until the lentils are quite soft.

Meanwhile, use a small, sharp knife to remove the core from the tomatoes and score the opposite end with an 'X'. Place in a medium heatproof bowl and pour over enough boiling water to cover. Leave for just 2–3 minutes, then drain off the water and peel and discard the skins. Roughly chop the tomatoes into 2cm (¾in) pieces.

When the lentils are ready, add the tomatoes, stock cube, red onion, potatoes, spices, 1¼ teaspoons of salt and a generous grind of pepper. Cover with the lid, turn down the heat to medium and cook for 15–18 minutes, stirring a couple of times throughout, or until the potatoes are nice and soft. Take off the heat and stir in the lime juice and fresh coriander.

Towards the last 10 minutes of cooking, make the topping by heating the oil in a medium sauté pan over a medium-high heat. Add the onions and fry for 10–12 minutes, stirring occasionally, until nicely golden. Stir in the ginger, garlic and green chilli and cook for 2 minutes more, stirring often, until fragrant. Lastly add the dried chillies, curry leaves, mustard and cumin seeds and fry for 1½ minutes more, stirring often, or until the leaves start to turn shiny and translucent and the onions are deeply brown. Immediately pour this into the finished dal, stirring to incorporate.

At this point, feel free to add a splash more water if you prefer a thinner dal. Serve warm.

Burnt Aubergines with Fenugreek Sauce, Tahini and Fried Shallots

I love to serve whole burnt aubergines in this way, where the punchy sauce is spooned over them, covering them generously like sauce blankets. This is quite a substantial vegetarian main so I would serve it with something light, like the Herby Leafy Salad (page 70).

Serves 4

4 aubergines (eggplants), pricked all over with a fork, about 8 times (1.2kg/2lb 10oz)

For the fenugreek sauce
2 tsp cumin seeds
1¼ tsp fenugreek seeds
½ tsp ground turmeric
4 tbsp olive oil
1 onion, finely chopped (180g/6¼oz)
40g (1½oz) fresh ginger, peeled and finely grated
40g (1½oz) tomato purée (paste)
2 tsp sugar
2 tbsp apple cider vinegar
fine sea salt and freshly ground black pepper

For the tahini
60g (2¼oz) tahini
1½ tbsp lemon juice

To serve
5g (⅛oz) coriander (cilantro), leaves and soft stems picked
60g (2¼oz) crispy onions or shallots, bought or homemade (see Note)

Start by burning the aubergines. If you have a gas hob, do this over an open flame. Turn the aubergines in the flame, using tongs if necessary, for about 15-20 minutes or until completely softened and charred on all sides. Alternatively, place a griddle (grill) pan over a high heat and ventilate your kitchen well. Grill the aubergines, turning as necessary, for about 40-45 minutes. When ready, transfer the aubergines to a colander set over a bowl and let sit for 30 minutes, to cool and drain off any liquid (discard the liquid). Carefully peel and discard the skin, leaving the aubergine and stem intact.

Meanwhile, make the fenugreek sauce. Add the cumin and fenugreek seeds to a small dry frying pan (skillet) and toast over a medium-high heat, shaking the pan a few times, until fragrant, about 2-3 minutes. Transfer to a spice grinder and blitz to a smooth powder (or use a pestle and mortar). Tip into a small bowl, stir in the turmeric and set aside.

Heat the oil in a large, lidded sauté pan over a medium-high heat. Add the onion and fry for about 6-7 minutes, stirring occasionally, until softened and browned. Add the ginger, tomato purée and the spices, turn down the heat to medium and cook for 2 minutes more, stirring often, until fragrant. Pour in 400ml (14fl oz) of water, add the sugar, vinegar, 1 teaspoon of salt and a good grind of pepper and bring to a simmer. Top with the lid, turn down the heat to medium-low and cook for 20 minutes, stirring halfway, until thickened slightly. Add the aubergines, top with the lid again and heat through for about 4 minutes.

Lastly, in a small bowl whisk together the tahini, lemon juice, 4 tablespoons of water and ¼ teaspoon of salt until smooth and pourable.

Place the aubergines on plates and spoon the sauce over the top of each one. Drizzle with the tahini and top with the coriander and crispy onions or shallots.

Note: You can simplify this recipe by buying crispy onions or shallots, but you can just as easily make your own. To do this, thinly slice 3 shallots into rounds and toss with a couple of teaspoons of flour or cornflour (cornstarch). Fry in two batches in plenty of vegetable oil at 180°C/350°F for about 4-5 minutes, or until browned and crisp.

Doh Piazeh Roast Potatoes

Doh piazeh means 'two onions' and refers to any dish that uses lots of onions in the base. I've had both Indian and Iranian versions of this dish, each delicious in their own right. This version with roast potatoes is my very own. Serve alongside roast chicken and a Herby Leafy Salad (page 70), for a complete meal.

Serves 4, as a side

- 1.2kg (2lb 10oz) floury potatoes, such as Maris Piper, peeled and chopped into rough 7cm (2¾in) chunks (so halved or quartered if larger)
- 120ml (4fl oz) olive oil
- 2 onions, finely chopped (360g/12½oz)
- 25g (1oz) fresh ginger, peeled and finely grated
- 5 garlic cloves, finely grated
- 3 green chillies, finely chopped – remove the seeds if you like less heat
- 2 tbsp tomato purée (paste)
- 1 tsp black mustard seeds
- 1 tsp ground turmeric
- 1½ tsp cumin seeds, roughly crushed using a pestle and mortar
- ½ tsp sugar
- ½ tsp dried mint
- 5 tbsp milk kefir (or coconut cream if vegan)
- 10g (¼oz) coriander (cilantro) leaves and soft stems, roughly chopped, to serve
- ½ lime
- fine sea salt and freshly ground black pepper

Preheat the oven to 190°C fan/210°C/410°F/Gas mark 6½.

Add the potatoes to a large saucepan and pour over enough water to cover by about 4cm (1½in). Season with 2½ teaspoons of salt and bring to the boil over a medium-high heat. Once boiling, cook for 5 minutes, or until three-quarters cooked through but still with a slight resistance when a knife is inserted through the centre. Drain through a colander set over the sink and then give the colander a good shake to fluff up the outsides.

Add 5 tablespoons of the oil to a large cast-iron frying pan (skillet) and place it on the middle rack of the oven to heat up for about 10 minutes. Carefully remove the hot pan, then gently add the potatoes and ½ teaspoon of salt and mix to coat in the fat. Bake for 50–55 minutes, turning about three times throughout, until golden and crisp.

Meanwhile, heat the remaining 3 tablespoons of oil in a medium sauté pan over a medium-high heat. Add the onions and cook for about 7 minutes, stirring often, until softened and browned. Add the ginger, garlic, chillies, tomato purée and spices and cook, stirring often, for about 3 minutes or until fragrant. Pour in 250ml (9fl oz) of water, season with the sugar, ½ teaspoon of salt and a good grind of pepper and turn down the heat to medium. Cook until thick and rich, stirring occasionally, for about 10 minutes. Take off the heat and stir in the dried mint.

When ready to serve, transfer the potatoes to a large plate, then spoon over the onion mixture. Drizzle with the kefir, sprinkle with the coriander and squeeze over the lime half. Serve right away.

Grilled Corn with Toumiya and Daqoos

For a long time I couldn't think of a way to incorporate Daqoos, the spice mix (page 272) into *Lugma*. This uniquely Bahraini mixture is often used as a finishing touch to sprinkle onto things like rice or fish. Then the sun came out, the seasons shifted, and sometimes that's all it takes for a brighter perspective – that and firing up an outdoor barbecue. Grilled corn is a common street food throughout the Middle East, typically eaten plain or with a dash of hot sauce, but I really love how both the daqoos and the *toumiya* (a vegan garlic sauce) complement the sweetness of the corn. You'll make more toumiya than you need here. Store refrigerated in a sterilized jar – it'll keep for up to three days and goes really well with grilled chicken or fried aubergines.

Serves 4

4 corn cobs
1½ tbsp sunflower oil
2½ tbsp Daqoos, the spice mix (page 272)
1 tbsp coriander (cilantro) leaves, roughly chopped, to serve

For the toumiya
200ml (7fl oz) water
2 tbsp cornflour (cornstarch)
15g (½oz) garlic cloves (about 5), finely chopped
1 lemon, halved; one half juiced to yield 1 tbsp, the other half for serving
½ tsp salt
100g (3½oz) sunflower oil (measure by weight not volume)

For the toumiya, add the water and cornflour to a small saucepan and whisk to combine. Place over a medium heat and cook, whisking constantly, for 3 minutes, or until the mixture thickens and appears translucent and there are no lumps (it will look a bit like Vaseline). Set aside to cool completely and solidify further. Once cool, transfer to a food processor with the garlic, lemon juice and salt. Pulse until nicely combined. With the machine still running, slowly drizzle in the oil in a very slow and steady stream. The mixture will start to turn white and take on a mayonnaise-like texture. Transfer to a small bowl – it will thicken as it sits. Stir in a tablespoon of cold water if you'd like a thinner consistency. You now have toumiya.

If your corn cobs come in the husk, then pull this down and tear at the silky threads and the husk with your hands to remove them. Don't worry if you can't get all the threads – they'll burn off as they grill. Preheat a large griddle (grill) pan over a medium-high heat. Drizzle the corn cobs with the oil and, once the pan is very hot, grill them for about 15 minutes, turning as necessary, until nicely charred on all sides. Preferably, do this on an outdoor barbecue (grill) when the sun is out (timings will vary). Transfer to a tray once they're ready. While the cobs are still warm, brush them all over with as much of the toumiya as you like (about 1–2 tablespoons per cob) then sprinkle all over with the daqoos. Transfer to a serving plate, squeeze over the lemon half, then sprinkle with the coriander. Serve right away.

Grilled Green Beans with Lemon and Feta

Vegetables cooked al dente are not really a thing in the Middle East; it's either raw or very cooked, and green beans are no exception. In fact, the first time I had to cook an al dente bean was while working in London and I was a little thrown: 'What do they mean by blanch for 90 seconds?' I grudgingly grew accustomed to them until I discovered grilled beans and, to my delight, found a halfway point between not overly soft and not overly crunchy either. That and the char, which gives these beans a lovely smoky flavour.

Serves 4, as a side

450g (1lb) green beans, trimmed
1 tbsp olive oil, plus an extra 1 tbsp to serve
75g (2½oz) feta, roughly crumbled
fine sea salt and freshly ground black pepper

For the lemon dressing
1½ unwaxed lemons
5 tbsp olive oil
1 onion, finely chopped (180g/6¼oz)
1 garlic clove, crushed
5g (⅛oz) oregano leaves, roughly chopped
5g (⅛oz) parsley leaves, roughly chopped
1 tsp maple syrup

Place a griddle (grill) pan over a medium-high heat (or use a large cast-iron pan). In a large bowl, toss the beans with the tablespoon of oil, ½ teaspoon of salt and a good grind of pepper. Once the pan is hot, add a third of the beans to the pan, spreading in a single layer, and cook for 5 minutes without turning. Carefully turn the beans over and cook for 3–4 minutes more or until charred and softened (don't worry if they're not perfectly charred). Transfer to a tray to cool, then continue in this way with the remaining beans. Keep the griddle pan on the heat.

For the dressing, first cut the lemon half into five 0.5cm (¼in) rounds, discarding any pips. Grill for about a minute on each side, until browned but not overly charred. Transfer to a cutting board and finely chop them, skins and all.

Add 2 tablespoons of the oil to a medium frying pan (skillet) and place over a medium-high heat. Once hot, add the onion, turn down the heat to medium and cook until softened and lightly browned, stirring occasionally, about 12 minutes. Remove from the pan and set aside to cool to room temperature, then stir in the chopped grilled lemon, garlic, herbs, maple syrup, remaining 3 tablespoons of oil, ¼ teaspoon of salt and a good grind of black pepper. Juice the remaining lemon to get 1½ tablespoons of juice and then stir this in too.

To serve, spread half the charred beans on a large platter, sprinkle with half the feta and spoon over half the dressing. Repeat with the remaining beans, feta and dressing and drizzle with the extra tablespoon of oil.

Hot Sauce Chickpeas with Turmeric Potatoes

There's a hole-in-the-wall shop in the souq (Manama's local market), that's been around for much longer than I have, called Aloo Basheer. They serve spicy chickpeas and spicy potato samosas, with the same spicy red sauce that is the perfect balance of chilli heat and acidity, and it's become an essential part of the Bahraini street-food scene. This dish is inspired by Aloo Basheer, which I have to say is not quite the real deal (souq not included, I'm afraid), but a close second. These chickpeas are not for the chilli-averse, but a spoonful of cold yoghurt often does the trick to temper their heat.

Serves 4

For the hot sauce
2 large red (bell) peppers, stems and seeds removed, quartered (320g/11¼oz)
60g (2¼oz) mild red chillies (about 3), left whole
2 plum tomatoes (240g/8½oz), halved
1 tbsp olive oil
5 tbsp apple cider vinegar

For the potatoes
350g (12oz) floury potatoes such as Maris Piper, peeled and cut into 3–4cm (1¼–1½in) chunks
½ tsp ground turmeric
3 tbsp olive oil
10 fresh curry leaves (from 1–2 stems)
½ tsp black mustard seeds
juice of ½ lime
10g (¼oz) coriander (cilantro) leaves and soft stems, roughly chopped, to serve
fine sea salt and freshly ground black pepper

For the chickpeas
3 tbsp olive oil
5 garlic cloves, crushed
1½ tsp cumin seeds, roughly crushed using a pestle and mortar
1 tsp paprika
1 jar of chickpeas (garbanzo beans), drained (500g/1lb 2oz), or 2 x 400g (14oz) cans, drained (440g/15½oz)
½ tsp sugar

Preheat the oven to 230°C fan/250°C/500°F/Gas mark 9 (or as high as your oven will go). Place the peppers, chillies and tomatoes on a medium tray lined with baking paper and drizzle over the tablespoon of oil, arranging the peppers and tomatoes skin-side up. Bake for 22–25 minutes, turning halfway, or until softened and charred in places. Set aside to cool slightly and, once cool enough to handle, peel and discard the pepper and tomato skins, and discard the chilli stems (remove the seeds too if you prefer it less hot). Add everything to a blender with the vinegar and blitz until completely smooth. Set aside.

Add the potatoes to a saucepan and pour over enough water to cover by about 3cm (1¼in). Add 2 teaspoons of salt and the turmeric and bring to a simmer. Cover with a lid, turn down the heat to medium, and cook for 10 minutes, or until cooked through.

Meanwhile, make the chickpeas. Add the oil to a medium sauté pan over a medium-high heat. Add the garlic, cumin and paprika and cook for 1 minute, until fragrant but not browned. Stir in the chickpeas, sugar and ¾ teaspoon of salt and cook for 2 minutes more, stirring occasionally, until nicely coated in the spices. Stir in the hot sauce and 3 tablespoons of water, turn down the heat to medium and cook over a medium heat for a further 5 minutes, stirring occasionally, until the chickpeas are nicely coated in the sauce and everything is heated through.

Once the potatoes are cooked, drain well and set aside. Rinse out and dry the pan and return it to a medium-high heat with the 3 tablespoons of oil. Once hot, add the curry leaves and fry for about a minute until the leaves turn translucent. Add the mustard seeds – they should sizzle right away – and remove the pan from the heat. Stir in the drained potatoes and the lime juice.

Divide the chickpeas between shallow bowls and top each with the turmeric potatoes and the chopped coriander.

VEGETARIAN

Photos from the iconic Aloo Basheer shop in Bahrain's Manama souk, which inspired the Hot Sauce Chickpeas on page 158.

Jewelled Pumpkin

This is one to pull out with the first signs of autumn, just as the leaves start changing colour and the sun starts setting sooner. Feel free to swap out the Crown Prince pumpkin for Kabocha or butternut squash, if you like. Serve as a main with some lightly cooked greens.

Serves 4

1 medium Crown Prince pumpkin (1kg/2lb 4oz), washed, halved, deseeded then cut into 8 wedges
2 tbsp olive oil
1 tsp ground cinnamon
fine sea salt and freshly ground black pepper

For the topping
25g (1oz) barberries
2 tsp caster (granulated) sugar
2 spring onions (scallions), green parts only, halved widthways then julienned (10g/¼oz)
5g (⅛oz) tarragon leaves, to serve

For the sauce
3 tbsp olive oil
1 large onion, thinly sliced (220g/8oz)
2 fresh bay leaves
1 cinnamon stick
8 cardamom pods, roughly bashed open
⅓ teaspoon loosely packed saffron threads
300ml (10½fl oz) good-quality chicken bone broth or stock (or vegetable stock if veggie)
1 tbsp apple cider vinegar

Preheat the oven to 220°C fan/240°C/475°F/Gas mark 9.

Line a large baking tray with baking paper, then add the pumpkin, oil, cinnamon, ¾ teaspoon of salt and a good grind of pepper and toss to combine. Arrange the pumpkin wedges so they're lying on their sides and are nicely spread out, then roast for 30–35 minutes, turning halfway, until cooked through and browned in places.

Meanwhile, prepare the topping. Add the barberries, sugar and 2 tablespoons of hot water to a small heatproof bowl, stirring to dissolve the sugar. Set aside to plump up.

Add the spring onions to a small bowl filled with ice-cold water and refrigerate until ready to use.

Make the sauce by adding the oil to a medium sauté pan over a medium-high heat. Once hot, stir in the onion, bay leaves, cinnamon, cardamom and ¼ teaspoon of salt, then turn down the heat to medium and cook for 15 minutes, stirring occasionally, until softened and only lightly coloured (turn down the heat if it's getting too brown). Stir in the saffron, stock, vinegar and another ¼ teaspoon of salt and bring to a simmer over a medium-high heat. Cook for 5 minutes, until very slightly reduced but still brothy. Keep warm over a low heat.

When ready to serve, pour the sauce onto a large, lipped plate, then arrange the pumpkin on top, overlapping the wedges slightly. Drain the barberries from their liquid and spoon these all over the pumpkin. Drain the spring onions from their water and pile these and the tarragon leaves on top. Serve warm.

Cinnamon-spiced Freekeh with Chickpeas and Tahini

This easy one-pot dish is a meal in its own right but will also go well with the Sautéed Greens with Yoghurt, Fried Onions and Turmeric Oil (page 178) or with some roasted chicken.

Serves 4

For the freekeh
20g (¾oz) dried ancho chilli, stem and seeds removed
4 tbsp olive oil
1 large onion, finely chopped (220g/8oz)
5 garlic cloves, crushed
2 tbsp tomato purée (paste)
2½ tsp ground cinnamon
440g (15½oz) jarred chickpeas (garbanzo beans), drained (or 2 cans)
300g (10½oz) cracked freekeh, picked of any stones, washed and drained well
fine sea salt and freshly ground black pepper

For the toppings
1½ tbsp apple cider vinegar
½ tsp caster (granulated) sugar
2 small banana shallots, thinly sliced into rounds (60g/2¼oz)
1 tbsp olive oil
30g (1oz) flaked almonds
¼ teaspoon paprika
40g (1½oz) tahini
1 garlic clove, crushed
1 tbsp lemon juice
5g (⅛oz) mint leaves, roughly torn

Add the ancho chilli to a large bowl and pour over 400ml (14fl oz) boiling water. Leave to rehydrate for about 15 minutes, then, reserving the soaking liquid, remove the chilli, finely chop and set aside.

Heat the oil in a large, lidded sauté pan over a medium-high heat. Add the onion and fry for about 5 minutes, or until softened and golden. Stir in the garlic, tomato purée, cinnamon, chopped chilli and the chickpeas and fry for 3 minutes more, stirring occasionally. Pour the reserved soaking liquid into a measuring jug/cup, and add enough boiling water to make 700ml (24fl oz) in total. Stir the freekeh, 1½ teaspoons of salt and a generous grind of black pepper into the pan, then pour over the liquid. Bring to a simmer, top with the lid, then turn down the heat to low and leave to cook, undisturbed, for 18 minutes. When ready, and without removing the lid, take off the heat and let steam gently for a further 10 minutes.

Meanwhile, make the toppings. In a small bowl, mix the vinegar, sugar and a tiny pinch of salt. Add the shallots and stir everything together. Set aside to soften and pickle gently.

Heat the oil in a small frying pan (skillet) over a medium-high heat. Add the almonds and a tiny pinch of salt and fry, stirring constantly, for about a minute or until golden. Stir in the paprika and immediately transfer to another small bowl.

Lastly, in a medium bowl whisk together the tahini, garlic, lemon juice, 3 tablespoons of water and a pinch of salt until smooth and pourable.

When the freekeh is ready, fluff up with a fork. Drizzle all over with the tahini sauce, then spoon over the shallots and their pickling liquid, the fried almonds and the mint. Serve warm, directly from the pan.

Macarona Béchamel

I'm not sure when béchamel landed in the Middle East, but once it arrived it was there to stay. You won't find any Arab household that doesn't have some sort of béchamel pasta bake on frequent rotation. This veggified version uses roasted aubergines in a spiced tomato sauce in place of a more typical beef or lamb mince. I like to have this with a big pile of rocket, dressed simply with lemon juice and olive oil.

Serves 6–8

400g (14oz) penne pasta or mezze penne

For the aubergine sauce
3 medium aubergines (eggplants), trimmed, cut into 4–5cm (1½–2in) cubes (700g/1lb 9oz)
6 tbsp olive oil
1 small onion, finely chopped (150g/5½oz)
1 small carrot, peeled and finely diced (100g/3½oz)
1 medium green (bell) pepper, stem and seeds removed, finely diced (120g/4¼oz)
4 garlic cloves, crushed
1½ tsp ground cinnamon
1½ tsp ground allspice
2 tsp cumin seeds, roughly crushed using a pestle and mortar
1 tsp Aleppo chilli flakes
1 tsp dried oregano
1½ x 400g (14oz) cans peeled plum tomatoes (600g/1lb 5oz), crushed by hand
½ tsp caster (granulated) sugar
1 tbsp apple cider vinegar
20g (¾oz) coriander (cilantro) leaves and soft stems, finely chopped
fine sea salt

For the béchamel
70g (2½oz) unsalted butter
90g (3¼oz) plain (all-purpose) flour
750ml (26fl oz) whole milk
generous pinch of freshly ground nutmeg
⅛ tsp ground white pepper
250g (9oz) Greek yoghurt
3 egg yolks
30g (1oz) parmesan or vegetarian alternative, finely grated

Preheat the oven to 220°C fan/240°C/475°F/Gas mark 9 and line a large baking tray with baking paper.

In a large bowl, toss the aubergine pieces together with 3 tablespoons of the oil and ½ teaspoon of salt. Spread in a single layer on the lined tray and roast for 25 minutes, or until softened and golden. Set aside.

Meanwhile, make the sauce by heating the remaining 3 tablespoons of oil in a large sauté pan over a medium-high heat. Add the onion, carrot and green pepper and cook for 8 minutes, stirring occasionally, until softened and starting to colour. Add the garlic, spices and oregano and cook for 1 minute more, until fragrant. Stir in the tomatoes, sugar and ½ teaspoon of salt, turn down the heat to medium and let simmer, stirring frequently, for 15 minutes or until thick and rich. Take off the heat and stir in the vinegar, coriander and roasted aubergines.

Make the béchamel by melting the butter in a medium saucepan over a medium-high heat. Whisk in the flour and cook for a couple of minutes, until starting to smell nutty. Slowly pour in the milk, a little at a time, whisking all the while, until fully incorporated and smooth. Stir in the nutmeg, white pepper and ¾ teaspoon of salt. Turn down the heat to medium and cook for 5 minutes, stirring occasionally to prevent it from catching. Take off the heat and whisk in the yoghurt and 2 of the egg yolks.

Turn the oven back on to 180°C fan/200°C/400°F/Gas mark 6.

Boil the pasta in plenty of salted boiling water until about three-quarters cooked (shave a few minutes off the timing on the packet instructions). Drain well through a colander set over the sink, then transfer it back into the pot with half the béchamel, stirring to coat. Transfer half the pasta mixture to a baking dish measuring 20 x 30cm (8 x 12in) with sides at least 8cm (3¼in) deep. Cover with all of the aubergine mix, pressing to evenly distribute, then top with the remaining pasta mixture. Stir the parmesan into the remaining béchamel, then spread this over the top. Use a pastry brush to brush the top of the béchamel with the remaining egg yolk. Place the dish on a large baking tray and bake for 35–40 minutes, or until nicely browned on top. Let rest for at least 20 minutes before serving.

Macaroni among Friends

'What shall I have for dinner tonight?' Ava asks, as I listen to her down the phone, mouth full while she munches on a pickle. 'What are the options?' I reply, as she lists what's in her fridge and matches them against her true heart's desire. 'I want what you made yesterday,' she says. I point out that it's a time-consuming dish, and she also doesn't have any chicken. 'Oh yes,' she sighs, and I know she's already moved on to thinking about her mother, what she would make if she were with her, that it would probably be what Ava calls 'village food', or *dahati* in Farsi. I understand this term too, even though I'm not Persian, but I know Ava's family well enough to call them my own. The food that graces their tables – 'nothing fancy,' Ava will point out – is some of the best I've ever eaten. It's food that's travelled – from Iran to Kuwait on her mum's side, from Iran to Bahrain on her dad's side – and now, as Ava settles into her new-found home with her husband, it travels all the way to Paris.

'I really want macaroni,' Ava says with breathless excitement down the phone. I know now that the idea has landed and, also, that it's not just any macaroni. 'Be sure to add the turmeric,' I say, but I don't really need to. Ava cooks with her breath. By this I mean that she cooks with all that her mother has ingrained in her, along with all the generations before that. She cooks with touch, taste, feel and is mostly driven by emotion. 'It's what I want to eat,' she'll say. 'It's what I'm craving.' I sometimes wish I could go back to that feeling, before cooking became a job and recipe-testing a rigorous process of measurement and precision. Ava's cooking is exactly what cooking should be: fluid, free, imperfect.

Back to the macaroni in question, though, and the day I finally sat down to try it. I've been sitting at Ava's family table for the past three decades, eating one tasty dish after another, sometimes Persian, sometimes Arabic, mostly unapologetically a mixture of the two. Herb-heavy, spice-generous, pickles optional but highly encouraged, and salad a must. Often Ava's mum will offer me a sheepish caveat like: 'It's not chef-worthy,' or, 'It's just my way but I'm sure there's better.' I'll always brush this off as unnecessary because, really, it is. As Ava's mum flipped her pot onto a large platter and lifted it to expose the most perfectly browned bread topping and burnt macaroni edges, I caught her eyes sparkle. She knew she'd succeeded, and I knew it was going to be a delicious day.

Later that night, and many hours after the phonecall, Ava sent me a photo of the macaroni she'd made. 'Hit the spot,' she wrote. 'You should put this in your book ya know.' It took me about 48 hours to put this into action. I'd like to say I need to thank Ava for sharing this dish, but in all honesty I probably need to thank her for sharing with me every dish before that: every unwanted lunchbox sandwich through our childhood, every late-night shawarma in our adolescence, every box of chocolates shared over birthdays, schoolgirl crushes and giggly sleepovers, every plate licked clean over our wins, every plate left untouched over our losses, our heartbreaks, our mournings. As we both left the island we call home to create new ones abroad, we took with us what we could. And, it turns out, what we could was mostly edible.

This is a story about friendship, migration and the food that travels along the way. Here's to endless plates of macaroni among friends.

Macaroni with Bread Tahdig and Marinated Feta

I might need to ask my fellow Italian cooks to look away for this one, but to me this dish is pure comfort. Our love of carbs means pasta is very popular in the Middle East, but it also means that concepts such as 'al dente' or 'subtly spiced' are absolutely not adhered to. This iconic Persian pasta dish gets half boiled and then steamed in the pot, which makes it slightly softer than what is typical, but then there's this wonderful crispy bread *tahdig* (or crispy bottom) that is just pure joy. Be sure to use the thin Lebanese pita bread here, not the thicker, fluffier ones; you want the pita to be roughly the same diameter or slightly larger than the base of your pan (22–24cm/8½–9½in). You can find Lebanese pita bread in most Middle Eastern grocery stores. Otherwise, you can also use a flour tortilla. This might require a little trial and error for the perfect doneness on your tahdig; it will vary depending on how powerful your hob (stovetop) is, or whether it's gas or electric.

Serves 6

For the macaroni
4 tbsp olive oil, plus extra for drizzling
3 onions, finely sliced (540g/1lb 3oz)
225g (8oz) elbow macaroni
225g (8oz) spaghetti, broken in half
6 garlic cloves, crushed
2½ tsp cumin seeds, finely crushed using a pestle and mortar
2½ tsp coriander seeds, finely crushed using a pestle and mortar
1 tsp Aleppo chilli flakes
1 tsp ground turmeric
4 tbsp tomato purée (paste)
300g (10½oz) plum tomatoes (about 3), puréed in a blender
fine sea salt

For the tahdig
3 tbsp olive oil
1 Lebanese pita bread (*khobez Lebnani*), 22cm (8½in) in diameter

For the feta
4 tbsp olive oil
1 jalapeño, finely chopped, seeds and all
20g (¾oz) coriander (cilantro), leaves and soft stems finely chopped
¾ tsp coriander seeds, toasted then roughly crushed using a pestle and mortar
200g (7oz) feta, diced into 1.5cm (⅝in) cubes
1 tbsp lime juice

For the macaroni, heat the oil in a large sauté pan over a medium-high heat. Add the onions and ¼ teaspoon of salt, stirring to coat in the oil, then turn down the heat to medium and cook for 20 minutes, stirring occasionally, until very soft and lightly golden.

Meanwhile, bring a large saucepan of water to the boil and season with 2½ teaspoons of salt. Add the macaroni and spaghetti and cook for just 4 minutes, or until halfway cooked. Ladle out 250ml (9fl oz) of the cooking water and drain the pasta through a strainer set over the sink. Lightly drizzle with oil to prevent it from sticking together.

Add the garlic, spices and tomato purée to the cooked onions and cook for 3 minutes more, stirring often, until fragrant and deeply red. Stir in the puréed tomatoes, the measured pasta water and 1 teaspoon of salt. Bring to a simmer over a medium-high heat, then cook for 5 minutes or until you have a thick and rich sauce. Take off the heat and stir in the cooked pasta until evenly coated.

To make the tahdig, add the 3 tablespoons of oil to a lidded, non-stick, deep-sided saucepan roughly 20–23cm (8–9in) in diameter. Use your hands to wipe some of the oil up the sides of the pan, then press the whole Lebanese pita into the pan so that it covers the base (and maybe slightly up the sides, depending on the size of your pan). Spoon in the pasta mixture, pressing down to compact. Top with a clean tea towel, followed by the lid, then pull the towel ends over the lid, tying them together or securing them in place with a rubber band. This is to ensure no steam escapes. Place over a medium-high heat and cook for exactly 7 minutes, then turn down the heat to low and cook, undisturbed, for 40 minutes more.

Meanwhile, marinate the feta. Add the oil, jalapeño, fresh coriander and coriander seeds to a medium bowl and stir to combine. Gently stir in the feta and lime juice and set aside.

Take the pasta off the heat, remove the lid and towel, and let sit for about 10 minutes. Then, with gusto and a tiny prayer, place a large plate over your pan and, in one swift movement, invert the whole thing onto it. Serve warm, with the feta alongside.

Melt-in-your-mouth Okra

This dish is inspired by a Jazan delicacy called *makshan bamiya* that I tried in Saudi Arabia. It came in a sizzling stoneware pot and for a moment I couldn't tell that it was okra, because the strands had become these melt-in-your-mouth greens and, hands down, it was the best thing I ate that day. If you're disheartened by some okra sceptics out there, then this dish might just convert them; it breaks every rule we've ever been taught about cooking okra, from soaking in vinegar to frying over high heat, and I really love it for that. You can serve this as a side, but I'd happily have it as a veggie main with some rice and a spoonful of Cucumber Yoghurt (page 78).

Serves 4

400g (14oz) fresh okra, topped, tailed and cut widthways into thirds
5 tbsp olive oil
1 onion, finely chopped (180g/6¼oz)
4 garlic cloves, finely chopped
3 green chillies, finely chopped, seeds and all (30g/1oz)
2½ tbsp tomato purée (paste)
2 tsp cumin seeds, finely crushed using a pestle and mortar
2 tsp coriander seeds, finely crushed using a pestle and mortar
1 tsp paprika
½ tsp ground turmeric
2 ripe plum tomatoes, roughly grated (shredded) on a box grater, skins discarded (165g/5¾oz)
2 tsp white miso
1½ tbsp fresh coriander (cilantro), finely chopped
fine sea salt and freshly ground black pepper

Bring a large, lidded pan of water to a simmer, then add the okra, top with the lid and turn down the heat to medium. Cook for 20 minutes, until very soft – you should be able to easily squeeze a piece between your fingers and for it to come apart. Drain through a sieve (strainer) set over the sink, run under cold water, then leave to drain completely. Return to the pan and use the bottom of a jar to mash the okra until it resembles pulled strands – you don't want any whole pieces. Set aside until needed.

Meanwhile, heat 3 tablespoons of the oil in a large, lidded sauté pan over a medium-high heat. Add the onion and cook, stirring occasionally, for about 7 minutes, until softened and browned. Add two-thirds of both the garlic and the green chilli, along with all the tomato purée and spices, and cook for 1½ minutes until nicely coloured. Add the grated tomato, miso, 400ml (14fl oz) of water, 1 teaspoon of salt and a good grind of pepper and bring to a simmer. Cook for 5 minutes, stirring occasionally, then stir in the okra, top with the lid and turn down the heat to medium-low. Cook for 20 minutes, stirring three or four times throughout, until thick and rich. Transfer to a large shallow serving bowl.

Add the last 2 tablespoons of oil and the remaining garlic and chilli to a small pan and place over a medium heat. As soon as it starts to bubble, cook for 30 seconds then add the fresh coriander and cook for 30 seconds more. Immediately pour the hot oil all over the okra and serve warm.

Mujadara with Yoghurt and Shirazi Salad

This Levantine dish of bulgur with lentils (or otherwise rice with lentils) is one of my favourite things to eat when I'm craving something both comforting and nourishing. I prefer the nuttiness that bulgur gives here, as opposed to rice, which is softer and requires some soaking. I'll also sometimes cheat when I'm running low on time, and use a packet of precooked Puy (French) lentils – which you're welcome to do here. The most important thing is never to skimp on the fried onions and, in my opinion, the Shirazi salad and yoghurt are both a must.

Serves 6

For the mujadara
200g (7oz) green or brown lentils, washed well
135ml (4½fl oz) olive oil
4 onions, 3 halved and cut into 0.5cm (¼in) slices (540g/1lb 3oz), 1 finely chopped (180g/6¼oz)
¾ tsp ground turmeric
1½ tsp ground cinnamon
1½ tsp ground cumin
1 tsp ground allspice
200g (7oz) bulgur wheat
fine sea salt and freshly ground black pepper

For the yoghurt
220g (7¾oz) natural (plain) yoghurt
1 garlic clove, crushed

For the Shirazi salad
400g (14oz) Lebanese cucumbers (about 3–4), halved, seeds removed, finely diced
1 large vine tomato, finely diced (150g/5½oz)
½ red onion, finely chopped (75g/2½oz)
2 tsp dried mint
2 tbsp lemon juice
1 tbsp olive oil
1½ tsp sumac

Fill a medium saucepan three-quarters full with water and bring to the boil. Add the lentils and cook for 12–15 minutes, or until just cooked through but not mushy. Drain well and set aside.

Meanwhile, heat 105ml (3½fl oz) of the oil in a large, lidded, deep-sided sauté pan over a medium-high heat. Once hot, add the sliced onions and turmeric and fry for 20–22 minutes, until deeply browned and crisp. Stir occasionally at first, then stir more often for the last 10 minutes or so, to ensure even browning and prevent burning. Use a slotted spoon to transfer the onions to a plate lined with paper towels, leaving any excess oil in the pan. Sprinkle the onions lightly with salt.

Return the pan to a medium-high heat with the remaining 2 tablespoons of oil, the finely chopped onion and ¼ teaspoon of salt. Fry for about 6 minutes, stirring often, until softened and browned. Add the cinnamon, cumin and allspice and cook for 30 seconds more, until fragrant, then stir in the cooked lentils, the bulgur, 1¼ teaspoons of salt and a good grind of pepper. Pour in 350ml (12fl oz) of hot water, bring to a simmer, cover with a lid, then set over a low heat and leave to cook, undisturbed, for 18 minutes. Take off the heat and leave to steam gently, lid on, for another 10 minutes.

Meanwhile, combine the yoghurt, garlic and ⅛ teaspoon of salt in a medium bowl and set aside.

Make the salad by adding all the ingredients except the sumac to a bowl and mix to combine.

To serve, spread half the mujadara out on a wide serving platter and top with half the fried onions. Top with the remaining mujadara, then follow with spoonfuls of the yoghurt, half the salad, the remaining fried onions and the sumac. Serve the extra salad in a bowl alongside.

VEGETARIAN

Musaqa'a: Aubergines in Spicy Tomato Sauce with Fried Potatoes

This Egyptian dish is one of my favourite vegan mains to cook and serve. The fried potatoes are my own little touch. Some will also add lamb mince or chickpeas, so it's really quite versatile. The most important thing is to have some plain rice or fluffy pita bread to eat with – you'll want something to soak up the melty aubergines and spiced sauce.

Serves 4

4 large aubergines (eggplants), trimmed, cut into 3–4cm (1¼–1½in) rounds (1.2kg/2lb 10oz)
4 tbsp olive oil, plus 1 tsp
1 large green (bell) pepper, stem and seeds removed, cut into 5–6cm (2–2½in) pieces (200g/7oz)
fine sea salt

For the sauce
3 tbsp olive oil
1 onion, finely chopped (180g/6¼oz)
6 garlic cloves, crushed
2 red chillies, 1 finely chopped (seeds and all), 1 left whole
1½ tsp cumin seeds, finely crushed using a pestle and mortar
1½ tsp coriander seeds, finely crushed using a pestle and mortar
1 tsp ground cinnamon
500g (1lb 2oz) ripe plum tomatoes, roughly grated (shredded) on a box grater and skins discarded (380g/13oz)
2½ tbsp apple cider vinegar
½ tsp sugar
15g (⅛oz) fresh coriander (cilantro), roughly chopped, plus a handful of picked leaves, to serve
150g (5½oz) cherry tomatoes

For the shoestring potatoes
about 700ml (24fl oz) sunflower oil, for deep frying
400g (14oz) red potatoes (about 2)

Preheat the oven to 220°C fan/240°C/475°F/Gas mark 9. Line a large baking tray and a small baking tray each with baking paper.

In a large bowl, toss the aubergines with the 4 tablespoons of oil and ¾ teaspoon of salt. Arrange on the large tray so they're lying flat. Add the green pepper to the bowl and toss with the teaspoon of olive oil and ⅛ teaspoon of salt, then arrange on the small tray. Place both trays in the oven and roast for 15 minutes. Remove the peppers, which should be softened and charred in places. Carefully turn over each aubergine and return to the oven for 15 minutes more, or until golden. Set aside and turn down the heat to 180°C fan/200°C/400°F/Gas mark 6.

Meanwhile, make the sauce by heating 2 tablespoons of the oil in a large sauté pan over a medium-high heat. Add the onion and cook for 5 minutes, stirring occasionally, until softened and golden. Add the garlic, chopped chilli and the spices and cook for 1½–2 minutes, stirring often, until fragrant. Stir in the grated tomato, vinegar, sugar and ½ teaspoon of salt, turn the heat to medium and cook for 5 minutes. Stir in the chopped coriander, cherry tomatoes and whole chilli and remove from the heat.

Arrange the aubergine and pepper pieces in a 25cm (10in) diameter baking dish (or use a 20 x 30cm/8 x 12in one), overlapping them slightly – they don't need to be perfect. Pour over the tomato sauce, evenly distributing the cherry tomatoes, then drizzle over the remaining tablespoon of oil. Bake for 30 minutes, or until the sauce is bubbling and has taken on some colour.

Meanwhile, for the potatoes, pour the sunflower oil into a medium, deep-sided saucepan, ensuring the oil doesn't come more than a quarter of the way up the sides. Place over a medium-high heat. While the oil heats, peel the potatoes, then use a mandoline to thinly slice them lengthways about 0.25cm (⅛in) thick. Stack the slices on top of one another and then cut into thin matchsticks. Transfer to a clean tea towel and press to remove some moisture. Test the oil is hot enough by dropping in a strip of potato – it should sizzle but not colour right away. Working in batches, a third at a time, fry the potato strips for 3–4 minutes, using a slotted spoon to move them around and prevent them from clumping together. Transfer to a tray lined with paper towels and sprinkle lightly with salt. Let the oil come back up to temperature and continue in this way with the remaining two batches.

When ready to serve, pile the fried potatoes on top of the musaqa'a and sprinkle with the extra handful of coriander. Serve right away, while the potatoes are crisp.

Potato and Sour Spinach Galette

I like to use a cast-iron pan here, as it gives the base and sides of this dish a really lovely crust. You can of course use a regular baking dish, but it won't give you quite the same texture. This works really well as a side dish to stewed meats in the winter months, but is also a really delicious vegan main and needs nothing more than a side salad.

Serves 4–6

For the filling
2 tbsp olive oil
2 onions, thinly sliced (360g/12½oz)
300g (10½oz) baby spinach
3 garlic cloves, crushed
25g (1oz) dill fronds, roughly chopped
2½ tsp sumac
1 large (25g/1oz) preserved lemon, seeds removed, flesh and skin finely chopped
2 tbsp lemon juice
fine sea salt and freshly ground black pepper

For the galette
1.6kg (3lb 8oz) waxy potatoes, peeled and cut into 0.25cm (⅛in) slices, preferably using a mandoline
2 tbsp cornflour (cornstarch)
5 tbsp olive oil, plus extra for greasing

First make the filling. Heat the oil in a large (about 28cm/11¼in diameter), cast-iron sauté pan over medium-high heat. Add the onions and ¼ teaspoon of salt, turn down the heat to medium and cook, stirring occasionally, for about 18 minutes or until softened and golden. Transfer to a medium bowl, then return the pan to the heat with the spinach and 1 tablespoon of water and cook just until wilted, about 3 minutes. Transfer to a sieve (strainer) and use the back of a spoon to squeeze out as much moisture from the spinach as possible. Add the spinach to the onion bowl with the remaining ingredients, ½ teaspoon of salt and a good grind of pepper and stir well to combine. Wipe out the pan and set aside to use again later.

Preheat the oven to 180°C fan/200°C/400°F/Gas mark 6.

Add the potatoes, cornflour, 2 tablespoons of the oil, 1¼ teaspoons of salt and a good grind of pepper to a very large bowl and use your hands to toss everything together. Pour another 2 tablespoons of oil into the sauté pan and use your hands to spread it up the sides. Divide the potato mixture into two and cover the bottom of the pan with half the potato slices, arranging them so they're lying flat and come about 3cm (1¼in) up the sides. Next, top with all of the spinach filling, spreading it evenly over the potatoes but leaving about a 2cm (¾in) border around the sides. Top with the remaining potato, this time overlapping the slices, starting from the rim of the pan and creating concentric circles to the centre. You should have some starchy liquid left in the bowl – pour this all over the potatoes.

Grease a large piece of foil with some oil and then use it to cover the sauté pan, greased side down. Bake for 30 minutes, then remove the foil and drizzle the top with the remaining tablespoon of oil. Turn up the heat to 200°C fan/220°C/425°F/Gas mark 7 and bake for 30–35 minutes more, rotating the pan halfway, or until nicely browned on top and around the edges. Leave to settle for about 10 minutes or so before serving, directly from the pan.

Sautéed Greens with Yoghurt, Fried Onions and Turmeric Oil

The lovely Claudine Boulstridge, who cross-tested most of the recipes in this book, told me that I really needed to sell this dish more. '"Greens" sounds too boring and healthy,' she said. 'Tell them it's a delicious way to eat lots of greens!' They're definitely not boring, even if they are quite healthy, so I stand by Claudine in saying that this is a very tasty way to get your greens in. I would happily eat this with some fluffy rice or alongside the Pan-fried Tomatoes with Za'atar, Pine Nuts and Halloumi (page 91). Feel free to change up the greens here, using more or less of any as you see fit.

Serves 4, as a side

- 1 tbsp apple cider vinegar
- 25g (1oz) golden raisins
- 135ml (4½fl oz) olive oil
- 3 onions, 2 halved and cut into 0.5cm (¼in) slices (360g/12½oz), 1 finely chopped (180g/6¼oz)
- ¾ tsp ground turmeric
- ¾ tsp dried mint
- 200g (7oz) Swiss chard leaves only, roughly shredded (save the stems for another use)
- 100g (3½oz) cavolo nero leaves only, roughly shredded
- 200g (7oz) baby spinach
- 3 garlic cloves, crushed
- 15g (½oz) fresh mint leaves, roughly chopped
- 300g (10½oz) Greek yoghurt, at room temperature
- 1 tbsp lemon juice
- fine sea salt and freshly ground black pepper

Add the vinegar and golden raisins to a small bowl and set aside while you continue with the rest.

Add 6 tablespoons of the oil to a medium frying pan (skillet) and place over a medium-high heat. Once hot, add the sliced onions and turmeric and fry, stirring often to prevent them burning, for about 12–15 minutes, or until deeply browned and starting to crisp up. Use a slotted spoon to transfer the onions to a plate lined with paper towels, leaving the oil in the pan. Set the onions aside to cool and crisp up further. Return the pan to a medium-high heat, add the dried mint and cook for just 20–30 seconds, or until fragrant. Immediately pour the oil into a small heatproof bowl and set aside.

Meanwhile, heat the remaining 3 tablespoons of olive oil in a large sauté pan over a medium-high heat. Add the finely chopped onion and cook, stirring occasionally, for about 5 minutes, or until softened and lightly coloured. Add big handfuls of the chard, kale and spinach, stirring to wilt a little before adding more. Once all the greens are in the pan, add the garlic, ¾ teaspoon of salt and a good grind of pepper, turn up the heat to high and cook for about 3–4 minutes, or until the greens are soft and no liquid remains in the pan. Take off the heat and stir in the fresh mint.

In a bowl mix together the yoghurt, lemon juice and ¼ teaspoon of salt. Spread half of this on a large platter and top with half the greens, half the fried onions and half the golden raisins. Repeat with the remaining yoghurt, greens, onions and golden raisins. Drizzle over the turmeric oil and serve warm, or at room temperature if you prefer.

Stewed Mung Beans and Greens with Saffron Rice

I published a similar recipe for these humble mung beans in *Shelf Love*, but as it's such a nostalgic dish for me, I feel it deserves a special place here in *Lugma*. Mung beans are highly underrated in my opinion; they're nourishing and satiating as much as they are delicious. If you don't do too well with spice, then feel free to use one or two chillies instead of the three specified in the recipe. The saffron rice could be optional but I'd love for you to enjoy this meal the way I would at home, with Torshi Makhlout (page 267) to eat alongside.

Serves 4–6 · Soaking time: 1 hour

150g (5½oz) whole dried green mung beans
6 tbsp olive oil
2 large onions, finely chopped (450g/1lb)
6 garlic cloves, finely grated
25g (1oz) fresh ginger, peeled and finely grated
3 green chillies, finely chopped, seeds and all
1 tbsp tomato purée (paste)
2 tsp cumin seeds, roughly crushed using a pestle and mortar
1½ tsp mild curry powder
1 tsp ground turmeric
70g (2½oz) tamarind pulp (from a block), soaked in 400ml (14fl oz) boiling water
400g (14oz) green leaves without stalks (I used a mixture of Swiss chard, spinach and cavalo nero), roughly shredded
40g (1½oz) coriander (cilantro) leaves and soft stems, finely chopped
120g (4¼oz) natural (plain) yoghurt, or kefir yoghurt
fine sea salt and freshly ground black pepper
Saffron Rice, to serve (page 127)

Pick out any stones from the mung beans and wash the beans very well. Place in a bowl and pour over enough boiling water to cover by about 3cm (1¼in). Leave to soak for about an hour, then drain.

Heat 4 tablespoons of the oil in a large, lidded sauté pan over a medium-high heat. Once hot, add the onions, turn down the heat to medium and cook, stirring occasionally, for about 25 minutes, or until softened and golden. Spoon out a third of the onions into a medium bowl and set aside. Turn up the heat to medium-high and stir in the garlic, ginger, two-thirds of the green chillies, the tomato purée and spices and cook for about 2 minutes, stirring often, until fragrant. Add the drained mung beans and 900ml (31fl oz) of water and bring to a simmer. Top with the lid, turn down the heat to medium and leave to cook for about 35 minutes, stirring once or twice throughout, or until the beans are cooked through but not mushy.

Meanwhile, strain the tamarind mixture through a fine-mesh sieve (strainer) set over a bowl and push down on the solids with your fingers to try to release as much of the pulp as possible. Discard the solids.

When the mung beans are ready, stir in the tamarind mixture, 1¼ teaspoons of salt and a generous grind of black pepper. Stir in the greens, a little at a time until wilted, cover and leave to cook for a further 10 minutes. Remove the lid, and simmer for 5 minutes, or until thickened ever so slightly. Stir in 30g (1oz) of the coriander and remove from the heat.

To the bowl with the reserved onion, add the remaining green chilli, 10g (¼oz) of coriander and 2 tablespoons of oil, then stir to combine.

Season the yoghurt with the tiniest pinch of salt. Transfer the mung bean mixture to a large shallow bowl (or serve directly from the pan) and top with the onion mixture. Serve warm with the yoghurt and saffron rice alongside.

Tomato Bulgur with Charred Courgettes

I like to eat this dish as is, with a big spoonful of yoghurt and some leaves, but you could also serve it alongside the Loomi Lemon Chicken (page 220) or stir in some pulses for a heartier meal. If you can't find white courgettes, feel free to use regular green ones.

Serves 4, as a side

For the bulgur
2 large plum tomatoes (240g/8½oz)
3 tbsp olive oil
1 onion, very finely chopped (180g/6¼oz)
4 garlic cloves, crushed
2 tbsp tomato purée (paste)
1 tsp paprika
1¼ tsp ground cinnamon
90g (3¼oz) bulgur wheat (medium grain variety)
70g (2½oz) fine bulgur wheat
fine sea salt and freshly ground black pepper

For the charred courgettes
750g (1lb 2oz) white courgettes (zucchini), trimmed and then cut at an angle into 5–6cm (2–2½in) chunks (700g/1lb 9oz)
3 tbsp olive oil
15g (½oz) basil leaves, picked
1 garlic clove, crushed
1 tbsp lemon juice

To serve
30g (1oz) walnuts, well toasted and roughly chopped
1½ tbsp pomegranate molasses

Use a small, sharp knife to core the tomatoes, then score the opposite end with an 'X'. Place in a medium heatproof bowl and pour over enough boiling water to cover. Leave for 2–3 minutes, then remove from the water and peel and discard the skins. Roughly chop into 2.5cm (1in) pieces and set aside.

Preheat the oven to its highest setting.

For the bulgur, heat the oil in a large, lidded sauté pan over a medium-high heat. Add the onion and a tiny pinch of salt, turn down the heat to medium and cook, stirring occasionally, for 10 minutes, until nicely softened but not at all coloured (turn down the heat if necessary). Add the garlic, tomato purée and spices, turn the heat back up to medium-high and fry for 2 minutes, stirring often, until fragrant. Stir in both bulgurs, the chopped tomatoes and 1 teaspoon of salt, then pour in 620ml (21½fl oz) of water. Bring to a simmer, then top with the lid, turn down the heat to its lowest setting and leave to cook, undisturbed, for 15 minutes. When ready, remove the lid and give everything a good stir (it should be a bit wet).

Meanwhile, spread out the courgettes on a medium baking tray and mix with 2 tablespoons of the oil, ½ teaspoon of salt and a good grind of pepper. Roast for 15–18 minutes, or until nicely charred and softened. Transfer to a bowl and mix with the basil, garlic and lemon juice.

Spread the bulgur out on a large platter with a lip, sprinkle over the walnuts, then spoon over the courgette mixture. Lastly, drizzle over the molasses and the last tablespoon of oil.

Zahra Bilaban: Cauliflower with Warm Yoghurt and Paprika Butter

I once bonded with a fellow Arab chef I barely knew over a heated discussion concerning warm yoghurt. His stance was that it simply didn't suit 'London palates' and so it was best to steer clear completely. 'But surely it's just a familiarity thing,' I had argued. 'It's simply one of the best tastes in the world!' On this last part we both agreed. Yoghurt is a huge part of most Middle Eastern diets, whether it's used for breakfast, hung for labneh, fermented into *jameed* (a dried and fermented sheep or goat's yoghurt) or used in sauces, as it is here. I add parmesan, which is very untraditional, but for me this adds a welcome funk – you can eliminate it if you like.

Serves 4

1 large head of cauliflower, trimmed and cut into large florets (700g/1lb 9oz)
4 tbsp olive oil
300g (10½oz) natural (plain) yoghurt
2½ tsp cornflour (cornstarch)
25g (1oz) parmesan or a vegetarian alternative, finely grated
5 garlic cloves, thinly sliced
15g (1oz) unsalted butter
½ tsp paprika
¾ tsp nigella seeds
1 tbsp mint leaves, roughly chopped
1 tbsp coriander (cilantro) leaves, roughly chopped
½ lemon
2 tbsp pomegranate seeds, to serve
fine sea salt

Preheat the oven to its highest setting and line a medium baking tray with baking paper.

Add the cauliflower, 2 tablespoons of the oil and ½ teaspoon of salt to the lined tray and toss to coat. Bake for 20 minutes, or until nicely browned and cooked through but still with a slight bite.

Meanwhile, add the yoghurt, 6 tablespoons of water, the cornflour and ½ teaspoon of salt to a small saucepan and whisk to combine. Place over a medium-low heat and cook for 10 minutes, whisking often, until nicely warmed through. Turn down the heat if necessary; you don't want the mixture to split at all. Stir in three-quarters of the parmesan and keep warm over a very low heat until needed.

Add the remaining 2 tablespoons of oil and the garlic to a small frying pan (skillet) and place over a medium heat. Cook for 10–12 minutes, stirring occasionally, until golden and crisp. Add the butter, paprika, nigella seeds and a tiny pinch of salt and cook for a couple more minutes, until melted and bubbling. Stir in the mint and coriander and immediately remove from the heat.

Arrange the roasted cauliflower in a large shallow bowl and pour over the warm yoghurt. Squeeze over the lemon, then spoon over the garlic and butter mixture. Lastly sprinkle with the remaining parmesan and the pomegranate seeds. Serve warm.

FISH

Fried Kingfish with Browned Butter and Crunchy Salad

Kingfish is one of my favourite fish, as it's meaty enough to lend really well to high-heat cooking methods, such as frying or grilling, without completely disintegrating. It also loves to be well-spiced, so don't be shy about getting creative with other spice mixes you might have. It's worth asking your fishmonger to source kingfish for you, but if you can't find it, monkfish will work just as well. Feel free to experiment with other types of fish too, such as swordfish or cod, altering cooking times as necessary (you want them cooked through and no longer translucent). For a traditional spread, serve with some buttery white rice (see page 127) and the Tomato Achar (page 269), but some simple roasted potatoes or grilled vegetables would go nicely here, as well.

Serves 4 · Marinating time: 1 hour +

1 tsp ground turmeric
1 tsp paprika
½ tsp Aleppo chilli flakes
2 tsp cumin seeds, finely crushed using a pestle and mortar
2 tsp coriander seeds, finely crushed using a pestle and mortar
seeds from 18 cardamom pods, finely crushed using a pestle and mortar
4 kingfish steaks (about 800g/1lb 12oz), about 2.5cm (1in) thick, or 4 monkfish fillets (about 650g/1lb 7oz)
120ml (4fl oz) sunflower oil
30g (1oz) unsalted butter
2 limes: 1 juiced to yield 1½ tbsp, 1 cut into 4 wedges to serve
fine sea salt and freshly ground black pepper

For the crunchy salad
4 tbsp apple cider vinegar
2 tsp caster (granulated) sugar
2 banana shallots, finely chopped (50g/1¾oz)
12 Lebanese or Persian cucumbers, peeled and seeds removed, chopped into 0.5–1cm (¼–½in) cubes (160g/5¾oz)
200g (7oz) mooli (daikon), peeled and chopped into 0.5–1cm (¼–½in) cubes (160g/5¾oz)
1 red chilli, stem and seeds removed, finely chopped
15g (½oz) coriander (cilantro) leaves and soft stems, roughly chopped
1 tbsp sesame seeds, well toasted

In a small bowl, combine all the spices, 1 teaspoon of salt (or ¾ teaspoon if using monkfish) and a generous grind of pepper. Lay the fish on a tray and pat them well dry with paper towels. Sprinkle the flesh all over with the spice mix and set aside to marinate for an hour at room temperature, or refrigerated for longer, if possible.

Just before you want to start cooking the fish, place all the salad ingredients into a medium bowl with ½ teaspoon salt and mix to combine. You don't want to do this too far in advance as you want everything stays nice and crunchy.

Line a tray with paper towels and heat the sunflower oil in a large, high-sided sauté pan over a medium-high heat. Once hot, fry the fish (in batches, if they don't all fit), for 2 minutes on each side, or until nicely browned and just cooked through. You may need to adjust these timings, depending on the type and thickness of your fish; thicker fillets of monkfish could need 1–2 minutes longer per side. Transfer to the lined tray to absorb any excess oil.

Meanwhile, melt the butter in a small frying pan (skillet) over a medium heat. Cook until browned and starting to smell nutty, about 7 minutes, stirring occasionally, then (careful, it might spit!) stir in the lime juice and ⅛ teaspoon salt.

Divide the fish, salad and lime wedges between four plates, pouring the browned butter over the fish. Serve warm.

Chbab Rubyan: Prawn Dumplings in Tamarind and Tomato Broth

This is quite an old, traditional recipe, one that not many people make any more, as it does involve quite a bit of work. I remember having this at my grandparents' dinner table when I was very little, and then not having it again until I made it myself many years later. It's a labour of love, for sure, and I'd recommend making it when you have a good stretch of time to get lost in the stuffing of dumplings and the cooking of prawn-based elixirs. I've taken a few liberties, such as adding chard to the broth and leaving out the split peas that would typically go into the stuffing. For me, the final result is pure magic, and reminds me time and time again how some traditions really do need to be kept alive.

Serves 4

For the dumpling shell

1kg (2lb 4oz) shell-on, heads-on extra-large raw king prawns (jumbo shrimp)
1 small onion, roughly grated (shredded) (65g/2¼oz)
1 tsp ground turmeric
1 tsp cumin seeds, finely ground using a pestle and mortar
100g (3½oz) rice flour (not the glutinous kind)

For the stuffing

2½ tbsp olive oil, plus extra for shaping
3 red onions, finely chopped (360g/12¾oz)
1 hot green chilli, finely chopped, seeds and all
1 black lime, halved, pips removed, and finely chopped by hand
¾ tsp ground turmeric
seeds from 15 cardamom pods, finely crushed using a pestle and mortar
1½ tsp cumin seeds, finely crushed using a pestle and mortar
¾ tsp ground cinnamon
40g (1½oz) coriander (cilantro), leaves roughly chopped (stems reserved for broth)
30g (1oz) dill fronds, roughly chopped (stems reserved for broth)
55g (2oz) golden raisins

Continued ingredients on page 194

First, peel and devein the prawns, reserving the shells and heads. Refrigerate the peeled prawns until ready to use.

For the broth, add 2 tablespoons of the oil, the tomato purée and the reserved prawn shells and heads to a medium, lidded saucepan and place over a medium-high heat. Fry for about 3–4 minutes, stirring often, until deeply red. Add the tamarind and head of garlic, the reserved herb stems, 900ml (30fl oz) of water and 1 teaspoon of salt and bring to the boil. Top with the lid, turn down the heat to medium-low and leave to cook for 30 minutes. Remove the lid, turn off the heat and use a wooden spoon to push the solids against the sides of the pan, breaking apart the tamarind and squeezing the juice from the prawn shells. Do this for a couple of minutes at least. Strain through a sieve (strainer) into a large bowl, pushing down on the solids to release all the flavour. Discard the solids. You should be left with about 700ml (24fl oz) of prawn broth. Wipe out the pan for later use and set the strained prawn broth aside.

Make the stuffing by adding the oil to a medium sauté pan over a medium-high heat. Once hot, add the onions and cook, stirring occasionally, until softened and browned, about 12 minutes. Stir in the chilli, black lime and spices and cook for another 2 minutes, stirring often, until fragrant. Add the herbs, golden raisins, ¾ teaspoon of salt and a good grind of pepper, cook for a minute, then set aside to cool completely.

Make the dumpling shell by adding the peeled prawns, grated onion, turmeric, cumin and 1 teaspoon of salt to a food processor and blitzing into a paste. Add the flour and pulse a few more times until combined and completely smooth. It will be quite sticky so use oiled hands to transfer to a large bowl. Keep a small bowl of oil beside you and, using oiled hands, roll out 30–35g (about 1oz) balls of the prawn mixture and place on a tray sprayed with a little water (this will prevent any sticking). You should make 18 balls.

Continued on page 194

For the broth
4 tbsp olive oil
3 tbsp tomato purée (paste)
90g (3¼oz) tamarind pulp (from a block)
1 head of garlic, halved widthways, plus 4 cloves, crushed
2 green chillies, pierced a couple of times with a knife
3 plum tomatoes (about 360g/12¾oz), roughly chopped and puréed in a food processor
375g (13oz) Swiss chard, leaves very finely shredded (175g/6oz), stems reserved for another use
fine sea salt and freshly ground black pepper

Working one at a time and using oiled hands, make an indentation into the centre of the ball with your index finger and then swivel your finger to create a large opening, so the ball is now shaped into a cup with a thin 0.5cm (¼in) rim. Add a tablespoon of the stuffing into the centre and then seal by pinching together the sides. Roll into a neat ball and continue this way with the remaining balls and filling.

Return the wiped-out saucepan to a medium-high heat with the last 2 tablespoons of oil and the crushed garlic. Cook for about 1 minute, until fragrant, then add the chillies and blitzed tomatoes and cook for 6 minutes more, stirring occasionally, until concentrated. Stir in the chard and ½ teaspoon of salt and cook until wilted, about 3 minutes. Pour in the prawn stock and bring to a simmer, then, once simmering, turn down the heat to medium-low and gently lower in each dumpling. Top with the lid and leave to cook for 15 minutes. Off the heat, let sit for 15 minutes more, for the dumplings to drink in all the flavours. Divide between 4 bowls and serve warm.

Baked Prawn Scampi with Fennel, Arak and Feta

It's no surprise that Bahrainis love their seafood, but Gulf prawns are truly something else: salty, delicate, they really are my favourite prawn. There's a shrimping ban for a good half of the year so, when it's lifted, my dad will buy extra at the fish market to freeze and use throughout the year. With this my mum would often reach into the freezer and make baked prawn scampi on skewers. Although I've majorly diverted here, this dish is an ode to those days, for the love of all things prawn and all things breadcrumbed. Be sure to use extra-large prawns here so that they stay nice and juicy when baked.

Serves 4

60g (2¼oz) unsalted butter, cut into 4 pieces
1 onion, halved and thinly sliced (180g/6¼oz)
1 fennel bulb, trimmed, quartered and thinly sliced (170g/6oz)
6 garlic cloves, crushed
1½ tbsp tomato purée (paste)
2½ tsp caraway seeds, roughly crushed using a pestle and mortar
4 tbsp arak (or raki)
3 limes: 2 juiced to yield 2 tbsp, 1 cut into wedges to serve
25g (1oz) panko breadcrumbs
2 tbsp crispy fried onions, bought or homemade (see page 151), roughly crushed
¾ tsp paprika
2 tbsp olive oil
400g (14oz) peeled and deveined extra-large raw king prawns (jumbo shrimp), patted dry
10g (¼oz) dill fronds, finely chopped, plus 1 tsp extra to serve
10g (¼oz) parsley, finely chopped, plus 1 tsp extra to serve
100g (3½oz) feta, roughly crumbled
fine sea salt and freshly ground black pepper

Add the butter, onion, fennel, garlic, tomato purée, caraway, ½ teaspoon salt and a good grind of black pepper to a medium, lidded, ovenproof sauté pan. Place over a medium heat, top with the lid and cook for about 15–18 minutes, stirring two or three times throughout, until softened and fragrant and only lightly coloured. Remove the lid, pour in the arak and lime juice, cook for just a minute, then set aside to cool for about 20 minutes.

Preheat the oven to 230°C fan/250°C/500°F/Gas mark 9.

In a small bowl, stir together the panko, fried onions, paprika, oil and ⅛ teaspoon salt.

Gently stir the prawns, herbs, feta, ½ teaspoon salt and a good grind of pepper into the fennel mixture until combined, arranging the prawns so they are sitting in one layer. Sprinkle evenly with the panko mixture and bake on the top shelf of your oven for 8–10 minutes, or until nicely golden and bubbling and the prawns are cooked through.

Sprinkle with the extra herbs and serve directly from the pan, with the lime wedges to squeeze alongside.

Salmon Harra

Samaka harra, which literally translates as 'spicy fish', is typically eaten in coastal towns through the Levant (Syria, Lebanon and Palestine). I first had it in the Syrian port city of Latakia, and was blown away by how tasty it was, despite its simplicity. The secret, I was told, was in the sea bream caught fresh that morning from the Mediterranean. 'You can't replicate it,' the waiter told me, and he was right: nothing will ever taste as good as that from its home origin. I've made a few changes here, namely with the fish used, but the essence is in the hot pepper paste, which you can find in most Turkish/Middle Eastern grocery stores.

Serves 4

8 garlic cloves
2 tbsp olive oil, plus 1 tsp extra for the herbs
1 tsp cumin seeds, roughly crushed using a pestle and mortar
1 tsp coriander seeds, roughly crushed using a pestle and mortar
2½ tbsp hot red pepper paste, biber salçasi
1 tbsp tomato purée (paste)
¾ tsp sugar
½ lemon, sliced into 4 x 0.5cm (¼in) rounds, pipes removed
½ small onion, thinly sliced into half-moons (75g/2½oz)
4 unskinned salmon fillets, or trout fillets if you prefer
2 tbsp coriander (cilantro), leaves and soft stems picked
2 tbsp parsley, leaves and soft stems picked
15g (½oz) walnuts, well toasted and roughly chopped
fine sea salt and freshly ground black pepper

Preheat the oven to 200°C fan/220°C/425°F/Gas mark 7.

Roughly crush the garlic into pieces using a pestle and mortar (you don't want the cloves whole but you don't want them puréed either). Heat the oil in a medium ovenproof sauté pan over a medium-high heat. Fry the garlic for 30–60 seconds, stirring occasionally, until fragrant and lightly coloured. Add the cumin and the coriander seeds and both pastes and cook for another 2 minutes, stirring all the while, until slightly darkened. Pour in 320ml (11fl oz) of water and season with the sugar, ¼ teaspoon salt and a generous grind of pepper. Bring to the boil and simmer for about 5 minutes, for the flavours to infuse (it will still be a bit loose). Chop each lemon round into four pieces, then stir these and the onion slices into the sauce. Remove from the heat.

Pat dry, then season the salmon all over with ½ teaspoon of salt and a good grind of pepper. Lower the fillets into the sauce, skin-side down, and use a spoon to scoop up the sauce and solids to coat the salmon. Transfer to the oven and bake for 8–10 minutes, or until cooked through (add only a couple more minutes if you prefer your salmon more well done, or if the fillets are particularly large).

Add the fresh coriander and parsley to a bowl and toss with the extra teaspoon of oil.

When ready, gently transfer the salmon and all of the sauce to a large platter and top with the herbs and the walnuts.

Spiced Mussels with Chickpeas and Coriander-Garlic Bread

You can take liberties here, if you don't want to use mussels, and swap them out for clams or hake or a mixture of fish and shellfish. The sauce is so flavourful and lends itself well to any seafood. Just be sure not to skip the bread, which you'll use to scoop and dip. You might make more butter than you need, so save any extra to toss with steamed vegetables or plain rice.

Serves 4

For the bread
1 tbsp olive oil
15g (½oz) coriander (cilantro), leaves and soft stems finely chopped
3 garlic cloves, roughly chopped
1½ tsp cumin seeds, toasted and finely crushed
1 tsp white miso
70g (2½oz) unsalted butter, softened at room temperature
1 medium ciabatta (I used a 400g/14oz loaf)

For the mussel sauce
½ tsp fenugreek seeds
1½ tsp cumin seeds
1½ tsp coriander seeds
seeds from 8 cardamom pods
½ tsp ground turmeric
¾ tsp Aleppo chilli flakes
2 tsp soft light brown sugar
200g (7oz) cherry tomatoes
1 onion, roughly chopped (180g/6¼oz)
4 garlic cloves, roughly chopped
30g (1oz) ginger, peeled and roughly chopped
1 green chilli, roughly chopped, seeds and all
4 tbsp olive oil
1 tbsp tomato purée (paste)
240g (8½oz) jarred chickpeas (garbanzo beans), drained weight (or 1 x 400g/14oz can, drained)
450ml (16fl oz) chicken stock
6 tbsp single (light) cream
fine sea salt and freshly ground black pepper

1kg (2lb 4oz) unshelled mussels, washed of any grit

Preheat the oven to 180°C fan/200°C/400°F/Gas mark 6.

Prepare the coriander butter for the bread by adding the oil, coriander, garlic, cumin, miso and a small pinch of salt to the bowl of a small food processor and blitzing until very finely chopped. Add the butter and pulse until well combined, scraping down the sides of the bowl as necessary.

Use a serrated knife to open up the ciabatta loaf through the middle, so you have 2 long rectangular halves. Spread the insides liberally with the butter (if you have more than you need, save this for another use). Place, buttered side-up, on a medium baking tray while you make the base for the mussels.

Add the fenugreek, cumin, coriander and cardamom seeds to a small frying pan (skillet) and place over a medium-heat. Toast until fragrant, shaking the pan often, about 3–4 minutes. Transfer to a spice grinder and blitz into a fine powder (or use a pestle and mortar and plenty of perseverance!). Stir in the turmeric, Aleppo chilli and sugar and set aside.

Heat a large, lidded sauté pan over a medium-high heat. Once very hot, add the tomatoes and cook for 4 minutes, turning as necessary, until charred and blistered but still retaining their shape. Transfer to a bowl and rinse and wipe out the pan.

Meanwhile, add the onion, garlic, ginger and green chilli to the bowl of a small food processor and blitz to a rough paste.

Heat the oil in the clean sauté pan over a medium-high heat. Add the onion mixture and cook for 6–7 minutes, stirring occasionally, until softened and very lightly coloured. Add the tomato purée, chickpeas and the spice mixture and fry for 2–3 minutes more, stirring occasionally, until fragrant. Pour in the stock and cream, add back the charred tomatoes and season with ½ teaspoon salt and a good grind of pepper. Bring to a simmer, then lower the heat to medium and cook gently for 10 minutes, for the flavours to infuse. Turn the heat back up to medium-high, stir in the mussels, top with the lid and leave to cook for 4 minutes, until the mussels have opened up and are cooked through. Discard any mussels that haven't opened.

While the broth is cooking, toast the bread in the oven for 10–12 minutes, until nicely browned. Transfer to a cutting board and slice as you like. Ladle the mussels and broth into large shallow bowls and serve with the warm bread alongside.

Sweet Date and Sour Tamarind Sea Bass

I adore sweet and sour flavours together but especially the combination of dates and tamarind, which is a match made in (food) heaven. This is a wonderfully easy dish to make, with super-punchy flavours. Serve as a light lunch with some lightly dressed greens, or with the Tomato, Potato and Saffron Rice (page 116) for a more substantial meal.

Serves 2

60g (2¼oz) tamarind pulp (from a block)
220ml (7½fl oz) boiling water
60g (2¼oz) pitted Medjool dates (about 3)
1 small red onion, very finely chopped (90g/3¼oz)
1 small green (bell) pepper, stem and seeds removed, finely chopped into 0.5cm (¼in) cubes (120g/4½oz)
2 garlic cloves, finely chopped
1–2 green chillies, finely chopped, seeds and all (depending on your heat preference)
30g (1oz) coriander (cilantro) leaves and soft stems, finely chopped
3½ tbsp olive oil, plus extra to serve
4 medium unskinned sea bass fillets
1 tsp mild curry powder
½ lime
fine sea salt and freshly ground black pepper

Preheat the oven to 210°C fan/230°C/450°F/Gas mark 8. Line a shallow baking dish (roughly 30 x 20cm/12 x 8in) with baking paper.

Place the tamarind in a small heatproof bowl and pour over 120ml (4fl oz) of the boiling water. In a separate small heatproof bowl, add the dates and the remaining 100ml (3½fl oz) of the boiling water. Set both aside for 15 minutes.

Meanwhile, in a medium bowl mix together the onion, green pepper, garlic, chilli, coriander, 2 tablespoons of the oil, ¼ teaspoon salt and a good grind of pepper.

When ready, remove the dates from their water and place them in the bowl of a small food processor along with 2 tablespoons of their water, then blitz until the dates are finely chopped and you have a paste (you can also do this with a hand-held blender).

Use your fingers to loosen the tamarind pulp from the seeds, then pour this through a fine-mesh sieve (strainer) set over a separate bowl. Push down on the solids to extract as much of the tamarind liquid as possible, scraping at the bottom of the sieve as well. Discard the solids and then mix in the date paste.

Pat dry the sea bass fillets and place them, skin-side down, in the lined baking dish (don't worry if they're slightly overlapping). Sprinkle the flesh all over with the curry powder, ¾ teaspoon salt and a good grind of pepper. Spoon over all the tamarind and date mixture, using your fingers to coat the flesh, then pour over the remaining 1½ tablespoons of oil. Lastly, spoon the onion and pepper mixture down the fillets. Bake for 17–20 minutes, or until cooked through and lightly coloured. Transfer to a plate, squeeze over the lime and drizzle with some extra olive oil.

Tuna Jacket Potatoes with Lime Yoghurt and Herbs

People often ask me if I'm constantly cooking elaborate dishes for myself, and the truth is, I'm really not. There's a time and place for the more time-consuming rice dishes, or the slow-cooked lamb cuts, but I tend to reserve this for weekends and when I'm feeding others. Most of the time I crave and cook comfort foods, like dal or buttery rice or a really good baked potato. These are not your average baked potato; they're packed full of flavour and the tuna sauce itself can be used to stir into pasta or to spoon over rice. You only really need some steamed greens or a side salad to go with them.

Serves 4

4 medium baking potatoes (800g/1lb 12oz)
6 tbsp olive oil
1 onion, finely chopped (180g/6¼oz)
5 garlic cloves, crushed
1 red chilli, finely chopped, seeds and all
2 tbsp tomato purée (paste)
2 tsp dried oregano
1 tbsp coriander seeds, finely crushed using a pestle and mortar
1½ tsp paprika
1 tsp Aleppo chilli flakes
2 x 320g (11¼oz) cans good-quality tuna in olive oil, drained but not rinsed (210g/7½oz)
½ tsp sugar
fine sea salt and freshly ground black pepper

For the toppings
100g (3½oz) Greek yoghurt
1½ tbsp lime juice
1 small garlic clove, crushed
2 spring onions (scallions), trimmed
10g (¼oz) fresh coriander (cilantro), leaves and soft stems picked
about 2 preserved lemons, flesh and seeds discarded and skin finely sliced (20g/¾oz)

Preheat the oven to 220°C fan/240°C/475°F/Gas mark 9.

Poke the potatoes a few times all over with a fork, then toss them in a tablespoon of the oil, ½ teaspoon of salt and a generous amount of pepper. Set a wire rack over a baking tray and place your potatoes on the rack. Bake for about 50 minutes in the middle of the oven, until crispy on the outside and cooked through the centre.

While the potatoes are baking, make the tuna sauce. Heat the remaining 5 tablespoons of oil in a large sauté pan over a medium-high heat. Add the onion and cook, stirring occasionally, for about 5 minutes, or until softened and lightly coloured. Stir in the garlic, chilli, tomato purée, oregano and spices and cook for 2 minutes more, stirring often, until deeply red and fragrant. Add the tuna, using a wooden spoon to finely break apart the chunks, then pour in 375ml (13fl oz) of water and season with the sugar, ¾ teaspoon salt and about 50 grinds of black pepper. Turn the heat down to medium and simmer for 12–15 minutes, stirring occasionally, until thick and rich. Keep warm until ready to serve.

For the toppings, mix together the yoghurt, lime juice, garlic and a small pinch of salt in a small bowl and set aside.

Chop the spring onions widthways into 3 pieces, then slice into very fine julienne strips. Place in a bowl and cover with very cold water. Leave for 10 minutes (or longer if you like) to crisp and curl up. Drain and pat dry, then combine in a bowl with the fresh coriander and preserved lemon.

When the potatoes are ready, use a small knife to split them down the middle without completely cutting through and give them a little squeeze to expose the insides. Fluff them up with a fork and then season with salt and pepper. Set on a large platter and top each one with the tuna sauce, drizzle with the yoghurt and pile the spring onion mixture on top.

MEAT

Coffee, Cardamom and Chipotle-rubbed Lamb Chops

Coffee isn't the first thing you think of when marinating meats, but the combination of fragrant cardamom, bitter coffee and smoky chipotle chillies complement each other really nicely, and the coffee itself acts as a tenderizer, as well as a flavour enhancer. This recipe is easy to double or triple up on amounts if needed. If serving it Bahraini style, then the lamb with some sort of flatbread (like tanour) is dinner, but I prefer to serve this with something fresh and crunchy like Springtime Fattoush (page 71).

Serves 4 · Marinating time: 1–3 hours

8 lamb cutlets
3 tbsp olive oil
½ lemon
4 spring onions (scallions), trimmed and sliced lengthways in half (60g/2¼oz)
1 green chilli, left whole
fine sea salt

For the rub
1 tbsp finely ground coffee beans
seeds from 15 cardamom pods, finely crushed
1 tsp cumin seeds, finely crushed using a pestle and mortar
5g (⅛oz) dried chipotle, stem and seeds removed, finely crushed, or 1¼ tsp chipotle chilli flakes
¾ tsp paprika
1 tsp soft light brown sugar

For the sumac onions
½ red onion (75g/2½oz), finely sliced
2 tsp sumac
1½ tbsp lemon juice

Combine all the ingredients for the rub in a medium bowl. Pat the lamb well dry on paper towels and season all over with ¾ teaspoon salt. Coat well with the rub, then leave to marinate at room temperature for 1 hour, or refrigerated for up to 3 hours (but not much longer).

Make the onions by placing all the ingredients in a bowl with a pinch of salt and using your fingers to massage everything together. Set aside to pickle gently while the lamb is marinating (you can do this hours ahead).

If you've refrigerated the lamb, be sure to bring it back up to room temperature before cooking. When ready, place a large cast-iron sauté pan over a medium-high heat. Toss the lamb with the oil. Once the pan is hot, cook the cutlets for 2–3 minutes on each side, for medium-rare. Adjust the cook time if you prefer your cutlets more or less well done (or if they're smaller or larger in size). Arrange them on a serving plate and pour over all but a couple teaspoons of the fat left in the pan, then squeeze over the ½ lemon.

Return the pan to a medium-high heat with the spring onions, chilli and a tiny pinch of salt and cook for about 3 minutes, flipping over as necessary, until softened and lightly browned. Pile the spring onions onto one side of the serving plate with the whole green chilli alongside. Top the cutlets with the sumac onions and serve right away.

Chicken Koftas with Fresh Tomato Sauce

These koftas are super tender thanks to the fresh tomato sauce that goes both in the mixture and is spooned on top. I know I often repeat myself by saying 'serve with yoghurt', but I would have a bowlful of yoghurt at the ready here, along with some crunchy raw veg and pita or *saj* bread, and build the ultimate kofta sandwich.

Serves 4

For the fresh tomato sauce
2 mild red chillies, roughly chopped, seeds and all (30g/1oz)
½ red onion, roughly chopped (75g/2½oz)
2 garlic cloves, roughly chopped
2 large ripe tomatoes (250g/9oz), roughly chopped
20g (¾oz) coriander (cilantro), leaves and soft stems, roughly chopped, plus an extra 1 tbsp to serve
1½ tbsp apple cider vinegar
1½ tbsp olive oil

For the koftas
500g (1lb 2oz) minced (ground) chicken
1 tbsp caraway seeds, toasted and finely crushed using a pestle and mortar
1 tbsp coriander seeds, toasted and finely crushed using a pestle and mortar
2 spring onions (scallions), finely chopped
45g (1¾oz) panko breadcrumbs
5 tbsp olive oil, plus extra for shaping
2 garlic cloves, thinly sliced
2 tsp tomato purée (paste)
2 tsp pomegranate molasses
fine sea salt and freshly ground black pepper

First make the sauce. Add the chillies, onion and garlic to a food processor and pulse until finely chopped. Add the tomatoes, coriander and 1 teaspoon salt and pulse a few more times until the tomato is puréed but the sauce is not completely smooth. Strain through a sieve (strainer) set over a bowl for about 5 minutes, pushing down lightly to help it along. Discard the liquid collected. Add two-thirds of this mixture to a large mixing bowl. Put the remaining third in a separate bowl, stir in the vinegar and oil and set aside.

Add to the large mixing bowl the chicken, spices, spring onions, panko, 2 tablespoons of the oil, 1¼ teaspoons of salt and a good grind of pepper. Mix very well to combine.

Pour a little olive oil into a small bowl and use oiled hands to divide the mixture into 12 balls, roughly 60–65g (2½oz) each. Form each ball into a torpedo shape (or round patties, if you prefer).

Place a large, lidded sauté pan over a medium-high heat with another 1 tablespoon of the oil. Once hot, add the koftas and fry for about 6–7 minutes, turning as necessary, until nicely browned all over (they won't be cooked all the way through). If necessary, you can fry in batches. Transfer the koftas to a plate and let the pan cool slightly. Return to a medium heat with the remaining 2 tablespoons of oil, add the sliced garlic and cook for about 1 minute, stirring often, or until nicely coloured and fragrant. Stir in the tomato purée and cook for another minute, then add the pomegranate molasses and 1½ tablespoons of water. Return the koftas to the pan and stir gently to coat in the mixture. Turn the heat down to medium-low, top with the lid and leave to cook for 4 minutes, or until the koftas are just cooked through. Transfer to a plate, then spoon over the reserved fresh tomato sauce and sprinkle with extra coriander.

Baked Lamb Koftas with Peppers, Feta and Oregano

I adore koftas in all forms but especially done like this, where you don't have to fry them separately and the onions and peppers form a deliciously rich base for the meat to sit in. I added panko to the mix here, which isn't traditional but it does help keep the baked kofta nice and soft – leave this out if gluten free.

Serves 4

1 large onion, peeled, halved and sliced into 0.5cm (¼in) half-moons (220g/7¾oz)
1 medium green (bell) pepper, stem and seeds removed, cut into 1.5cm (⅝in) strips (150g/5½oz)
1 medium red (bell) pepper, stem and seeds removed, cut into 1.5cm (⅝in) strips (150g/5½oz)
1 tbsp fresh thyme leaves
3 tbsp olive oil, plus extra for shaping
1½ tsp sweet paprika
200g (7oz) Datterini or cherry tomatoes
150g (5½oz) tomato passata (strained tomatoes)
2 tbsp apple cider vinegar
¾ tbsp maple syrup
120g (4¼oz) feta, broken into random large chunks

For the koftas
500g (1lb 2oz) minced (ground) lamb (15–20% fat) or beef (or a mixture of both)
40g (1½oz) panko breadcrumbs
20g (¾oz) parsley, leaves and soft stems finely chopped, plus an extra 1 tbsp to serve
10g (¼oz) oregano leaves, finely chopped, plus an extra 1 tbsp to serve
3 garlic cloves, crushed
1 tsp ground cinnamon
1 tsp ground cumin
¼ tsp bicarbonate of soda (baking soda)
1 onion, halved (180g/6¼oz)
1 large ripe plum tomato (130g/4¾oz)
fine sea salt and freshly ground black pepper

Preheat the oven to 200°C fan/220°C/425°F/Gas mark 7.

First make the koftas. Add the meat, panko (if using), herbs, garlic, spices, bicarbonate of soda, 1 teaspoon salt and a generous grind of pepper to a large mixing bowl. Using the coarse side of a box grater, grate the onion halves and then use your hands to squeeze out the excess liquid – you should get about 85g (3oz) of squeezed-out flesh. Add this to the bowl, then grate the tomato in the same way, straining off the juices through a sieve (strainer) to leave 70g (2½oz) pulp. Add to the bowl.

Pour a little oil into a small bowl and use oiled hands to knead the mixture very well for about 4 minutes. Set aside to rest for 20 minutes.

Meanwhile, add the sliced onion, the red and green peppers, thyme, 2 tablespoons of the oil and ½ teaspoon salt to a large cast-iron skillet or ovenproof sauté pan and mix to combine. Bake for 15 minutes, or until the onion and peppers are softened and browned in places. Carefully remove from the oven and turn up the temperature to 220°C fan/240°C/475°F/Gas mark 9.

Divide the meat mixture into 12 pieces, roughly 55–60g (2oz) each and, using oiled hands, form into torpedo-shaped koftas.

Stir the paprika and tomatoes into the pan with the peppers. In a jug, whisk together the passata, vinegar, maple syrup and ¼ teaspoon salt and pour this into the pan. Add the koftas, moving the peppers around them, then drizzle over the final tablespoon of oil. Return to the oven for 8 minutes, then turn each kofta over. Dot with the feta and bake for 12 minutes more, or until nicely browned and bubbling.

Sprinkle over the extra chopped herbs and serve directly from the pan.

Allspice Chicken with Herby Bulgur-stuffed Tomatoes

Of all the vegetables suitable for stuffing, tomatoes are perhaps the easiest and quickest and don't require much preparation. I love how they soften and collapse ever so slightly, and how the tomato liquid provides the perfect broth-like sauce for the dish. Serve with Springtime Fattoush (page 71), if you like.

Serves 4–6

1½ tbsp tomato purée (paste)
2½ tsp ground allspice
2 tsp Aleppo chilli flakes
5 tbsp olive oil
6 chicken legs, bone in, skin on (1.5kg/3lb 5oz)
130g (4¾oz) coarse-grain bulgur wheat
6 large ripe beef tomatoes (1.1kg/2lb 7oz)
20g (¾oz) parsley, roughly chopped, plus an extra 1 tbsp, chopped, to serve
20g (¾oz) mint leaves, roughly chopped
3 spring onions (scallions), trimmed and finely sliced
1½ tsp ground cinnamon
2 tbsp lemon juice
1 tbsp pomegranate molasses, plus 1½ tsp extra to serve
fine sea salt and freshly ground black pepper

In a large bowl mix together ½ tablespoon of the tomato purée, 1 teaspoon of the allspice, all the chilli, 1 tablespoon of the oil, 1¼ teaspoons of salt and a good grind of pepper. Pat dry the chicken legs on paper towels and add them to the bowl, turning so that they're evenly coated. Set aside to marinate.

Add the bulgur to a small, lidded saucepan with ¼ teaspoon of salt and 250ml (9fl oz) of water. Bring to the boil over a medium-high heat, then top with the lid, turn down the heat to low and cook for 15 minutes. Set aside to cool.

Meanwhile, using a small, sharp knife, slice off the stem end of the tomatoes, about 1.5cm (⅝in) thick, saving the tops. Core the tomatoes, taking care not to pierce the skin. Using a small spoon, scrape out the seeds and pulp into a sieve (strainer) set over a bowl to catch the juices, leaving a 1cm (½in) border of flesh on each cored tomato. Once the pulp has drained, weigh out 100g (3½oz) of it (use the remaining pulp for something else), finely chop and add to a large mixing bowl. Place the cored tomatoes and their tops, cut-side down, on a tray lined with paper towels to absorb any excess liquid.

Preheat the oven to 200°C fan/220°C/425°F/Gas mark 7.

To the mixing bowl add the cooked bulgur, herbs, spring onions, cinnamon, the remaining 1½ teaspoons of allspice, the lemon juice, another tablespoon of the oil, ½ teaspoon salt and a good grind of pepper. Mix well to combine. Season the insides of the tomatoes with a little salt and pepper, then divide the bulgur mixture between them and top with their lids. Place in a large roasting tin (about 30 x 40cm/12 x 16in). Arrange the chicken legs in the tin, skin-side up, shifting the tomatoes around so everything is evenly spaced in a single layer.

Pour the strained tomato juices into a measuring jug/cup and, if needed, top up with water to get to 200ml (7fl oz). Whisk in the remaining tablespoon of tomato purée, the pomegranate molasses, 2 tablespoons of the oil and ¼ teaspoon salt. Pour the mix into the tin, avoiding pouring on top of the chicken – you want the skin to crisp up. Drizzle over the last tablespoon of oil and roast for 50–55 minutes, basting halfway through, until the chicken is tender and golden and the tomatoes are softened but not completely falling apart. Check the tomatoes at the 45-minute mark – if they look like they're starting to collapse, gently remove them and return the chicken to the oven. When ready to serve, return the tomatoes to the tin if necessary, then sprinkle with the extra parsley, add a drizzle of molasses and serve from the tin, or transfer to a very large serving platter.

Fasoolia for the Heart

'He was so handsome, sort of like Tom Selleck back in the day,' she said with a youthful giggle. 'Oh, but I sure didn't make it easy for him.' She flicked her ponytail and grinned at me with a cheeky glimmer in her eyes. It's not difficult to imagine Mama Hala turning heads in her twenties. Forty years on and she still holds herself with grace and glamour as only a woman of great taste would.

That day she wore pink sweats, a white T-shirt and her house slippers. Her blonde hair was slicked back neatly, her nails perfectly manicured, her kitchen well organized and pristine. She was buzzing, excited, ready and eager to show me that sentimental dish I had asked her for.

'There's nothing to it really,' she said, 'but he told me it's the best dish he'd ever eaten. Personally, I think it's because I add a lot of garlic.' Garlic, coriander and fresh tomato, she repeated several times, the necessary ingredients for this dish but also for all Lebanese stews. I watched as she set to work, her bowls of ingredients arranged neatly alongside the cooker, *a mise en place* set-up any chef would dream of. To the back was another pot, also pink and also steaming. '*Ruz bil sha'ariyah*, rice with vermicelli,' she confirmed as she caught me looking. 'It's not necessary but they just go so well together,' she beamed, 'especially when you add butter.' She paused for just a moment and then reiterated, 'Yes, lots of butter.'

It was *fasoolia bi lahme* that Mama Hala was preparing, a dish of stewed lamb and white beans that she'd learnt to make from her mother – a staple dish in any Lebanese household. Upon her eldest daughter's request she'll make it every year on her late husband's birthday. Just as it was his favourite dish back then, now in his absence, it is his daughter's favourite dish too. Mama Hala smiled as she recalled him stealing bites of the stew before it was even on the table, a sneaky embrace with a motive. 'He could eat it for weeks on end and never tire of it,' she said proudly. 'But surely he's had it before, a Syrian version perhaps?', I'd asked. 'Yes,' she confirmed, 'but he'd never had mine. I make it special,' she said with conviction. She went on to explain how he referred to the stew as '*inkha'at*' or '*batoon*' which mean 'goat's brain' and 'a full stomach' respectively. '*Le'ana be aby el mukh*,' she said by way of explanation, because it fills the mind.

Sat at the kitchen table, observant and amused, was Mama Hala's daughter, my dearest friend. In this moment we exchanged glances. Some Arabic sayings are hard to translate into English. I understood, though, what he had meant in his words, only because I've felt it before too, a dish so wholesome that it fills the mind, fills the belly and the soul. *Fasoolia* for the heart.

Later that day, myself full after two helpings of *fasoolia*, Mama Hala made me a strong cup of Arabic coffee, with instructions to leave the last dregs behind. When I was done, she flipped my cup onto a saucer and as we waited for the dregs to empty, we spoke at length about love and lust, relationships and loss, broken hearts and empty promises. 'So, the *fasoolia*,' I recapped, 'it's a love story?' I held her gaze – sadness, defiance, acceptance, peace – 'Yes,' she said softly, 'it's a story about love.' She picked up my coffee cup and let out a gasp, '*Oh!*' she exclaimed with such joy that I was curious enough to want to hear all about it too. Whatever the coffee dregs had to say, they sure sounded wonderful. I listened as Mama Hala launched into the tellings of my future with animated enthusiasm, her eyes shiny, her smile bright. It's not difficult to see how she pours love into her daily actions, be it a coffee reading, or a big old pot of lamb and white bean stew. 'Love is coming your way,' she said excitedly, with as much certainty as she had when adding butter to her rice, when stirring coriander into her beans. I gazed over at her daughter, my friend – whose stories and woes and pains I've felt as my very own. That day though, also full up with garlic-heavy *fasoolia*, she was smiling.

This is a story about love, loss and all the dishes made to fill our hungry hearts. In loving memory of the Syrian Tom Selleck: may he rest in eternal peace.

Fasoolia bi Lahme: White Bean and Lamb Stew

This dish is dedicated wholeheartedly to Mama Hala (see pages 216–217), who cooked for me her version of this in a way only someone who has made it countless times before would: effortlessly, and with lots of love. Besides the cooking method, I haven't steered too far away from traditional flavours for this one. I quite like the simplicity of this dish, the comfort it brings, especially when it's cold or miserable outside and you really just need a hug in food form. I like to sprinkle this with feta and have it with white or vermicelli rice, or *ruz bil sha'areeyah*.

Serves 4–6

25g (1oz) ghee
500g (1lb 2oz) boneless lamb neck fillet, cut into roughly 4cm (1½in) cubes
1 red onion, roughly chopped (150g/5½oz)
3 fresh bay leaves
1 cinnamon stick
8 garlic cloves, crushed
2 tbsp tomato purée (paste)
2 plum tomatoes (220g/7¾oz), roughly grated (shredded) and skins discarded (130g/4¾oz)
2 x 400g (14oz) cans cannellini beans, drained (480g/1lb 10oz)
1 tbsp cumin seeds, finely crushed using a pestle and mortar
30g (1oz) coriander (cilantro), finely chopped, plus an extra 5g (⅛oz) to serve
2 jalapeños, thinly sliced into rounds, seeds and all
2 tbsp apple cider vinegar
fine sea salt and freshly ground black pepper

Preheat the oven to 150°C fan/170°C/340°F/Gas mark 3½.

Melt the ghee in a large, heavy-based, lidded saucepan over a medium-high heat. Pat the lamb dry with paper towels and season all over with ½ teaspoon salt and a good grind of pepper. Once the ghee is hot, add the lamb to the pan and sear for about 5 minutes in total, turning as necessary, until nicely browned. Add the onion, bay leaves and cinnamon and cook for about 3 minutes, stirring often, until softened and lightly coloured. Add three-quarters of the garlic and all the tomato purée and cook for just a minute more, stirring all the while. Pour in 600ml (21fl oz) of water, add ½ teaspoon salt and a good grind of pepper and bring to the boil.

Top with the lid and transfer to the oven for 1 hour and 40 minutes, stirring halfway, or until the lamb is tender. Remove the lid and stir in the grated tomatoes, the beans, cumin, coriander, the remaining garlic, another 100ml (3½fl oz) of water, ½ teaspoon salt and a good grind of pepper. Replace the lid and bake for 30 minutes more. Let settle for 10 minutes before serving.

While the lamb is cooking, add the jalapeños to a small bowl with a pinch of salt and the vinegar and mix to combine.

When ready to serve, transfer the stew to a large shallow bowl, and serve the pickled jalapeños alongside.

Loomi Lemon Chicken

I love this dish for two reasons: the first is that spatchcocking a chicken means super-juicy meat every time. The second is that it celebrates *loomi* (aka black limes) in its very dramatic-looking appearance, and I really appreciate that. Serve with some lightly dressed greens or the Pan-fried Tomatoes with Za'atar, Pine Nuts and Halloumi (page 91).

Serves 4 · Marinating time: 2 hours to overnight

1 whole large chicken (1.8kg/4lb)
2 black limes (10g/¼oz)
2 tsp cumin seeds, finely crushed using a pestle and mortar
1¼ tsp paprika
1½ tsp dried oregano
2 tsp soft light brown sugar
1 head of garlic, halved widthways, plus 1 extra clove, crushed
1 lemon, cut into 8 x 1cm (½in) rounds, seeds removed
2½ tbsp olive oil
25g (1oz) unsalted butter
75g (2¾oz) natural (plain) yoghurt
1½ tbsp parsley, roughly chopped
fine sea salt and freshly ground black pepper

Pat the chicken well dry with paper towels, then flip it over, breast side down, so the backbone is facing you. Use a pair of poultry shears (or a very sharp knife) to cut along each side of the backbone to remove it (save it for making stock or gravy!). Flip the chicken back over and push down firmly on the breast to flatten the bird – you want to snap the wishbone. Pat the chicken dry again and season all over with 1½ teaspoons salt, using your fingers to push some salt in between the skin and flesh. Set aside.

Use your hands to press down on the black limes to roughly crush them. Open them up and pick out and discard any pips (these are bitter). Add the black lime to a spice grinder and blitz to finely crush (you can also do this in a small food processor with a large quantity of black limes). Measure out 1½ tablespoons (store any extra in a sealed jar) and add to a small bowl with the cumin, paprika, oregano, sugar, ¼ teaspoon salt and a generous grind of black pepper and mix well. Rub this all over the chicken (try to get some underneath the skin as well), making sure it is well coated. Transfer to a plate and refrigerate, uncovered, for at least a couple of hours, or up to overnight. If the latter, remove the chicken from the refrigerator an hour before roasting.

When ready to cook, remove the chicken from the refrigerator and then preheat the oven to 190°C fan/210°C/410°F/Gas mark 6½.

Place the garlic halves, the lemon slices and 100ml (3½fl oz) of water in a large cast-iron skillet. Place the chicken on top, breast-side up, and drizzle all over with the oil. Transfer to the oven and roast for 25 minutes, then carefully remove and use a spoon to baste the chicken. Return to the oven, rotating the dish, and roast for another 15 minutes.

Meanwhile, melt the butter in a small pan. When ready, remove the chicken and pour the butter all over the skin. Return to the oven for about another 10 minutes or until the juices run clear and the internal temperature reads 75°C (167°F) on a digital thermometer. Set aside to rest for about 10 minutes, then carefully transfer the chicken to a large platter.

Pick out 3–4 lemon slices and the roasted garlic. Squeeze the garlic flesh into a medium bowl, discarding the papery skins, and use a fork to mash until smooth. Finely chop the lemons, peel and all, and add to the bowl along with the yoghurt, the crushed clove of garlic, the parsley and a tiny pinch of salt.

Pour the pan juices and remaining lemon slices all over the chicken and serve with the yoghurt alongside.

Middle Eastern Bolognese

You can't rush a good bolognese; it needs that time to cook low and slow, for the ingredients to melt into each other and for the whole thing to transform into a silky, rich sauce. Every Middle Eastern household will have a version of this, and there's never really any hard and fast rules besides one, very non-Italian rule: it should be heavily spiced, and spicy. You can have this bolognese any way you please – on a baked potato, spooned over rice or as a delicious pasta bake (see page 224).

Serves 6

2 tbsp olive oil
1 onion, finely chopped (180g/6¼oz)
1 carrot, peeled and finely chopped (120g/4¼oz)
1 green (bell) pepper, stem and seeds removed, finely chopped (150g/5½oz)
4 garlic cloves, finely chopped
300g (10½oz) minced (ground) beef (5–10% fat)
300g (10½oz) minced (ground) lamb (15–20% fat)
2 cinnamon sticks
3 fresh bay leaves
1 black or regular dried lime, poked a couple of times with a sharp knife
2 mild red chillies, pierced a couple of times with a sharp knife
seeds from 15 cardamom pods, finely crushed using a pestle and mortar
1 tbsp cumin seeds, finely crushed using a pestle and mortar
2 tsp coriander seeds, finely crushed using a pestle and mortar
1 tsp Aleppo chilli flakes
1½ tsp dried oregano
1½ tbsp tomato purée (paste)
1 chicken stock cube (bouillon cube)
400g (14oz) can plum tomatoes, puréed
150ml (5½fl oz) whole milk
20g (¾oz) coriander (cilantro), roughly chopped
fine sea salt and freshly ground black pepper

Heat the olive oil in a large, deep-sided, lidded sauté pan over a medium-high heat. Add the onion, carrot and pepper and cook, stirring occasionally, for about 5 minutes, or just until softened. Add the garlic and cook for 2 minutes more. Stir in the minced beef and lamb and cook for 10 minutes, using a spoon to break apart any clumps until finely crumbled. It will release lots of liquid at first; allow this to cook down and the meat to start to brown. Stir in the cinnamon, bay leaves, dried lime, chillies, spices, oregano, tomato purée, the stock cube, 1 teaspoon salt and a very generous grind of pepper and fry for a couple of minutes, until fragrant. Pour in the puréed tomatoes and 300ml (10½fl oz) of water, bring to a simmer, then turn down the heat to its lowest setting, cover with a lid and leave to cook for 2 hours, stirring every 25 minutes or so. At the end of this time, the sauce should be thick and rich.

Pour in the milk, replace the lid and cook gently for 25 minutes more. Set aside to cool slightly, then pick out and discard the cinnamon sticks and bay leaves. Remove the dried lime, squeezing its juices into the sauce, and either discard or, if you like its bitterness as I do, finely chop and stir back into the sauce, along with the chopped coriander. The sauce is now ready to use.

Middle Eastern Bolognese Pasta Bake

This is my favourite way to showcase the Middle Eastern bolognese (see previous page), especially with the addition of feta and pine nuts. I tested this the same day I made the Labneh with Slow-cooked Leeks and Peas (page 101) and the two recipes complemented each other really well.

Serves 4–6

300g (10½oz) rigatoni pasta
1 x quantity of Middle Eastern Bolognese (page 223)
125g (4½oz) feta, roughly crumbled
125g (4½oz) buffalo mozzarella, roughly torn
25g (1oz) pine nuts, well toasted
10g (¼oz) coriander (cilantro) or parsley, leaves and soft stems roughly chopped
fine sea salt

Preheat the oven to 200°C fan/220°C/425°F/Gas mark 7.

Bring a large pan of water to the boil over a medium-high heat. Season with 2 teaspoons of salt, add the pasta and cook for 12–14 minutes, or according to the packet instructions, until al dente. Measure out 130ml (4½fl oz) of the cooking water and drain the pasta through a colander set over the sink.

Select a baking dish measuring 23 x 33cm (9 x 13in) or a round one 28cm (11¼in) diameter. Add the drained pasta, the bolognese sauce and the reserved pasta water and mix to combine evenly. Pick out the whole chillies and lay these over the top, then sprinkle evenly with the feta and mozzarella. Bake for 30 minutes, or until crispy and browned around the edges.

Sprinkle over the toasted pine nuts and fresh coriander or parsley and serve warm.

Saloonat Dajaj: Chicken and Vegetable Stew

Saloona refers to any stew-like dish in Bahrain. It usually contains meat or fish, hearty veggies and is always tomato based. It is always quite saucy, the flavourful sauce generously poured onto rice, or the entire stew poured onto tanour bread to make a dish called *thareed*. I thought perhaps I wouldn't include a saloona recipe in this book, but my dad informed me in no uncertain terms that this would be sacrilege and so here we are with a very rustic version. Feel free to mix up the vegetables – other root veggies would be delicious, as well as big chunks of courgettes and aubergines. Just be sure not to cut the vegetables too small; you want nice chunks that don't disintegrate into the sauce.

Serves 4–6 · Marinating time: 1 hour to overnight

For the chicken

- 1 tbsp cumin seeds
- 1 tbsp coriander seeds
- 1½ tsp fenugreek seeds
- 3 dried mild red chillies (Middle Eastern or Kashmiri chillies), stems removed
- 6 whole cloves
- 10 cardamom pods, left whole
- 1 tsp ground turmeric
- 1 tsp paprika
- 1 tsp caster (granulated) sugar
- 50g (1¾oz) fresh ginger, peeled and finely grated
- 6 garlic cloves, finely grated
- 200g (7oz) Greek yoghurt
- 2 tbsp apple cider vinegar
- 1½ tbsp olive oil
- 4 chicken legs (1kg/2lb 4oz)
- fine sea salt and freshly ground black pepper

For the stew

- 3 tbsp olive oil
- 1 large red onion, finely chopped
- 1 green chilli, finely chopped, seeds and all
- 2½ tbsp tomato purée (paste)
- 350g (12oz) tomatoes, roughly grated (shredded) and skins discarded (200g/7oz)
- ½ tsp caster (granulated) sugar
- 30g (1oz) coriander (cilantro) leaves and soft stems, roughly chopped
- 350g (12oz) floury potatoes (about 2 medium ones), peeled and chopped into 6cm (2½in) chunks
- ½ butternut squash (500g/1lb 2oz), or 1 small squash, peeled, deseeded and cut into 7cm (2¾in) chunks (350g/12oz)
- 1 large carrot, peeled and cut at an angle into 5 pieces

Start by marinating the chicken. Toast the cumin, coriander and fenugreek seeds, the dried chillies, cloves and cardamom in a small dry frying pan (skillet) over a medium heat until fragrant – about 3–4 minutes, stirring occasionally. Transfer to a spice grinder and blitz until smooth (alternatively use a pestle and mortar and some strength!). Add half the mixture to a large bowl with the turmeric, paprika, sugar, half of both the ginger and garlic, the yoghurt, vinegar, oil, 1 teaspoon of salt and a generous grind of pepper. Mix well to combine. Use your hands to pull away at and discard the chicken skins and then, using a sharp knife, cut between the joints to separate the thighs from the drumsticks. Add these to the marinade and mix well to coat. Refrigerate for at least an hour or up to overnight if time allows. Remove from the refrigerator about 30 minutes before cooking.

To make the stew, add the oil to a large, lidded cast-iron casserole pan (Dutch oven) and place over a medium-high heat. Once hot, add the onion and cook for 4 minutes, stirring occasionally, until softened and lightly coloured. Add the chicken pieces and any marinade left in the bowl, stirring to coat in the onions, and cook for about 6 minutes, flipping a couple of times, until sealed (they won't colour much). Stir in the rest of the ginger and garlic, as well as the chilli, tomato purée and the remaining spice mix and cook for a minute more, until fragrant. Add the grated tomato, sugar, coriander, 800ml (28fl oz) of water, the vegetables and 1 teaspoon of salt and bring to a simmer. Once simmering, cover with the lid, turn down the heat to medium-low and leave to cook gently for 40 minutes. Remove the lid, give everything a stir and cook for 30 minutes more, or until the chicken is very tender and the vegetables soft (the stew will still be quite saucy). When ready, transfer to a large serving bowl and serve warm.

Slow-cooked Fenugreek Lamb with Pickled Chillies

Slow-cooked meats are commonly eaten throughout the Gulf countries, particularly lamb, mutton, goat and sometimes camel. The spicing though, is where things really get interesting: every household has their own secret mix and it's often a concoction of more spices than you'll forgive me for on one recipe page. This is one of my favourite lamb recipes to date, perfect for feeding a crowd, and it's pretty hands off once you get it into the oven.

Serves 6 · Marinating time: 1 hour to overnight

12 cardamom pods, left whole
2 tsp fenugreek seeds
1 tbsp cumin seeds
1 tbsp coriander seeds
5 cloves
⅓ tsp black peppercorns
½ tsp ground turmeric
½ tsp chilli flakes
2 tsp soft light brown sugar
1 small onion, roughly chopped (150g/5½oz)
½ carrot, washed and roughly chopped into 2cm (¾in) cubes (60g/2¼oz)
5 garlic cloves, roughly chopped
30g (1oz) fresh ginger, peeled and roughly chopped
20g (¾oz) coriander (cilantro), roughly chopped
50g (1¾oz) tomato purée (paste)
1 tbsp olive oil
1.8kg (4lb) bone-in lamb shoulder
250g (9oz) plum tomatoes, blitzed in a food processor to a purée
4 tbsp apple cider vinegar
3 cinnamon sticks
2 dried limes (black or regular), pierced a couple of times with a sharp knife
2 green chillies, left whole
fine sea salt

For the pickled chilli topping
2 tbsp apple cider vinegar
1 tsp caster (granulated) sugar
2 mild red chillies, finely sliced at a slight angle, seeds and all
10g (¼oz) coriander (cilantro) leaves and soft stems, picked

Toast the cardamom, fenugreek, cumin, coriander, cloves and black peppercorns in a small dry frying pan over a medium heat until fragrant – about 3–4 minutes, stirring occasionally. Transfer to a spice grinder and blitz until fine (alternatively, use a pestle and mortar and some strength!). Stir in the turmeric, chilli flakes, sugar and 1 teaspoon salt. Set aside.

Add the onion, carrot, garlic, ginger and coriander to a food processor and pulse until finely chopped. Add the tomato purée, oil and the spice mixture and pulse to a coarse paste.

Pat the lamb well dry with paper towels and use a sharp knife to make about 12 incisions all around. Rub the meat with 1 teaspoon of salt, then place on a tray. Rub evenly all over with the onion–spice mixture and leave to marinate for at least an hour, or refrigerated overnight if you are getting ahead. (If marinated overnight, sit the lamb at room temperature for at least an hour before cooking.)

Preheat the oven to 150°C fan/170°C/340°F/Gas mark 3½.

Scrape the blitzed tomatoes into a large jug or bowl and mix with the vinegar, 600ml (21fl oz) of water and ½ teaspoon salt. Pour this into a large, lidded cast-iron casserole pan (Dutch oven) about 28cm (11¼in) in diameter and add the cinnamon sticks, dried limes and green chillies. Slowly lower in the lamb, skin-side up. Roast, uncovered, for 45 minutes, then remove from the oven, baste, cover and cook for about 3½ hours, basting twice throughout, or until the meat easily pulls away from the bone. Take out of the oven and remove the lid, basting once again. Turn up the temperature to 170°C fan/190°C/375°F/Gas mark 5 and return to the oven, uncovered, for 20 minutes, or until nicely coloured on top. Set aside to cool slightly, then carefully transfer the lamb and sauce to a large lipped serving platter, discarding the bones.

While the lamb is cooking, pickle the chillies by adding the vinegar, sugar and ⅛ teaspoon salt to a small bowl and whisking to combine. Add the red chillies and leave to pickle gently.

To serve, spoon the fresh coriander and the chillies and their pickling liquid all over the lamb.

HALAWA (SWEETS)

Chocolate and Coffee Granita with Tahini Cream and Halva

As far as desserts go, granitas are probably the easiest to put together. The most crucial piece of equipment you'll need for this is a fork (and a bit of patience) to create those nice, fluffy ice crystals that granitas are so known for. This is a very grown-up dessert, but one that contains some of my favourite ingredients: namely coffee, tahini and chocolate.

Serves 4, generously · Freezing time: 6 hours +

For the granita
1 tbsp instant espresso powder
55g (2oz) cocoa powder
¼ tsp fine sea salt
125g (4½oz) caster (superfine) sugar

For the tahini cream
30g (1oz) tahini
2 tbsp maple syrup
2 tsp vanilla bean paste
200ml (7fl oz) double (heavy) cream

To serve
90g (3¼oz) halva, roughly crumbled
1 tbsp roughly grated (shredded) dark (bittersweet) chocolate

Heat the espresso powder with 450ml (16fl oz) of water in a small saucepan over a medium heat until just starting to bubble. Whisk in the cocoa powder, salt and sugar and cook over a medium-low heat for just a few minutes, or until nicely dissolved. Pour into a shallow container, then leave to cool to room temperature. Once cool, freeze for about 1–1½ hours, or until the edges begin to solidify (the shallower the container, the faster this will happen). Use a fork to scrape at the mixture and separate the crystals and then freeze for another 45 minutes. Continue in this way, scraping at the mixture every 45 minutes for the next 4 hours, or until the granita is flaky with fine crystals throughout. Leave to freeze for longer as needed.

Meanwhile, in a medium bowl whisk the tahini, maple syrup and vanilla until smooth. Add the cream and whisk to soft peaks, then refrigerate before use (you want it very cold).

When ready to serve, divide the granita between small bowls and top with the tahini cream to one side. Sprinkle over the halva and chocolate shavings and serve right away, while still cold.

Al Nakhla

A date palm's Arabic name is *nakhla*. I prefer this name because it's feminine, and as much as I can admire the grandeur of all date palms, it is the female trees that generously bear their fruit, and there's nothing quite like the strong, commanding presence of a female date palm. Look down and her feet are in water, her roots deeply penetrating the earth in search of humidity, look up and her head is on fire, her leaves worshipping the sun for as many hours of the day that are given. The date palm is made to endure the harshest of conditions, arid deserts and insufferable heat, but even with this you'll watch her fruit gradually turn from vibrant green to golden yellow and amber. You'll know when she's ready to harvest; the dates will easily detach from the palm in kind surrender, and you'll have the sweetest of fruits, more kilos of dates than you could possibly know what to do with. You'll also have her leaves to weave baskets, her trunk to provide timber, her seeds to create prayer beads and whatever fruits remain to make rich molasses, delicious vinegar and strong liquor. There are many Arabic sayings that ask us to take heed of the date palm, for she is patient, enduring and forever generous in her offerings.

Growing up, dates always made a regular appearance in my day to day. They'd appear before breakfast with strong Bahraini coffee, or in the afternoon with barely sweetened red tea. They'd make their way to every family gathering, every *iftar*, every joyous wedding and tragic funeral. Through the good times and the bad, truly, there would be dates. In his later years my grandfather complained that his doctor advised him to eat fewer dates, which he flatly refused to do. They were the one life pleasure he would simply not give up, and none of us dared dispute it.

Nowadays, I wait patiently for September, the most crucial month for my dad and his personal date-harvesting project, as well as the month I finally get a restock of my beloved dates. There are eight date palms in my parents' garden. When it's time for their harvest and they are lovely ripe *rotab* – fresh dates that haven't yet been dried – it's time to give the date-man a call. He comes with his hooked knife and his basket and skilfully hacks at the trees to release their fruit. You could eat them at this point, if you wanted, but most people prefer them dark and sticky. Once upon a time, my dad would arrange a bunch of sunbeds out on the lawn and spread the dates across them for their flavours to concentrate and sweeten as the harsh desert sun did its magic.

Nowadays, he has upped his game a few notches, with a designated room where the dates are spread out on trays, a fan beside them to assist in the drying process. The rest of us listen, amused, as Dad goes on about ambient dehydration temperatures, proper vac-pac packaging and how to prevent skin separation for the perfect date. When he visits London in late September, he will come proudly brandishing his dates, sealed in their packaging, now equipped with a nutrition label as well as a quote, this one from the Quran, saying: 'And Allah said [unto Mary]: and shake the trunk of this palm tree towards you, it will drop fresh, ripe dates upon you.'

قوله تعالى وهُزِّي إليكِ بِجَذَعِ النَّخلةِ تُساقط عليكِ رُطَباً جَنِياً

It is his proudest moment and, for this reason, it is mine too. I might be biased, but these are some of the best dates I've had. Their variety is Al-Khalas, and they give the Medjool dates a run for their money. But it doesn't really stop at Khalas, the varieties of dates are countless, their personalities as diverse as the date palms they come from. If I were to list them all it would fill up each and every one of these pages, and so I've stuck to just a few.

As a child I didn't pay much attention to the abundant date varieties surrounding me. I knew that sometimes the dates were fresh *rotab*, their skins less desirable but their insides sweet like soft toffee. I knew that my dad liked the sticky kind, and kept them packed tight in a container on the kitchen table, ready to have with his morning coffee. Sometimes, though, I preferred the drier dates, that weren't sickly sweet, with more flesh and less seed, and of these I could eat quite a few. When I moved to the UK and started working in restaurant kitchens, the only word I heard when it came to dates was 'Medjool'. I also began incorporating Medjool dates into my recipes, as not only were they so widely available, but they were also great to cook with. They are large, chewy, delicious, and for this I understand their popularity – what's not to love? But they aren't the only dates I grew up knowing.

It's Khalas dates that sit proudly on my parents' kitchen table. Their sticky, chewy, fudge-like taste make them a firm favourite in many Middle Eastern households. They're also a lot smaller than a Medjool date, so you could comfortably eat 3–5 in one sitting. Even sweeter still are the fresh Sukkari dates (*rotab*). These beautiful, golden-brown dates are round and dimpled and you could easily squeeze the toffee-like flesh out of its skin with your fingers. I like to have these cold, right out of the fridge, like a sweet. There's also Safawi or Khidri dates, both drier than the Khalas variety and more moderately sweet. Safawi dates are slightly firm and dark brown, with a taste reminiscent of coffee, while Khidri dates are chewier, reddish-brown in colour and with a similar taste to raisins. There are also dates I came to know when I was older, such as those from Saudi's Medinah – Ajwa and Ambar, to name a couple. Ajwa dates, known as the 'holy date', resemble prunes both in their appearance and taste, but are much drier in texture. Ambar dates, on the other hand, are popular for having a good flesh-to-seed ratio, the flesh soft and rich and the date large. I love how when you place these dates side by side, you'll notice how wildly different they all are, how 'brown dates' feels like an unjust description when you pick up on their reds, their golds, their treacle blacks, or even their two-tone colours, like with the Sagai dates, which are light yellow and crunchy on their tops and soft and brown through their bodies.

I never really understood my grandfather's (and now my father's) obsession with dates until I left Bahrain. At that time I felt that I was forever searching, for a new home, a different path, a different purpose. When I settled, I found myself searching still, this time for the things that brought me comfort, like eating my three Khalas dates in the morning, sweet and sticky and cold from the fridge. These dates, from a *nakhla* in my parents' garden, I eat slowly, mindfully, aware that in the delicate balance of life and date palms, this *lugma*, this bite, is the most precious.

Dates with Tahini, Chilli and Salt

This is a non-recipe recipe that is a fancy version of what is a staple snack for many Bahrainis: dates with *harda* – basically dates dipped into tahini – a typical bite served with strong coffee. You can take as many liberties as you like here: stuff the dates with your favourite nuts, sprinkle them with nigella seeds, omit the chilli or salt – the choice is yours. I like to make these, then put them in the refrigerator to get really cold and chewy, but that's a personal preference.

Makes 12

12 Medjool dates, pitted
25g (1oz) shelled whole pistachios, lightly toasted
15g (½oz) tahini
1 tsp date molasses
1 tsp sesame seeds, well toasted
⅓ tsp Aleppo chilli flakes
A pinch of flaked salt

Stuff the dates with the pistachios and arrange them, cut side up, on a plate. Drizzle over the tahini and date molasses, then sprinkle with the sesame, chilli and salt.

Labneh and Loomi Flan

There's a real affinity for soft, dairy-based desserts like flans and crème caramels in the Arab world. Perhaps because there's a certain amount of comfort to them, or because anything cooling and creamy is the perfect antidote to the unforgiving heat. Either way, this flan is all of that, but it's also tangy from the addition of labneh and slightly bitter from the black lime (*loomi*) which counterbalance all the sweetness. There's also the texture here, which I adore, a sort of flan-meets-cheesecake.

Serves 8 · Draining time: overnight · Chilling time: 3 hours

For the labneh
450g (1lb) natural (plain) yoghurt
¼ tsp fine sea salt

For the caramel
140g (5oz) caster (superfine) sugar
1 black lime, pips removed, finely crushed in a spice grinder to give 1½ tsp, plus extra to serve

For the flan
180g (6¼oz) labneh, bought or homemade (see recipe)
250g (9oz) sweetened condensed milk
250ml (9fl oz) whole milk
120ml (4fl oz) double (heavy) cream
3 large eggs, plus 1 yolk
1 tsp vanilla bean paste
¾ tsp flaked salt, plus extra to serve

Begin by making the labneh the day before you want to serve the flan. Mix together the yoghurt and salt. Line a sieve (strainer) with cheesecloth or a clean tea towel with plenty of overhang and place over a clean bowl. Transfer the yoghurt to the lined sieve and fold over the overhang to encase the yoghurt. Top with a weight (a couple of cans will do) and place in the refrigerator overnight. The next day, unwrap the mixture, discarding the collected liquid – you now have labneh. Measure out 180g (6¼oz) and save any extra in a sealed container in the refrigerator (it will keep for up to 5 days).

Preheat the oven to 150°C fan/170°C/340°F/Gas mark 3½. You will need a 28cm (11¼in) diameter flan dish, or a 20cm (8in) square baking tin will also work.

To make the caramel, add the sugar to a medium saucepan with 3 tablespoons of water and place over a medium heat. Cook for about 6–7 minutes, resisting the urge to stir, until the sugar has dissolved and the mixture is bubbling but not yet coloured. Swirl the pan slightly, then sprinkle in the black lime and swirl to combine. Continue cooking for another 5–7 minutes, or until the mixture is a deep amber (don't be afraid to take it to the edge). Working quickly, pour the caramel into the flan dish, swirling to cover the base and a little up the sides. Place the flan dish in a larger roasting tin and leave to set.

Once set, add all the flan ingredients to a blender and blitz on high for about 30 seconds or until well combined. Pour this mixture into the flan dish.

Fill your kettle with water and bring to the boil. Once boiling, place the tin holding the flan dish in the middle rack of the oven and pour enough boiling water into the tin to come halfway up the sides of the flan dish, being very careful not to get any water into the flan itself. Bake for about 45–50 minutes, or until the custard is just set but with a nice jiggle in the centre. Carefully remove the tin from the oven and leave the flan to cool in its water bath. Once cool, remove from the tin and refrigerate for at least 3 hours.

When ready to serve, run an offset spatula or butter knife around the dish to gently loosen the flan from its edges. Place a large round plate on top and in one swift motion invert the whole thing onto it. Serve sprinkled with some extra salt and black lime, if you like.

Luqaimat with Date Molasses, Sesame and Fennel Salt

Luqaimat are a bit like doughnuts, but with a more crisp exterior. You'll find them at the dessert table during Ramadan, or on offer during winter fairs, where they're fried *à-la-minute* and eaten immediately. Nowadays, people douse them in sugar syrup after they're fried, but I find these too sweet, and much prefer the traditional way of tossing them in date molasses. I can't help but add the salt, which I think works really nicely here.

Serves 6/Makes about 45 · Resting time: 1 hour

180g (6¼oz) plain (all-purpose) flour
3 tbsp custard powder (I use Bird's)
1½ tbsp cornflour (cornstarch)
seeds from 20 cardamom pods, finely crushed using a pestle and mortar
½ tsp loosely packed saffron threads, finely ground
1 tbsp fast-action dried yeast
⅓ tsp fine sea salt
1 tbsp caster (superfine) sugar
190ml (6¾fl oz) lukewarm water
10g (¼oz) white sesame seeds
1½ tsp fennel seeds
¼ tsp flaked sea salt
700ml (24fl oz) sunflower oil, for deep frying, plus extra for oiling your hands
120g (4¼oz) date molasses

Add the first 8 ingredients to a large mixing bowl and whisk to combine and get rid of any lumps. Pour in the water, then switch to a rubber spatula and use this to beat the mixture together. Do this for about 3 minutes, really working the dough until there are no lumps; it will be quite thick and sticky. Cover with a plate and leave in a warm place in your kitchen until doubled in size, about 1 hour.

Meanwhile, add the sesame and fennel seeds to a small dry frying pan (skillet) and place over a medium heat. Toast for about 4–6 minutes, stirring often, until nicely browned. While still warm, transfer to a pestle and mortar with the flaked salt and grind until roughly crushed.

Heat the sunflower oil in a small deep-sided saucepan over a medium-high heat. While it heats, deflate the dough with a spatula, beating a couple times until smooth. Line a medium tray with paper towels and set aside. Whisk the date molasses and 1½ tablespoons of water together in a medium mixing bowl and set this aside too.

Keep a small bowl of oil beside you. Dip 2 dessertspoons into the oil bowl to grease them (you'll use these to form the luqaimat) then use 1 spoon to remove a marble-sized amount of dough from the bowl, using the other spoon to help you drop it into the oil. It should sizzle but not colour right away, and immediately start to puff up and rise to the surface – the oil is hot enough at this point. Immediately use a slotted spoon to turn the dough around in the hot oil – this'll help shape it and round it out. It should be about the size of a ping-pong ball once puffed up. Continue in this way, frying 8–10 luqaimat at a time, using a slotted spoon to turn them so they evenly brown all over. Fry for about 4 minutes, until browned, crispy and cooked through, and use the slotted spoon to transfer the fried luqaimat to the prepared tray to absorb the excess oil. While still hot, transfer them to the date molasses bowl, tossing with a spatula to roughly coat them, then immediately place them on a serving platter and sprinkle with the sesame and fennel salt. (This is a bit messy, and it can take some practice to shape the dough into nice round balls. Don't worry if they're not perfect though; they don't need to be.) You should make about 45 luqaimat, give or take a few.

Pile the luqaimat on top of each other, to create height. Drizzle any remaining molasses over the top and serve within 3 hours.

HALAWA

Pistachio Cake with Labneh Cream and Kataifi

My mum is a really good baker. She'd bake a cake every weekend and it would always come out perfect. So perfect, in fact, that she once made her signature Victoria sponge and went to answer the doorbell, only to return moments later to an empty plate, a trail of crumbs and our dog Max, gazing up at her with guilty eyes and a sugar-powdered nose. My journey into baking was not so smooth. I would be impatient, flustered and heavy-handed – all things that don't bode well in the world of desserts. With time, and perhaps a bit of maturity, I've learnt to find joy in desserts, so long as I get to be a little bit whimsical in the process. This cake is one I'm super proud of, especially the fun element that the crunchy kataifi topping adds. If you can't find kataifi in Turkish or Middle Eastern supermarkets, you can thinly shred some filo (phyllo) sheets to create the same effect.

Serves 10

For the cake
170g (6oz) shelled pistachios
190g (6½oz) self-raising (self-rising) flour
½ tsp ground cinnamon
seeds from 15 cardamom pods, finely crushed using a pestle and mortar
½ tsp bicarbonate of soda (baking soda)
½ tsp fine sea salt
280g (10oz) caster (superfine) sugar
170g (5¾oz) unsalted butter at room temperature, cut into 3cm (1¼in) cubes
190g (6½oz) egg whites, at room temperature (from about 5 large eggs)
120g (4¼oz) Greek yoghurt, at room temperature
1 tbsp vanilla bean paste
240ml (8fl oz) whole milk

For the topping
60g (2½oz) kataifi, defrosted if frozen, roughly cut into 4cm lengths
1 tsp caster (superfine) sugar
¼ tsp ground cinnamon
25g (1oz) unsalted butter

For the labneh cream
180g (6¼oz) Labneh, bought or homemade (see page 240)
130g (4¾oz) mascarpone
140g (5oz) cream cheese
50g (2oz) icing (confectioner's) sugar, sifted

Preheat the oven to 165°C fan/185°C/360°F/Gas mark 4½. Grease and line the base and sides of two 20cm (8in) diameter, loose-based cake tins with baking paper. (If you only have one tin, then you can bake one cake at a time.)

Pulse the pistachios in a food processor until they resemble ground (powdered) almonds. Tip 150g (5½oz) into a large bowl (reserve the rest for decorating) along with the flour, cinnamon, cardamom, bicarbonate of soda and salt and whisk to evenly combine.

Put the sugar and softened butter into a second large bowl and beat with a hand mixer on a medium-high speed until light and fluffy – about 3–4 minutes. Scrape down the sides with a spatula. Lower the speed to medium and add a third of the egg whites at a time, mixing until fully incorporated with each addition. Scrape down the sides with a spatula again, then increase the speed to medium-high and beat for 1 minute, until the mixture is nice and smooth. Add the yoghurt and vanilla and beat for 30 seconds, then scrape down the sides once more. Turn the speed down to low and add a third of the flour mixture and a third of the milk. Alternate these until combined, and the mixture is smooth.

Evenly divide the batter between your prepared tins (about 650g/1lb 7oz per tin). Bake for 37–40 minutes or until a cake skewer inserted into the centre comes out clean. Allow both cakes to cool completely in their tins. (Ideally, both cakes would cool in their tins, but if you only have one tin, allow the first cake to cool slightly after cooking and release it carefully from the tin. Re-line the tin and repeat with the remaining batter.)

With the oven still on, line a medium baking tray with baking paper. In a bowl toss together all the topping ingredients, using your fingers to separate the kataifi strands as much as possible so they aren't too clumped together. Spread out onto the prepared tray and bake for 15–20 minutes, stirring halfway, until golden. Set aside to cool completely.

Lastly, use a hand-held mixer (or a whisk and some arm power) to beat together the labneh cream ingredients in a medium bowl, for about 1 minute, or until soft peaks. If too thick, add a splash of milk to make it easier to work with. Refrigerate until needed.

Once cool, release the cakes from their tins and discard the baking paper.

To decorate the cake, place one of the cakes on a cake stand (a rotating one is easiest if you have one). Use an offset spatula to spread a little less than half the labneh cream on top of the cake, spreading it evenly all around. Next, top with the second cake, stacking it so that it's aligned. Use the remaining labneh cream to coat the top and sides (an offset spatula will help you most here). You're going for a rustic look so don't worry if it's not perfect. Lastly, sprinkle the top of the cake with the kataifi, followed by the reserved ground pistachios.

Qatayef with Ricotta, Apricots and Honey Syrup

I've always thought that qatayef are the result of pancakes meeting crumpets and then morphing into their own thing. They're soft and pliable, like a pancake, but yeasted and bubbly, like a crumpet. Here the qatayef are stuffed, folded, fried and doused in a lemony honey syrup, which all in all makes for a very delicious eating experience.

Serves 6–8/Makes 21 qatayef · Resting time: 80 minutes

700ml (24fl oz) sunflower oil, for deep frying, plus extra for greasing
2 tsp thyme leaves, picked, to serve

For the batter
180g (6¼oz) plain (all-purpose) flour
2 tsp caster (superfine) sugar
2 tsp milk powder
¾ tsp fast-action dried yeast
⅓ tsp baking powder
⅛ tsp salt
320ml (11fl oz) lukewarm water

For the honey syrup
150g (5½oz) runny honey
1 large lemon to yield 6 strips of finely shaved skin and 2½ tbsp juice
2 tbsp apricot jam
3 tbsp water

For the filling
160g (5¾oz) whole-milk ricotta
80g (2¾oz) feta, finely crumbled
80g (2¾oz) pitted soft dried apricots, finely chopped
30g (1oz) caster (superfine) sugar
1 tbsp apricot jam

First, make the batter by whisking together all the ingredients, except the water, in a medium bowl until evenly combined. Pour in half the water, whisking until smooth, then pour in the rest and whisk to a smooth batter with the consistency of double (heavy) cream. Cover the bowl with a plate and leave to rest at room temperature for 60–80 minutes, or until bubbly.

Meanwhile, make the syrup by adding the honey and lemon strips to a medium frying pan (skillet) and placing it over a medium-high heat. Cook for 4 minutes, stirring occasionally, or until bubbling and a deep amber colour. Take off the heat and immediately whisk in the jam, lemon juice and water until combined (careful, it might spit). Transfer to a large bowl and set aside to cool completely. It will thicken as it cools. Add a splash more water if needed – you want it to be the consistency of maple syrup.

Make the filling by mixing together all the ingredients in another medium bowl.

Heat a large, non-stick frying pan (or a flat griddle/grill pan) over a medium heat. Drizzle in a little oil and use a paper towel to wipe it all over the pan to lightly grease. Once hot, use a tablespoon measure (or a small ice-cream scoop) to pour 2 tablespoons of the batter into the pan to create a circle roughly 8cm (3¼in) in diameter. Repeat twice, to make 3 pancakes at a time (or as many as will fit into your pan without touching). Leave to cook, without flipping, for about 1½–2 minutes, or until lightly browned on the bottom and bubbles form on top to resemble crumpets. Once bubbles start to appear on top (do not flip) use a spatula to transfer the pancakes to a large tray, bubbly-side up, spacing them so they're not overlapping. Keep covered with a tea towel so they don't dry out. Continue with the remaining batter, making 21 pancakes in total. Lightly grease the pan as needed throughout the frying process, and adjust the heat as necessary.

Continued overleaf

To stuff the pancakes, place a heaped teaspoon of the filling in the centre of one pancake, bubbly-side up, and then fold it in half to encase the filling. Seal the ends by squeezing them together firmly – they should stick together easily. Keep them covered under a tea towel while you continue with the remaining pancakes and filling.

Fill a medium, high-sided saucepan with the sunflower oil and heat over a medium-high heat. To test the oil is hot enough, dip in a corner of one of your qatayef – it should sizzle immediately but not colour right away. Fry the qatayef in batches, so about 7 at a time, for about 4 minutes per batch or until nicely golden. When ready, use a slotted spoon to transfer to a tray lined with paper towels. Then, while the qatayef are still hot, drop them into the honey syrup bowl, tossing gently to coat, then arrange nicely on a large platter.

Pour the remaining honey syrup all over the qatayef and sprinkle with thyme. Serve warm. You can also serve qatayef at room temperature but they will soften up as they sit, so it's best to eat them within a couple of hours of frying.

Arab Mess

This dessert is a perfect amalgamation of the two parts of me: the classic British dessert, Eton Mess, with an Arab twist. I love the addition of acidity here, thanks to the sumac, lime and pomegranate molasses, which cuts through the rich mascarpone cream and sweet meringue. The Persian candy floss is a bit of a whimsical addition – in Bahrain we call it *sha'ar banat*, which translates as 'girls' hair'. You can find it in most Middle Eastern or Turkish grocery stores. You'll make more meringue than you need here, so store any extra in an airtight container in the refrigerator.

Serves 6

For the meringue
115g (4oz) caster (superfine) sugar
65g (2¼oz) egg whites (from 2-3 eggs), at room temperature
⅛ tsp cream of tartar
1 tsp rosewater
40g (1½oz) pistachios, finely crushed using a pestle and mortar

For the cardamom cream
200g (7oz) mascarpone
200ml (7fl oz) whipping (heavy) cream
30g (1oz) caster (superfine) sugar
seeds from 10 cardamom pods, finely crushed using a pestle and mortar

For the macerated berries
300g (10½oz) strawberries, hulled, then halved or quartered if larger
120g (4½oz) blueberries
120g (4½oz) blackberries
120g (4½oz) raspberries
1½ tsp sumac, plus an extra 1 tsp to serve
1½ tbsp caster (superfine) sugar
1 tbsp pomegranate molasses
zest and juice from 1 large lime, to yield 1½ tsp zest and 1½ tsp juice
30g (1oz) Persian candy floss (*sha'ar banat*), white or pink, to serve (optional)

Preheat the oven to 160°C fan/180°C/350°F/Gas mark 4. Line a large 30 x 40cm (12 x 16in) baking tray and a smaller one with baking paper.

Start with the meringue. Spread the sugar out on the smaller tray and transfer to the oven to heat up for 10 minutes. Towards the last 2 minutes, add the egg whites and cream of tartar to the bowl of a stand mixer fitted with the whisk attachment and beat on medium speed until it starts to turn frothy. When ready, remove the sugar from the oven and turn down the heat to 100°C fan/120°C/250°F/Gas mark ½.

With the mixer turned to medium-low speed, use the baking paper to help you slowly pour the sugar into the mixer. Once incorporated, turn the speed up to high and beat until glossy and stiff peaks form, about 5-6 minutes. Towards the last 30 seconds, add the rosewater. Use a spatula to evenly spread the meringue out to the dimensions of the large tray. Sprinkle all over with the crushed pistachios and transfer to the oven for 70-80 minutes, or until completely dried out. Set aside to cool completely, then break apart into random 5-6cm (2-2½in) shards.

Meanwhile, make the cream by adding all the ingredients to a bowl and use a hand-held mixer (or a stand mixer fitted with the whisk attachment) to beat into soft peaks. Refrigerate until ready to serve – you want it nice and cold.

Put all the berries in a large bowl. Weigh out 100g (3½oz) and place these in a food processor with the sumac, sugar, molasses and lime juice and blitz until completely smooth. Pour this over the berries and gently toss to coat. Refrigerate until ready to serve.

To serve, divide half the cream between 6 shallow dessert bowls. Top with half the berry mixture, then sprinkle over some of the meringue shards. Repeat with the remaining cream, berries and more of the meringue. Divide the candy floss (if using) between the bowls, then sprinkle with the extra sumac and the lime zest.

HALAWA

Rose and Vanilla Rice Pudding with Filo

This dessert is a mash-up of two very warming things, the first being rice pudding and the second being *Um Ali*, the Middle East's answer to bread and butter pudding. The filo topping here ends up being a bit soft through the centre and crispy around the edges, and the two together make the whole eating experience quite nostalgic. Make sure the rosewater you use is a Middle Eastern or Mediterranean brand; some supermarket brands can be overly concentrated, unlike the delicate rosewater we'd typically cook with.

Serves 6

For the rice
10g (¼oz) unsalted butter, for greasing
80g (2¾oz) pudding rice
800ml (28fl oz) whole milk
300ml (10½fl oz) single (light) cream
60g (2¼oz) caster (superfine) sugar
⅛ tsp salt
2 tsp rosewater
1 vanilla pod, split down the middle, seeds scraped (reserve the pod for the syrup)

For the syrup
40g (1½oz) caster (superfine) sugar
1 fresh bay leaf
40ml (1½fl oz) water
1 tsp rosewater
1 tbsp lemon juice
2 tbsp dried rose petals

For the filo
4 sheets good-quality filo (phyllo)
30g (1oz) unsalted butter, melted
¾ tsp ground cinnamon

Preheat the oven to 140°C fan/160°C/325°F/Gas mark 3. Use the butter to grease the base and sides of a 24cm (9½in) diameter baking dish and place this on a larger baking tray.

Add the rice, milk, cream, sugar, salt, rosewater and vanilla seeds (minus the pod) to a large bowl and mix to combine. Carefully transfer the rice mixture to the prepared dish, stirring to evenly distribute the rice, then cover the surface with a piece of baking paper. Wrap the dish tightly in foil, carefully transfer to the oven and bake for 2 hours.

Meanwhile, make the syrup by adding the sugar, bay leaf, water and reserved vanilla pod to a small saucepan. Place it over a medium heat and cook gently until the sugar dissolves. Take off the heat and stir in the rosewater and lemon juice. Set aside.

About 10 minutes before the rice is ready, trim the filo sheets to about 28cm (11¼in) square. Lay one sheet onto a clean work surface and brush it liberally with melted butter, then sprinkle all over with ¼ teaspoon of the cinnamon. Repeat with the remaining sheets and cinnamon, brushing the last sheet with just the butter. When the rice pudding is ready, remove from the oven and turn the heat up to 170°C fan/190°C/375°F/Gas mark 5. Remove the foil and baking paper and drape the filo over the top, pulling and scrunching in the sides to form a round border. Brush the scrunched-up sides with any remaining butter and bake for 20–25 minutes more, or until golden and bubbling. Let settle for about 10 minutes and then stir the rose petals into the syrup and pour it over the top of the filo. Serve warm.

Sunrise Clementines with Hibiscus and Orange Oil

We ate a lot of cooling fruits growing up – things like marinated oranges, saffron-poached pears or refreshing strawberry and rhubarb 'soups'. I'm not sure if it was my mum's way of getting her kids to eat desserts that were somewhat healthy, or if it was simply to override the relentless heat. Either way it's stuck with me through the years, and I'll often turn to chilled fruit to spoon over yoghurt or ice cream, or to eat as is with a spoon. Get ahead by making the hibiscus syrup and the orange oil up to two days in advance, but don't mix in the clementines until the day you want to serve them.

Serves 4 · Refrigeration time: 2 hours +

1 very large unwaxed orange, or 2 medium ones
3 tbsp olive oil
130ml (4½fl oz) water
15 dried hibiscus flowers
50g (1¾oz) caster (superfine) sugar
2 tsp orange blossom water
1 tbsp lemon juice
7 medium clementines or tangerines, seedless (650g/1lb 7oz)

Finely shave the skin of the orange to give you 15g (½oz) of peel. Use a small, sharp knife to scrape away any of the white pith. Roughly chop the peel, then add to a small food processor with the olive oil and blitz until finely chopped. Transfer to a small bowl and set aside to infuse while you continue with the rest.

Squeeze the orange and measure off 120ml (4fl oz) of juice. Add to a small saucepan with the water, hibiscus and sugar. Bring to a simmer over a medium-high heat, stirring to dissolve the sugar, and simmer for just 1 minute. Take off the heat, stir in the orange blossom water and lemon juice, and set aside to infuse and cool down completely, about 45 minutes. Once cool, strain through a sieve (strainer) into a wide shallow bowl, discarding the solids.

Peel the clementines (or tangerines) and slice them into 1–1.5cm (½–⅝in) rounds (don't worry if some fall apart a little, but try to keep most slices intact). Gently add them to the hibiscus liquid, then refrigerate for at least 2 hours, or until very cold.

Strain the orange oil through a small sieve set over a bowl, pushing down on the solids to extract as much of the oil as possible (discard the solids).

Just before serving, spoon the orange oil over the fruit and serve cold.

HALAWA

Really Soft Date Loaf with Cardamom, Fennel and Nigella Seeds

This date loaf is inspired by a multitude of things. The idea landed while eating a Welsh bara brith, similar to an English tea loaf, where dried fruit is soaked in tea to create a bread loaf that's then sliced and slathered in butter. I knew then that this would be the perfect template for a cardamom date cake, which I had wanted to include in *Lugma* somehow. Then there's the topping, which sets this loaf apart in a very lovely way. The combination of fennel, sesame and nigella seeds is often sprinkled onto *khobez hamar*, a type of date-based flatbread made in Bahrain but perfected in Al-Ahsa in eastern Saudi Arabia. This really is a special loaf, so easy to make and one that improves with time, so make it a day before you want to serve it if you can. I like to have it drizzled with tahini and date molasses, which is quite rich, so feel free to just spread it with lashings of salted butter.

Serves 8

320g (11¼oz) pitted Medjool dates, finely chopped
400ml (14fl oz) boiling-hot strong brewed tea
1 tsp bicarbonate of soda (baking soda)
110g (3¾oz) olive oil (by weight not volume), plus extra for greasing
140g (5oz) dark soft brown sugar
2 eggs
2 tbsp date molasses
275g (9¾oz) plain (all-purpose) flour, sifted
1 tsp baking powder
seeds from 25 cardamom pods, finely crushed using a pestle and mortar
¼ tsp fine sea salt

For the topping
1 tbsp sesame seeds
1 tsp fennel seeds, roughly crushed using a pestle and mortar
1 tsp nigella seeds

To serve
tahini or salted softened butter
date molasses

Put the dates in a medium heatproof bowl and add the tea and bicarbonate of soda. Mix to combine and set aside to soften for 20 minutes.

Preheat the oven to 170°C fan/190°C/375°F/Gas mark 5. Grease and line the base and sides of a standard 1-litre loaf tin (about 23 x 13 x 6cm/9 x 5 x 2½in) with a piece of baking paper.

In a large bowl, vigorously whisk together the oil, sugar, eggs and molasses until smooth, aerated and without lumps, about 2 minutes.

In a separate bowl, whisk together the flour, baking powder, cardamom and salt.

Use a fork (or your hands) to roughly mash the dates into the tea, then whisk this into the sugar mixture until combined. Switch to a spatula and gently fold in the flour mixture, just until evenly combined (do not overmix). Transfer the mixture to the prepared tin and place it on a baking tray. Sprinkle the top with the sesame, fennel and nigella seeds, then bake on the middle rack of your oven for 65–70 minutes, or until a skewer inserted into the centre comes out clean. Check your loaf at the 35-minute mark; if it looks too dark on top, cover loosely with foil. When ready, lift the loaf out the tin using the baking paper to help you and leave to cool completely on a wire rack.

Serve sliced with a drizzle of tahini or a generous amount of softened butter, followed by some date molasses.

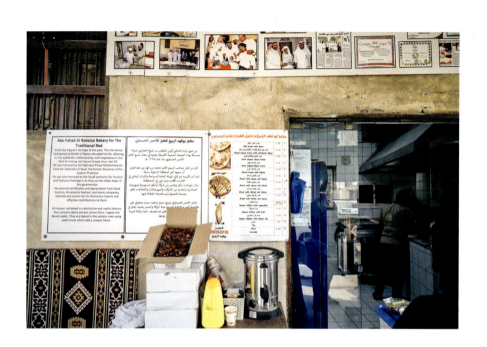

HALAWA

A bakery in Al Ahsa making traditional *khobez hassawi ahmar*, or Hassawi red bread, a date-based flatbread topped with sesame, fennel and nigella seeds and sometimes served with various fillings and toppings.

CONDIMENTS

Middle Eastern Chilli Crisp

I first made this as part of a Christmas gift hamper consisting of different chilli-based condiments. Out of it came this chilli crisp, which isn't a true Chinese chilli crisp as we know it, but an 'inspired by the Middle East' version yielding quite a different result. Ironically this condiment, being the mildest of them all, was the resounding favourite. It goes really well with just about anything – try it stirred into soups, spooned onto rice, hummus or labneh or onto Yoghurty Butter Beans (page 110). Stored in a sealed jar and topped up with enough oil to cover, it'll keep for up to 6 weeks.

Makes 1 small jar

5 tbsp sunflower oil
5 tbsp olive oil
2–3 shallots, thinly sliced into rounds, preferably on a mandoline (100g/3½oz)
8 garlic cloves, thinly sliced
25g (1oz) pine nuts
2 tsp sesame seeds
1 tsp chilli flakes
2 tsp Aleppo chilli flakes
½ tsp paprika
1 tsp fennel seeds, roughly crushed using a pestle and mortar
1 tsp caraway seeds, roughly crushed using a pestle and mortar
1 tsp coriander seeds, roughly crushed using a pestle and mortar
fine sea salt

Add both oils and the shallots to a medium frying pan (skillet) and place it over a medium-low heat. Let cook and bubble gently, stirring occasionally, until crisp and lightly browned, about 20–22 minutes. Turn down the heat if the shallots starts to colour too soon; you really want to give them this time to slowly crisp up. When ready, strain through a sieve (strainer) set over a bowl to catch the oil.

Transfer the shallots to a plate lined with paper towels, and return the oil to the pan, again over a medium-low heat. Add the garlic and cook for about 5 minutes, stirring occasionally, or until lightly golden. Be sure not to get it too dark as garlic can quickly turn bitter, so do keep your eye on it. Strain once again through the same sieve set over the bowl and put the garlic with the shallots. Return the oil to the pan again and place over a medium heat with the pine nuts. Cook for 2–3 minutes, stirring, until lightly golden. Strain once again through the sieve set over the bowl and put the pine nuts on the same plate with the shallots and garlic.

Add the sesame, all the spices and ¼ teaspoon salt to a medium heatproof bowl and mix to combine. Pour the oil back into the pan one last time and heat on medium until shimmering, but not smoking. Quickly pour this over the spices – they should sizzle immediately. Leave to cool completely. Once the spices are completely cool, stir in the fried shallots, garlic and pine nuts and transfer to a small sterilized jar, if not using right away.

CONDIMENTS

Torshi Makhlout

Torshi are pickled vegetables of which there are many variations. *Makhlout* means 'mixed' and can include all the vegetables listed here, along with celery, onions, garlic, turnips, aubergines, green peppers and more to your heart's desire (or to what's in your refrigerator). The spicing and pickling liquids can also vary; some will include tamarind and date vinegar, or molasses and plenty of herbs. Here I've gone with a happy medium. I've stuck to apple cider vinegar for its availability, but if you do stumble upon date vinegar, then feel free to use that instead. Serve a bowl of this alongside a mezze spread or with grilled meats or vegetables.

Makes two 1-litre (35fl oz) jars

2 large carrots, peeled and sliced into 0.5cm (¼in) rounds (250g/9oz)
1–2 pickling cucumbers, halved and sliced into 2cm (¾in) half-moons
⅓ of a large cauliflower (300g/10oz), cut into small (3cm/1¼in) florets, thicker stems reserved for use in another recipe
250g (9oz) hispi cabbage (about 1 small head), core removed, cut into 4–5cm (1½–2in) cubes
450ml (16fl oz) apple cider vinegar
4 tbsp sugar
1½ tsp ground turmeric
2 tsp coriander seeds
1 tsp cumin seeds
½ tsp fennel seeds
¾ tsp allspice berries
¼ tsp black peppercorns
¾ tsp ground ginger
1 tsp nigella seeds
3 green chillies, left whole
3 red chillies, left whole
flaked sea salt

Put the prepared vegetables into a large bowl and toss with 2 tablespoons of flaked salt. Transfer to a colander set over the bowl and leave to soften and drain for 1 hour.

Meanwhile, add 1 litre (35fl oz) of water, the vinegar, sugar, turmeric and 1½ tablespoons of flaked salt to a large pan and bring to the boil over a high heat. Once boiling, remove from the heat and set aside to cool to room temperature.

Add the coriander, cumin and fennel seeds along with the allspice and the peppercorns to a small dry frying pan (skillet) and toast over a medium heat until fragrant, about 4 minutes. Transfer to a spice grinder (or use a pestle and mortar) and grind until fine. Stir in the ground ginger and nigella seeds.

When ready, discard the accumulated liquid from the salted vegetables. Have 2 sterilized 1 litre (35fl oz) jars at the ready. Add a sixth of the spices and 1 chilli to each jar, then follow with a sixth of the vegetables. Continue in this way, compacting the spices, chillies and vegetables into the jars. Lastly, pour over the cooled pickling liquid. Weight the tops down with a small saucer and seal the jars. Leave to pickle at room temperature for at least 2 weeks before opening. Refrigerate once opened; they will keep for up to 3 months.

Aubergine Maabouch

Maabouch is a chilli condiment from Kuwait that comes in various forms – red, green, mixed, etc. Some will make it very spicy with dried chillies and oil, others a bit milder with fresh chillies, tomatoes and vinegar. This version uses meaty aubergines, which I really love, as it's substantial enough to spread onto sandwiches or slather over some cheese. My favourite way to eat this is alongside fried fish and white rice.

Enough for a 500ml (17fl oz) jar

2 aubergines (eggplants), cut into roughly 3cm (1¼in) cubes (500g/1lb 2oz)
4 tbsp olive oil, plus extra to seal the jar
120g (4¼oz) mild green chillies (or jalapeños), stem and seeds removed, roughly chopped
3 mild dried red chillies, stem and seeds removed, roughly chopped
3 garlic cloves, roughly chopped
1 plum tomato, roughly chopped (100g/3½oz)
1 tbsp coriander seeds, toasted and roughly crushed using a pestle and mortar
20g (¾oz) fresh coriander (cilantro), roughly chopped
1 tsp sugar
2 tbsp apple cider vinegar
1 tbsp lemon juice
fine sea salt

Preheat the oven to 200°C fan/220°C/425°F/Gas mark 7.

Line a large baking tray with baking paper. Add the aubergines, 2 tablespoons of the oil and ½ teaspoon salt. Toss to coat the aubergines evenly. Bake for 30–35 minutes, or until nicely browned and cooked through. Set aside to cool completely.

Put both types of chilli, the garlic, tomato, coriander seeds, fresh coriander, sugar and ½ teaspoon salt into the bowl of a small food processor. Pulse a few times, scraping the bowl as you go, until everything is finely chopped. Strain through a sieve (strainer), discarding the liquid, then transfer the solids to a large bowl with the vinegar, lemon juice and remaining 2 tablespoons of oil. Roughly chop the roasted aubergines, then stir them into the chilli mixture.

Transfer to a sterilized jar and top with enough oil to seal. You can eat this right away but it will become more mild as it sits. Refrigerate for up to 3 days.

Tomato Achar

This traditional Bahraini pickle is often served with fish and rice. The ingredients can vary but the main ones are chillies and garlic, which subtly infuse themselves into the tomatoes in a very lovely way. Unlike Indian achar, which is more concentrated and punchy, the Bahraini version has a more delicate flavour that I really enjoy. I urge you to keep a jar of it in your fridge; it's so simple to put together and really makes an impact. Once opened, keep refrigerated for up to 3 weeks.

Enough for a 1-litre (35fl oz) jar · Salting time: overnight · Preserving time: 5 days

750g (1lb 10oz) large Datterini tomatoes, or large cherry tomatoes
50g (1¾oz) flaked sea salt
9 garlic cloves
1 tbsp cumin seeds, toasted and roughly crushed using a pestle and mortar
1 tbsp coriander seeds, toasted and roughly crushed using a pestle and mortar
6 dried red chillies, toasted
3 tbsp caster (granulated) sugar
1 fresh green chilli
200ml (7fl oz) distilled white vinegar

Wash the tomatoes and dry them really well. Use a small sharp knife to cut through the tomatoes from the stem end, stopping short about 1cm (½in) from the bottom (so you only cut them about three-quarters of the way through). Gently push some flaked salt into the middle and then place each tomato, stem-side up, into a colander set over a bowl. Continue in this way with all the tomatoes and salt. Cover with a plate and leave to sit overnight, at room temperature. The next day, discard the water drained from the tomatoes.

Bring a small pan of water to the boil. Add the garlic and blanch for just 30 seconds. Drain and run under cold water to stop the cooking, then dry the garlic very well on paper towels. This is to prevent it from discolouring in the pickle.

Begin assembling the achar into a sterilized 1-litre (35fl oz) jar. Add a third of the cumin and coriander seeds followed by a third of the tomatoes, 2 dried chillies, 3 garlic cloves, a third of the sugar and the fresh green chilli. Continue in this way with the remaining ingredients (except the green chilli and vinegar), then very lightly press down to gently compress. Pour over the vinegar, then add enough filtered water, if needed, until everything is completely submerged. Make sure the jar is tightly sealed, then leave to pickle at room temperature for 5 days, turning the jar every now and then to redistribute the spices. It will keep, refrigerated, for up to 3 weeks.

Cheat's Mehyawa

Of all the condiments that exist in the world, *mehyawa* has to be one of my favourites. You can find it throughout the Gulf countries, but Bahrain is renowned for having the best. It was brought to Bahrain via the Holi community, Arabs who migrated to Iran and spent some time there. Upon their return, they introduced many Persian influences, including some delicious foods like mehyawa.

The elusive thing about mehyawa is you can only really find the authentic sauce made in people's homes, which you can either buy from local bakeries or directly from source. As for the recipe, well, after asking more people than I care to admit, I've found it to be one of Bahrain's most closely guarded secrets. So I set to work in creating my own. Pretty soon though, I encountered one major problem. Mehyawa is made using a local dried sardine called *matoot*, which is one of the sardine family only smaller. *Matoot*, combined with a mixture of toasted ground spices and a five-day fermentation in Bahrain's scalding sun, produces the most unique, funky-tasting condiment. After stuffing bags of *matoot* into my suitcase and trying my hand at making mehyawa in my small London kitchen I came to the humbling realization that the likelihood of finding *matoot* outside of the Gulf is zero to none, therefore the likelihood of anyone trying their hand at the recipe might also be the same. But what, I wondered, if I tried to make mehyawa more simply, using ingredients that are readily available in supermarkets and by cutting the production time substantially? The next question that ran through my mind was, if I do this, will I ever be forgiven?

This cheat's mehyawa is for those of you who have yet to try the condiment, and for those of you who, like me, are hundreds if not thousands of miles away from the taste of home. Traditionally, mehyawa is spread onto a type of flatbread called *falazeen* but it's also delicious drizzled over labneh or fried eggs. It's intense and quite salty, so use it sparingly. I love it, and I hope you will too.

Makes: 1 small jar

1 tsp coriander seeds
1 tsp cumin seeds
½ tsp fennel seeds
½ tsp flaxseeds
¼ tsp black mustard seeds
30g (1oz) anchovies in olive oil, drained weight
1 tbsp apple cider vinegar
1 tsp date molasses
1½ tbsp olive oil
1½ tbsp water

Add all the seeds to a small dry frying pan (skillet) and place it over a medium heat. Cook for about 3 minutes, shaking the pan a few times, until fragrant and the seeds begin to pop. Transfer to a spice grinder and blitz to a smooth powder. Otherwise, do this using a pestle and mortar while the seeds are still warm – just crush them as finely as you can. Add this to the bowl of a small food processor along with the remaining ingredients and blitz until completely smooth and pourable.

Transfer to a small sterilized jar and store, sealed, in the refrigerator for up to 2 weeks. It will thicken as it sits, so thin it out with a little water to get it to a pourable consistency.

Daqoos, the Sauce

There are two types of daqoos, this saucy version and a dry spice mix. The sauce is sharp and slightly spicy, which lends itself well to all types of rice dishes (see Emmawash page 121).

Makes 250g (9oz)

2 tbsp olive oil
3 garlic cloves, finely grated
1 hot green chilli, destemmed and finely chopped – seeds and all
1 tsp ground coriander
1 tbsp tomato purée (paste)
2 large ripe vine tomatoes (240g/8½oz), blitzed to a purée
1½ tbsp apple cider vinegar
½ tsp sugar
½ tsp fine sea salt

Add the oil, garlic, chilli, coriander and tomato purée to a small saucepan and place it over a medium-high heat. Cook for 2 minutes, stirring occasionally, or until fragrant and deeply red. Stir in the blitzed tomatoes, vinegar, sugar and salt. Bring to a simmer, then turn down the heat to medium and cook for 12 minutes, until thickened slightly but still pourable. Transfer to a bowl to cool to room temperature. If not using right away, keep sealed and refrigerated in a sterilized jar for up to 1 week. Serve alongside the rice dish of your choice.

Daqoos, the Spice Mix

Not to be confused with Daqoos, the sauce (above), which you'll often see paired with various rice dishes throughout the Gulf. The spice mix, however, I have yet to see outside of Bahrain. It is generally used as a finishing touch on dishes such as rice, fish or eggs. Keep a jar of this on your shelves to sprinkle onto anything that needs a bit of a lift.

Makes half a small jar

1 tbsp cumin seeds
2 tbsp coriander seeds
1½ tsp sesame seeds
½ tsp onion granules
½ tsp garlic granules
2 tsp pearl barley
3 tbsp Aleppo chilli flakes
1 tbsp paprika
½ tsp fine sea salt

Add all the seeds to a small dry frying pan (skillet) and place it over a medium heat. Toast until fragrant, about 3–4 minutes. Transfer to a spice grinder with the onion and garlic granules and blitz until finely crushed (or use a pestle and mortar). Empty into a small bowl, then return the pan to a medium-low heat and add the barley. Toast for 5–6 minutes, shaking the pan often, until browned and toasted. Transfer to a spice grinder and blitz into a fine powder (you can also do this using a pestle and mortar but it will require some perseverance!). Pass the ground barley through a fine-mesh sieve (strainer) into the spice-mix bowl and discard any of the solids that don't pass through. Stir in the chilli, paprika and salt. Store in a small jar for up to 6 months.

CONDIMENTS

Meal suggestions

Mezze party (serve with pita)
Cheesy filo rolls with burnt honey, chilli and mint (page 77)
Cauliflower mutabal (page 67)
Baby aubergines, two ways (pages 96–97)
Batata harra oo helwa (page 81)
Chicken koftas with fresh tomato sauce (page 209)

Picnic spread
The disappearing island's salad Olivieh (page 106)
Steamed carrots with harissa onions and herbs (page 64)
Grilled green beans with lemon and feta (page 157)
Sunrise clementines with hibiscus and orange oil (page 256)

Weekend brunch
Balaleet: sweet noodles and salty eggs (page 30)
Ful with chickpeas and tahini (page 40)
Chai karak (page 52)
Really soft date loaf with cardamom, fennel and nigella seeds (page 259)

Roast chicken dinner
Loomi lemon chicken
Pan-fried tomatoes with za'atar, pine nuts and halloumi
Doh piazeh roast potatoes
A herby leafy salad

Feeding a crowd (non-veg version)
Slow-cooked fenugreek lamb with pickled chillies (page 220)
Tomato, potato and saffron rice (page 116)
Sautéed greens with yoghurt, fried onions and turmeric oil (page 178)
Batata harra oo helwa (page 81)
Arab Mess (page 251)

Feeding a crowd (veg version)
Macarona béchamel (page 165)
Kebab nekh-y: chickpea and veg fritters with mango pickle (page 88)
Labneh with slow-cooked leeks and peas (page 101)
Springtime fattoush (page 71)
Qatayef with ricotta, apricots and honey syrup (page 249)

A rice feast (non-veg edition)
Fega'ata: bottom of the pot chicken and rice (page 122)
Cucumber yoghurt (page 78)
Tomato achar (page 269)
A herby leafy salad (page 70)

A rice feast (veg edition)
Machboos (page 132)
Melt-in-your-mouth okra (page 171)
Savoury trifle salad with aubergines, yoghurt and pita (page 84)

An autumnal spread
Jewelled pumpkin (page 163)
Baked mushroom rice with cinnamon and allspice (page 118)
Yoghurty butter beans with Middle Eastern chilli crisp (page 110)

BBQ season
Coffee, cardamom and chipotle-rubbed lamb chops (page 206)
Grilled corn with toumiya and daqoos (page 154)
Watermelon salad with cucumber, red onion and ricotta salata (page 109)

Weeknight meals
Tuna jacket potatoes with lime yoghurt and herbs (page 202)
Bahraini dal, with simple buttered rice (page 148)
Vermicelli chicken and rice with cardamom and cinnamon (page 128)
Mujadara with yoghurt and Shirazi salad (page 172)
Sweet date and sour tamarind sea bass (page 201)
Coffee, cardamom and chipotle-rubbed lamb chops (page 206)
Cinnamon-spiced freekeh with chickpeas and tahini (page 164)
Salmon harra (page 196)
Baked lamb koftas with peppers, feta and oregano (page 212)
Tomato bulgur with charred courgettes (182)
Hot sauce chickpeas with turmeric potatoes (page 158)
Melt-in-your-mouth okra, with simple buttered rice (page 171)
Spiced mussels with chickpeas and coriander-garlic bread (page 198)

Weekend cooking
Chbab rubyan: prawn dumplings in tamarind and tomato broth (page 196)
Onion and potato frittata with charred pepper salsa (page 44)
Mana'eesh, two ways (pages 47–50)
Macarona béchamel (page 165)
Middle Eastern bolognese pasta bake (page 223)
Mathrooba: beaten chicken and rice (page 136)
Emmawash: spiced rice with mung beans and prawns (page 121)
Herby meatball rice with kohlrabi and pistachio slaw (page 125)
A very green lasagne with fresh chilli sauce (page 144)
Fasoolia bi lahme: white bean and lamb stew (page 219)
Slow-cooked fenugreek lamb with pickled chillies (page 228)
Pistachio cake with labneh cream and kataifi (page 244)

Index

Note: page numbers in **bold** refer to illustrations.

achar, tomato 23, 269
aish (rice) 6
Akka 48
akkawi 48–50
Al Ahsa, bakery in **260-1**, 261
allspice 118, 213
Aloo Basheer shop, Manama souk **160-1**, 161
apricot, *qatayef* with **248**, 249–50
Arab mess 251, **252-3**
arak 195
arayes (meat-stuffed pita) 22
aruz (rice) 6
aubergine
  aubergine *maabouch* 268
  aubergine sauce 164
  baby aubergines with tomato and pepper salsa 97, **98-9**
  baby aubergines with walnuts, ricotta and herbs 96, **98-9**
  burnt aubergines with fenugreek sauce, tahini and fried shallots **150**, 151
  musaqa'a: aubergines in spicy tomato sauce with fried potatoes **174**, **175**
  savoury trifle salad with aubergines, yoghurt and pita **82-3**, 84

ba-gill (wild leek) 70
Bahrain 6, 10–11, 14, 17, 20–1, 26, 30, 34–5, 39, 52, 58, 60–1, 88, 95, 103–4, 122, 132, 134–5, 148, 154, 158, 161, 166, 195, 206, 227, 234, 237, 239, 251, 259, 269–70, 272
  farmland **68-9**, 69
baith oo tamat: eggs and tomatoes 26, **27**
balaleet: sweet noodles and salty eggs 6, 23, 30, **31**
barley and herb nourishing soup 61, **63**
batara harra oo helwa: hot and sweet potatoes **80**, 81
béchamel sauce 144–7, 164
beef, Middle Eastern Bolognese **222**, 223
beetroot, sesame beets with charred spring onions 86, **112**, 113
berries, macerated 251, **252-3**
Bolognese, Middle Eastern **222**, 223, **224**, **225**
Bombay mix 92, **93**
bread (ready-made) 106
  chickpea and bread soup with roasted garlic and coriander 60, **62**
  coriander-garlic bread 198, **199**
  liver and charred onions in a bun **42**, 43
  see also pita bread
breakfast 25–55
broad bean 40, 71
broccoli, roasted broccoli salad with lime and chilli dressing and Bombay mix 92, **93**
broth, tamarind and tomato 190–4, **191-3**
brunch 25–55
bukhoor (incense) 19
bulgur wheat 172
  allspice chicken with herby bulgur-stuffed tomatoes 213, **214-15**
  tomato bulgur, charred courgettes **182**, **183**
butter
  browned butter 188, **189**
  paprika butter **184**, 185
butter bean (lima bean), yoghurty butter beans with Middle Eastern chilli crisp 110, **111**

cakes
  pistachio cake with labneh cream and kataifi 244–5, **246-7**
  really soft date loaf with cardamom, fennel and nigella seeds **258**, 259
  walnut cake 6
cannellini bean
  Arabic baked beans **28**, 29
  fasoolia bi lahme: white bean and lamb stew **218**, 219
caramel 240, **241**
cardamom 21, 30, 52, 244–5
  cardamom cream 251, **252-3**
  cardamom pancakes with honey lime syrup 36, **37**
  coffee, cardamom and chipotle-rubbed lamb chops 206, **207**
  really soft date loaf with cardamom **258**, 259
  vermicelli chicken, rice and cardamom 128, **129**
carrot 58, 106, 164, 223, 227, 228, 267
  steamed carrots with harissa onions and herbs 64, **65**
cauliflower 267
  cauliflower mutabal **66**, 67
  zahra bilaban: cauliflower with warm yoghurt and paprika butter **184**, 185

chai 52–5
  chai hamar **54**, 55
  chai karak 52, **53**–4
  chai loomi **54**, 55
chbab rubyan: prawn dumplings in tamarind and tomato broth 190–4, **191**–3
cheese 29
  Arabic pizza 48–50
  'cheese and olives': halloumi with spicy olives and walnuts **32**, 33
  cheesy filo rolls with burnt honey, chilli and mint **76**, 77
  cheesy leek and za'atar *fatayer* **46**, 47
  see also specific cheeses
chen'ad (kingfish) 103
chicken
  allspice chicken with herby bulgur-stuffed tomatoes 213, **214**–15
  beaten chicken and rice 134–6, **137**
  bottom of the pot chicken and rice 122, **123**
  chicken koftas with tomato sauce **208**, 209
  chicken stock 58
  chicken and vegetable stew **226**, 227
  the Disappearing Island's salad olivieh 106
  loomi lemon chicken 220, **221**
  vermicelli chicken and rice with cardamom and cinnamon 128, **129**
  vermicelli chicken soup 58, **59**
chickpea (garbanzo bean) 84
  chickpea and bread soup with roasted garlic and coriander 60, **62**
  cinnamon-spiced freekeh with chickpeas and tahini 164
  ful with chickpeas and tahini 40, **41**
  hot sauce chickpeas with turmeric potatoes 158, **159**
  kebab nekh-y: chickpea and veg fritters with mango pickle 88, **89**
  spiced mussels with chickpeas and coriander-garlic bread 198, **199**
chilli
  cheesy filo rolls with burnt honey, chilli and mint **76**, 77
  fresh chilli sauce 144–7, **145**
  lime and chilli dressing 92, **93**
  Middle Eastern chilli crisp 110, **111**, 264, **265**
  pickled chillies 228, **229**
  tahini, dates with tahini, chilli and salt **238**, 239
chocolate and coffee granita with tahini cream and halva 232, **233**
cinnamon 118, **119**, 128, **129**
  cinnamon-spiced freekeh with chickpeas and tahini 164

Clementine, hibiscus and orange oil 256, **257**
coffee
  chocolate and coffee granita with tahini cream and halva 232, **233**
  coffee, cardamom and chipotle-rubbed lamb chops 206, **207**
  see also *gahwa*
condiments 263–72
coriander 21, 61, 144–7
  chickpea and bread soup with roasted garlic and coriander 60
  coriander-garlic bread 198, **199**
courgette
  charred courgettes with saffron, kefir and sticky onions 85
  tomato bulgur, charred courgettes 182, **183**
cream 240, 255
  cardamom cream 251, **252**–3
  labneh cream 244–5
  tahini cream 232, **233**
cream cheese 77, 244–5
cucumber 267
  cucumber yoghurt 78, **79**
  see also Lebanese cucumber
cumin 21

dal, Bahraini 148, **149**
daqoos (sauce) 272, **273**
daqoos (spice mix) 70, 154, 272
date molasses 139, 242
date(s) 19, 234–7, **236**
  date pickle **138**, 139
  dates with tahini, chilli and salt **238**, 239
  really soft date loaf with cardamom, fennel and nigella seeds **258**, 259
  sweet date and sour tamarind sea bass **200**, 201
doh piazeh roast potatoes 152, **153**
dressings 70, 113
  lemon **156**, 157
  lime and chilli 92, **93**
Dubai 14
dumplings, prawn 190–4, **191**–3

egg 36, 44, 47, 77, 106, 132, 164, 244–5, 251
  eggs and tomatoes 26, **27**
  fried eggs, *mehyawa* and crispy sage **38**, 39
  sweet noodles and salty eggs 30, **31**
Eid 132
emmawash: spiced rice with mung beans and prawns **120**, 121

falazeen (flatbread) 270
fasoolia bi lahme: white bean and lamb stew 216–17, **218**, 219
fatayer, cheesy leek and za'atar **46**, 47
fattoush 22

springtime fattoush 71, **72-3**
fega'ata: bottom of the pot chicken and rice 122, **123**
fennel
  baked prawn scampi with fennel, arak and feta 195
  fennel salt 242, **243**
  really soft date loaf with cardamom, fennel and nigella seeds **258**, 259
fenugreek seed 22
  fenugreek sauce **150**, 151
  slow-cooked fenugreek lamb with pickled chillies 228, **229**
feta 77, 144-7, 224, 249-50
  baked lamb koftas with peppers, feta and oregano **210-11**, 212
  baked prawn scampi with fennel, arak and feta 195
  grilled green beans with lemon and feta **156**, 157
  macaroni with bread *tahdig* and marinated feta **167**, 168, **169**
filo pastry 95
  cheesy filo rolls with burnt honey, chilli and mint **76**, 77
  rose and vanilla rice pudding with filo **254**, 255
finyal (coffee cup) 52
fish 187-203
flan, labneh and *loomi* 240, **241**
freekeh, cinnamon-spiced freekeh with chickpeas and tahini 164
frittata, onion and potato frittata with charred pepper salsa 44, **45**
fritters, chickpea and veg 88, **89**
ful with chickpeas and tahini 40, **41**

gahwa (coffee) 19, 52, 217
  see also coffee
galette, potato and sour spinach **176**, 177
garlic
  chickpea and bread soup with roasted garlic and coriander 60, **62**
  coriander-garlic bread 198, **199**
ghoozi/ghouzi (whole lamb over rice) 35, 132
ginger peaches 74, **75**
gram flour 88
granita, chocolate and coffee 232, **233**
Greek yoghurt 44, 60, 67, 88, 106, 164, 224-5, 227
  cucumber yoghurt 78, **79**
  green yoghurt **94**, 95
  lime yoghurt 202, **203**
  sautéed greens with yoghurt, fried onions and turmeric oil 178, **179**
  savoury trifle salad with aubergines, yoghurt and pita **82-3**, 84
  yoghurt béchamel 144-7

green bean with lemon and feta **156**, 157
Gulf, food of the 6, 10, 20, 21

hake with date molasses rice **138**, 139
halawa (sweets) 231-59
halloumi 144-7
  halloumi with spicy olives and walnuts **32**, 33
  pan-fried tomatoes with za'atar, pine nuts and halloumi **90**, 91
halva 232, **233**
hamour (grouper) 103
harees (mutton porridge) 35
harissa onions 64, **65**
hibiscus and orange oil 256, **257**
Holi community 270
honey
  cheesy filo rolls with burnt honey, chilli and mint **76**, 77
  honey lime syrup 36, **37**
  honey syrup **248**, 249-50
hummus 6, 23

Iran 10, 20, 85, 152, 166, 270
Iraq 20

jameed (dried/fermented yoghurt) 185
Jarada 102, 103-4, **105**, 106

kale (lacinato)
  sautéed kale with yoghurt, fried onions and turmeric oil 178, **179**
  stewed kale **180**, 181
kashk-e-bademjan (Iranian dish) 85
kataifi 244-5, **246-7**
kebab nekh-y: chickpea and veg fritters with mango pickle 88, **89**
kefir 58, 85
khobez hamar (date-based flatbread) 259
khobez hassawi ahmar (Hassawi red bread) 261
khobez Lebnani (Lebanese pita) 22, 71, 84, 168
kingfish fried with browned butter and crunchy salad 188, **189**
koftas
  baked lamb koftas with peppers, feta and oregano **210-11**, 212
  chicken koftas with fresh tomato sauce **208**, 209
kohlrabi and pistachio slaw **124**, 125-6
Kuwait 30, 166, 268

laban bil khiar (mezze) 78
labneh 29, 47
  labneh cream 244-5, **246-7**
  labneh and *loomi* flan 240, **241**
  labneh with slow-cooked leeks and peas **87**, 100, 101

lamb
  baked lamb koftas with peppers, feta and oregano **210-11**, 212
  coffee, cardamom and chipotle-rubbed lamb chops 206, **207**
  fasoolia bi lahme: white bean and lamb stew **218**, 219
  herby meatball rice with kohlrabi and pistachio slaw **124**, 125-6
  Middle Eastern Bolognese **222**, 223
  samboosa tikka with green yoghurt 95
  slow-cooked fenugreek lamb with pickled chillies 228, **229**
lasagne, a very green lasagne with fresh chilli sauce 144-7, **145**
Lebanese cucumber (Persian cucumber) 21, 106, 109, 172, 188
Lebanon 196, 216
leek
  cheesy leek and za'atar *fatayer* **46**, 47
  labneh, slow-cooked leeks, peas **87**, **100**, 101
lemon
  grilled green beans, lemon and feta **156**, 157
  lemon dressing **156**, 157
  lemony vine leaf rice **130**, 131
lentil(s) 61, 148, 172
lettuce 70, 84, 106
Levant 10, 172, 196
lime
  dried 20-1
  honey lime syrup 36, **37**
  lime and chilli dressing 92, **93**
  lime yoghurt 202, **203**
  see also loomi (black lime)
liver and charred onions in a bun **42**, 43
London 17, 19, 104, 157, 185, 235, 270
loomi (black lime) 17, 19, 20-1
  labneh and *loomi* flan 240, **241**
  loomi lemon chicken 220, **221**
luqaimat 6
  luqaimat with date molasses, sesame and fennel salt 242, **243**

maabouch, aubergine 268
maash (mung bean) 121
macarona béchamel 165
macaroni 166-7
  macaroni with bread *tahdig* and marinated feta **167**, 168, **169**
machboos 6, 21, 23, 132, **133**, 135
mana'eesh (fermented fish condiment) 35, 48
mango pickle 88, **89**
marinade, chicken 227
mascarpone 244-5, 251
mast-o-khiar (mezze) 78
mathrooba: beaten chicken and rice 6, 134-6, **137**

matoot (sardine) 270
meat 205-28
meatballs, herby meatball rice with kohlrabi and pistachio slaw **124**, 125-6
mehyawa 6, 35
  cheats *mehyawa* 270-1, **271**
  fried eggs with *mehyawa* and crispy sage **38**, 39
meringue 251, **252-3**
mezze 57-113
mozzarella 48-50, 144-7, 224
muhammar oo samak: date molasses rice with fish **138**, 139
Muharram 61
Muharraq 134
mujadara, yoghurt, *Shirazi* salad 172, **173**
mung bean(s)
  emmawash: spiced rice with mung beans and prawns **120**, 121
  stewed mung beans and greens with saffron rice **180**, 181
musaqa'a: aubergines in spicy tomato sauce with fried potatoes 174, **175**
mushroom rice baked with cinnamon allspice 118, **119**
Muslims 13, 235
mussels, spiced mussels with chickpeas and coriander-garlic bread 198, **199**
mutabal, cauliflower **66**, 67

nakhla (date palm) 234-7, **236**
New York 14

oil
  hibiscus and orange 256, **257**
  smoky 84
  turmeric 178, **179**
okra, melt-in-your-mouth **170**, 171
olive(s)
  halloumi, olives, walnuts **32**, 33
  marinated olives **49**, 50
Oman 20
onion
  fried onions 178, **179**
  liver and charred onions in a bun **42**, 43
  onion and potato frittata 44, **45**
  onion topping 148, **149**
  steamed carrots with harissa onions and herbs 64, **65**
  sticky onions 85
  sumac onions 206, **207**
  watermelon salad with cucumber, red onion and ricotta salata **108**, 109
orange and hibiscus oil 256, **257**
Ottolenghi 19

INDEX   283

Palestine 48, 196
pancakes 34–5
  cardamom pancakes with honey lime syrup 36, **37**
pasta 166–7
  green lasagne, fresh chilli sauce 144–7, **145**
  macaroni with bread *tahdig* and marinated feta **167**, 168, **169**
  Middle Eastern Bolognese pasta bake 224, **225**
peach, ginger 74, **75**
pea(s), slow-cooked 87, **100**, 101
pepper (green bell) 96, 132, 164, 174, 201, 223
  baked lamb koftas with peppers 210–11, 212
  charred pepper salsa 44, **45**
pepper (red bell) 33, 158
  Arabic pizza, red pepper, onions and *akkawi* 48–50, **49**
  baked lamb koftas with peppers 210–11, 212
  tomato and pepper salsa 97, **98–9**
pickles
  date pickle **138**, 139
  mango pickle 88, **89**
  pickled chillies 228, **229**
  tomato *achar* 23, 269
  torshi makhlout **266**, 267
pine nut 84, 91, 118, 264
pistachio 36, 239, 251
  kohlrabi and pistachio slaw **124**, 125–6
  pistachio cake with labneh cream and kataifi 244–5, **246–7**
pita bread 22
  bread *tahdig* **167**, 168, **169**
  fried pita 71, **82–3**, 84
pizza, Arabic pizza: *mana'eesh* with red pepper, onions and *akkawi* 48–50, **49**
pomegranate seed 71, 84, 131, 185
potato 58, 106, 122, 148, 227
  doh piazeh roast potatoes 152, **153**
  fried potatoes 174, **175**
  onion and potato frittata 44, **45**
  potato and sour spinach galette **176**, 177
  shoestring potatoes 174, **175**
  tomato, potato and saffron rice 116, **117**
  tuna jacket potatoes 202, **203**
  turmeric potatoes 158, **159**
prawn
  baked prawn scampi with fennel, arak and feta 195
  emmawash: spiced rice with mung beans and prawns **120**, 121
  prawn dumplings in tamarind and tomato broth 190–4, **191–3**
pumpkin, jewelled **162**, 163

Qatar 30
qatayef with ricotta, apricots and honey syrup **248**, 249–50

rice 6, 11, 21, 115–41, 141
  baked mushroom rice with cinnamon allspice 118, **119**
  beaten chicken and rice 134–6, **137**
  bottom of the pot chicken and rice 122, **123**
  date molasses rice with fish **138**, 139
  herby meatball rice with kohlrabi and pistachio slaw **124**, 125–6
  lemony vine leaf rice **130**, 131
  machboos 132
  plain buttery saffron rice 127
  saffron rice **180**, 181
  spiced rice, mung beans, prawns **120**, 121
  tomato, potato and saffron rice 116, **117**
  vermicelli chicken and rice 128, **129**
rice pudding, rose and vanilla rice pudding with filo **254**, 255
ricotta 91, 96, 109, 249–50

saffron 85, 116, 127, 181
safi (rabbitfish) 103, 139
sage, crispy **38**, 39
salads 57–113
  crunchy salad 188, **189**
  the Disappearing Island's salad olivieh 104, 106, **107**
  a herby leafy salad 70
  roasted broccoli salad with lime and chilli dressing and Bombay mix 92, **93**
  savoury trifle salad with aubergines, yoghurt and pita **82–3**, 84
  Shirazi salad 172, **173**
  springtime fattoush 71, **72–3**
  tomato and red onion 44
  watermelon salad with cucumber, red onion and ricotta salata **108**, 109
salmon harra 196, **197**
saloona (stew) 21
  saloonat dajaj: chicken and vegetable stew 6, **226**, 227
salsa 32, 33
  charred pepper 44, **45**
  tomato and pepper 97, **98–9**
salt 239
  fennel salt 242, **243**
samboosas 13
  samboosa tikka with green yoghurt **94**, 95
sauces
  aubergine sauce 164
  daqoos (sauce) 272, **273**
  fenugreek sauce **150**, 151
  fresh chilli sauce 144–7, **145**

fresh tomato sauce **208**, 209
hot sauce 158, **159**
macarona béchamel 165
mussel 198, **199**
spicy tomato sauce 174, **175**
yoghurt béchamel 144-7
Saudi Arabia 14, 141, 171, 237, 259
scampi, baked prawn scampi with fennel, arak and feta 195
sea bass, sweet date and sour tamarind sea bass **200**, 201
sesame seed 113, 242, 259, 264
shakshukas 17, 23
shawarma 22, 23
shillah 61
Shirazi salad 172, **173**
slaw, kohlrabi and pistachio **124**, 125-6
smoky oil 84
soups 57-113
   chickpea and bread soup 60, **62**
   nourishing herb and barley soup 61, **63**
   Vermicelli chicken soup 58, **59**
spinach 144-7
   potato and sour spinach galette **176**, 177
   sautéed spinach with yoghurt, fried onions and turmeric oil 178, **179**
   stewed mung beans and spinach with saffron rice **180**, 181
   spring onion, charred 86, **112**, 113
stews 21
   chicken and vegetable 6, **226**, 227
   stewed mung beans and greens **180**, 181
   white bean and lamb 216-17, **218**, 219
stock, chicken 58
sumac onions 206, **207**
sweet potato, hot and sweet **80**, 81
sweetcorn, grilled corn with *toumiya* and *daqoos* 154, **155**
Swiss chard 144-7, 190-4
   sautéed Swiss chard with yoghurt, fried onions and turmeric oil 178, **179**
   stewed **180**, 181
Syria 196, 216
syrup 255
   honey lime syrup 36, **37**
   honey syrup **248**, 249-50

tahdig 22, 125, 168, **169**
tahini 40, 67, 113, 151, 165, 239
   tahini cream 232, **233**
tamarind pulp 22, 181, 190-4, 201
tannour bread 60
thareed (dish) 227
tikka
   Bahraini Tikka 20
   samboosa tikka with green yoghurt **94**, 95
tomato 29, 40, 48-50, 58, 88, 116, 121-2, 131-2, 136, 147-8, 158, 164, 168, 171-2, 198, 212, 219, 223, 227-8, 268, 272
   allspice chicken with herby bulgur-stuffed tomatoes 213, **214-15**
   baith oo tamat: eggs and tomatoes 26, **27**
   chicken koftas and tomato sauce **208**, 209
   pan-fried tomatoes with za'atar, pine nuts and halloumi **90**, 91
   prawn dumplings in tamarind and tomato broth 190-4, **191-3**
   spicy tomato sauce 174, **175**
   tomato *achar* 23, 269
   tomato bulgur with charred courgettes 182, **183**
   tomato and pepper salsa 97, **98-9**
   tomato and red onion 44
torshi makhlout **266**, 267
toumiya 154, **155**
tuna jacket potatoes 202, **203**
turmeric
   turmeric oil 178, **179**
   turmeric potatoes 158, **159**
tzatziki 78

United Arab Emirates (UAE) 30
United States 14

vanilla and rose rice pud with filo **254**, 255
vegetarian dishes 143-85
vermicelli noodles (wheat) 23
   sweet noodles and salty eggs 30, **31**
   vermicelli chicken and rice 128, **129**
   vermicelli chicken soup 58, **59**
vine leaf 14
   lemony vine leaf rice **130**, 131

walnut 6, 33, 85, 96
watermelon salad with cucumber, red onion and ricotta salata **108**, 109

yellow split pea 122, 132
yoghurt 61, 101, 113, 181, 240
   cauliflower, warm yoghurt, paprika butter **184**, 185
   mujadara with yoghurt and *Shirazi* salad 172, **173**
   yoghurty butter beans with Middle Eastern chilli crisp 110, **111**
   see also Greek yoghurt

za'atar
   cheesy leek and za'atar *fatayer* **46**, 47
   pan-fried tomatoes with za'atar, pine nuts and halloumi **90**, 91
zahra bilaban: cauliflower with warm yoghurt and paprika butter **184**, 185

Acknowledgements

They say it takes a village, and this could not ring more true than with *Lugma*. I knew early on that no solo venture is a success without a supportive community, but I don't think I truly comprehended the community I've been blessed with.

The first thank you goes to my parents for instilling in me from a very young age that the sky's the limit, and for teaching me how to love mathrooba and buttered crumpets in equal measure.

To my very best friend, Maram, who knows me better than I know myself, thank you for always being by my side. Maram was the first to read my proposal before I'd even submitted it, and has since immersed herself in my project like it was her very own. She really is the definition of chosen family.

To Anthony, who helped me run up the steepest hill in Madeira, and has since stuck around to help me run through any and all of life's hurdles. Thank you for being my favourite human of all time, and for making sure no single rice grain goes to waste.

To my dear friend Amina, who's gentle and kind spirit has made its mark both in my own life but also in *Lugma*, thank you to you and your mum for opening up your home kitchen and your heart.

Thank you to the 'Foo(d) fighters', my WhatsApp group of friends from my local gym, who willingly gave my recipe 'trials and errors' a home. Thanks to them no food made ever went to waste, and I always felt like I had a group of fabulously fit cheerleaders rooting for me throughout the process.

A special thank you to the amazing Claudine Boulstridge, who has cross-tested almost every recipe of my publishing career to date, and whose palate and word I trust even more than my own.

To Sophie Allen and Emily Lapworth, who gave me the biggest gift of feeling heard. Thank you for honouring my vision for *Lugma*, and for injecting as much love into is as I have. You really are the dream team, along with Stephanie Evans and Stephen Lang and the larger team at Quadrille, a leading publisher that I can't rave about enough.

A big thank you to Daisy Parente for being the best agent and hype woman a girl could ask for (and to Felicity for leading me to her!).

I've been blessed with two Matts for this book. A big thank you to Matt Russell, who injected all the warmth and calm into *Lugma*, both in his cheerful presence and in his beautiful food photos. And thank you to my dear friend Matt Wardle, a secret honorary Bahraini from Liverpool, who captured the essence of *Lugma* through his travel photography. Thank you for crossing the border into Saudi on your motorcycle, all for a story about rice (worth it).

A special mention to Wei Tang, just the most wonderful all-round human, prop stylist and friend. And to Emma Cantlay, Lucy Cottle and Annabelle Davis, thank you for cooking your hearts out on some very hot summer days.

For the beautiful cover illustration, thank you to Ella Ginn. And for the stunning calligraphy, a big shukran to Karima Sharabi, who's mum was coincidentally my high school maths teacher – what a small, wild and wonderful world we live in.

And to anyone else who has been part of this journey in some way, perhaps without you even knowing it, a big, heartfelt thank you.

About the author

Noor Murad is a Bahraini-British chef and author. Born and raised in Bahrain to an Arab dad and an English mum, she began her journey into food at 16 years old with a summer job at a hotel in Bahrain with zero experience and much curiosity. She then went on to work at Käfer, a German catering company based at Bahrain's Formula 1 track, doing a short stint in Munich, before heading off to New York to earn a Bachelor's degree at the Culinary Institute of America. During her time in America, she spent 6 months working at a seafood restaurant in Maui and a year working at Jean George's Spice Market in NYC's Meat Packing district. In 2012 she headed back to Bahrain, worked in restaurants and offered catering and cooking classes to the community.

Her big leap of faith happened in 2016 when she applied to work at Ottolenghi in London. She worked for some time as sous chef at Ottolenghi's Spitalfields restaurant before moving to the Ottolenghi Test Kitchen, where she developed recipes for *The Guardian*, *New York Times*, Ottolenghi's MasterClass series and various online publications. She also developed recipes for Ottolenghi *Flavour* and *Falastin*. In 2020, Noor created and co-authored the Ottolenghi Test Kitchen cookbooks *Shelf Love* and *Extra Good Things* published in 2021 and 2022 respectively.

Noor draws on her Bahraini upbringing in her cooking, with Arabic, Persian and Indian flavours making their mark on her recipes. That said, she still enjoys a good jacket potato and a classic scone, thanks to her British roots.

Quadrille, Penguin Random House UK, One Embassy Gardens,
8 Viaduct Gardens, London
SW11 7BW

Quadrille Publishing Limited is part of the Penguin Random House group of companies whose addresses can be found at global.penguinrandomhouse.com

Copyright © Noor Murad 2025
Food Photography
© Matt Russell 2025
Location Photography
© Matt Wardle 2025
Cover illustration © Ella Ginn 2025
Cover and chapter script
© Karima Sharabi 2025

Noor Murad has asserted her right to be identified as the author of this Work in accordance with the Copyright, Designs and Patents Act 1988

Penguin Random House values and supports copyright. Copyright fuels creativity, encourages diverse voices, promotes freedom of expression and supports a vibrant culture. Thank you for purchasing an authorized edition of this book and for respecting intellectual property laws by not reproducing, scanning or distributing any part of it by any means without permission. You are supporting authors and enabling Penguin Random House to continue to publish books for everyone. No part of this book may be used or reproduced in any manner for the purpose of training artificial intelligence technologies or systems. In accordance with Article 4(3) of the DSM Directive 2019/790, Penguin Random House expressly reserves this work from the text and data mining exception.

Published by Quadrille in 2025

www.penguin.co.uk

A CIP catalogue record for this book is available from the British Library

ISBN 978-1-83783-201-9
10 9 8 7 6 5 4 3 2 1

Managing Director: Sarah Lavelle
Editorial Director: Sophie Allen
Design and Art Direction: Emily Lapworth
Illustrator: Ella Ginn
Script: Karima Sharabi
Photographers: Matt Russell and Matt Wardle
Props stylist: Wei Tang
Food stylists: Noor Murad, Emma Cantlay, Lucy Cottle and Annabelle Davis
Production Director:
Stephen Lang

Colour reproduction by F1

Printed in China by RR Donnelley Asia Printing Solutions Limited

The authorised representative in the EEA is Penguin Random House Ireland, Morrison Chambers, 32 Nassau Street, Dublin D02 YH68.

Penguin Random House is committed to a sustainable future for our business, our readers and our planet. This book is made from Forest Stewardship Council® certified paper.